Duʿā

The Weapon of the Believer

A treatise on the status and etiquette of duʿā in Islām

Abu Ammaar Yasir Qadhi

ISBN 1 898649 63 4

SECOND EDITION

British Library Cataloguing in Publication Data.

A catalogue record for this book is available from the British Library.

Published: Al-Hidaayah Publishing and Distribution Ltd

Printed in Turkey by Mega Printing

Distributed by: Al-Hidaayah Publishing and Distribution Ltd
P.O. Box 3332
Birmingham B10 0UH
United Kingdom

Tel: 0121 753 1889
Fax: 0121 753 2422
Website: www.al-hidaayah.co.uk
Email: mail@al-hidaayah.co.uk

وَقَالَ رَبُّكُمُ ٱدْعُونِىٓ أَسْتَجِبْ لَكُمْ
إِنَّ ٱلَّذِينَ يَسْتَكْبِرُونَ عَنْ عِبَادَتِى سَيَدْخُلُونَ جَهَنَّمَ
دَاخِرِينَ ﴿٦٠﴾

And your Lord has stated: Make *duʿā* to Me, I will (of a surety) respond to you. Verily, those who are too arrogant to worship Me will enter the Fire of Hell, humiliated.

Sūrah *Ghāfir, 60*

Duʿā is (the essence of) worship.

Prophetic ḥadīth

Duʿā and the seeking of protection from Allāh are like weapons, but the sharpness of a weapon is not sufficient for it to cause effect, for the person that handles it also plays a role. So whenever the weapon is a perfect one, having no flaw in it, and the forearm is strong, and there are no preventing factors, then it will cause an effect on the enemy…

Ibn Qayyim al-Jawziyyah

Duʿā

The Weapon of the Believer

A treatise on the status and etiquette of duʿā in Islām

CONTENTS

بِسْمِ ٱللَّهِ ٱلرَّحْمَٰنِ ٱلرَّحِيمِ

INTRODUCTION

All praise is due to Allāh. We praise Him, seek His aid, and ask His forgiveness. We also seek refuge in Allāh from the evil of our souls, and from our impious deeds. Indeed, whoever Allāh guides, none can misguide, and whoever He misguides, there is none that can guide him. I bear witness and testify that there is no deity worthy of worship except Allāh, all glory be to Him, and I bear witness and testify that Muḥammad is His final Messenger, and His perfect worshipper.

Verily, man has been created for a noble and great purpose – in fact, the most noble and dignified goal that can exist – and that is that he may worship Allāh alone, without any partners. Allāh has said in the Qur'ān:

وَمَا خَلَقْتُ ٱلْجِنَّ وَٱلْإِنسَ إِلَّا لِيَعْبُدُونِ ﴿٥٦﴾

And I have only created *jinn* and mankind to worship Me.[1]

And the greatest and most noble form of worship is *duʿā*. It is a plea from the very heart of a believer directed towards Allāh – the Hearer of all things[2], the Knower of all secrets. It is a confession that emanates from the heart of a believer that he is weak and helpless, that he cannot achieve anything without Allāh's help and aid. It is an implicit affirmation of every single Name and Attribute of Allāh, for it affirms that Allāh is the Creator, the Sustainer, the Controller of all Affairs, the Hearer, the Seer, the Merciful, the Great, the All-Powerful, the Ever-Capable. The concept of *duʿā* entails

---

1 Sūrah *al-Dhāriyāt*, 56.

2 It should be remembered that Allāh's Names and Attributes are only in Arabic, and that the translations used in this treatise – and in all English books – convey only a small fraction of the real Arabic meaning of the word. Therefore, these translations should not, and cannot, take the place of the actual Arabic Names and Attributes of Allāh.

complete submission to Allāh, and perfect recognition of His right to be worshipped. It also consigns man to his proper status – a poor, created being, who has no control of any matter by himself, but rather he is the one that is controlled. It is a confirmation and attestation from the worshipper that he is in need of his Creator at every instance, and that Allāh is independent of any need from him. It shows that man is in a dire state of poverty towards his Lord, and that he cannot live without Him in any circumstance. In fact, his need for his Lord is more than his need for food, drink and air, for it is his Lord that provides him with all this and more. In particular, he is in need of continual guidance from His Lord, and this is the most important of all his needs, and the most noble of all his wants.

Duʿā is the *essence* of worship. This can be seen by imagining the condition of one making *duʿā* – a worshipper repenting from his sins, humiliated in front of His Lord, in a state of fear, submitting himself to the will of Allāh, earnestly desiring Allāh's rewards, raising his hands, turning to Allāh with the best of hopes from Him, exemplifying the statement of Allāh:

إِنَّهُمْ كَانُوا يُسَارِعُونَ فِي الْخَيْرَاتِ
وَيَدْعُونَنَا رَغَبًا وَرَهَبًا ۖ وَكَانُوا لَنَا خَاشِعِينَ ﴿٩٠﴾

> "Verily, they used to hasten to do good deeds, and they used to make *duʿā* to Us with hope and fear, and used to humble themselves before Us."[3]

Such a person makes *duʿā*, keeping in mind the promise that Allāh has given him, hopeful of achieving that promise:

وَقَالَ رَبُّكُمُ ادْعُونِي أَسْتَجِبْ لَكُمْ
إِنَّ الَّذِينَ يَسْتَكْبِرُونَ عَنْ عِبَادَتِي سَيَدْخُلُونَ جَهَنَّمَ
دَاخِرِينَ ﴿٦٠﴾

---

[3] Sūrah *al-Anbiyā',* 90.

> And your Lord has said: "Call upon me, and I will answer you!" Verily, those who are (too) arrogant to worship Allāh will enter Hell, humiliated![4]

So when one visualises such a person, and the state that he will be in, one can understand the Prophet's (ﷺ) statement:

> *Duʿā* is worship.[5]

So the entire concept of worship, the purpose for which mankind was created, can infact, be summarised in one simple act: that of *duʿā*.

Duʿā is a noble, spiritual form of worship which allows the created to appreciate the majesty and eminence of the Creator. This is because the worshipper turns to his Lord at his time of need, after all other types of aid have been cut off, and all other sources have been despaired of. He turns to his Lord to obtain from Him contentment, peace and serenity, and he finds Beneficence which will never be found from other sources. And how can this not happen, when he is turning to the Lord of all lords, and the King of all kings, the One Who is Self-Sufficient from all wants, and Who is Praised at all times?

So with the noble status of this act of worship in mind, it becomes obligatory on every single believer, without exception, to become familiar with this great concept of *duʿā*. So many questions that abound in one's mind must be answered. What is *duʿā*? What are its blessings and its excellence? What is the proper etiquette that one must follow while making *duʿā*? Why is someone's *duʿā* responded to, and someone else's not? And how can one increase one's chances of getting one's *duʿā* accepted? And what are the factors that prevent one's *duʿā* from being accepted? Also, if everything is already predestined, then what is the purpose of making

---

4 Sūrah *Ghāfir*, 60.

5 Authentic, narrated by Aḥmad and the four *Sunans*, and others, from Nuʿmān ibn Bashīr, as reported in *Ṣaḥīḥ al-Jāmiʿ* # 3407.

du'ā, for surely, if it is already written, it will happen whether the *du'ā* is made or not, and if it is not written, then no matter how much *du'ā* one does, it will never occur?

All these questions, and more , are answered in the short treatise in your hands. Although there are many books in English about the concept and etiquette of *du'ā*, in this author's humble opinion, none of them have done justice to this topic. Most only deal with some of the etiquette of *du'ā*, and none actually discuss the importance and status of *du'ā* in a Muslim's life. Therefore, I felt a dire need for such a book in the English language, and compiled this short, yet insha-Allāh comprehensive, treatise, in which I pray that the reader will find essential information that is needed by every Muslim with regard to this greatest act of worship. I have deliberately not elaborated unnecessarily on many advanced points or difficult concepts, nor have I diverged to discuss obscure tangents, for the purpose of this book is not so that a person masters the many facets of *du'ā*, but rather that the reader obtains *practical* benefit, by applying what he has read in his daily life. This work is meant for the layman who wishes to learn more about *du'ā* so that he can worship Allāh properly; it is not for the scholar. Therefore, the chapter sections have deliberately been left short, for I have restricted myself to quoting some *āyāt* and *aḥādīth*, and the statements of scholars, along with short explanations where appropriate.

This book is not the result of any unique research on my part; rather, it is compiled from a number of sources that I felt were excellent references in this field. Therefore, the treatise in the reader's hand is merely a compilation, translation, and arrangement of material found primarily in the following works:

1. *Al-Du'ā: Mafhūmuh, Aḥkāmuh, Akhṭā' taqau' fīhi,* by Muḥammad ibn Ibrāhīm al-Ḥamad (with comments and editing by Imām 'Abd al-'Azīz ibn 'Abdullāh ibn Bāz – *raḥimahu Allāh*).

2. *Taṣḥīḥ al-Duʿā*, by the *ʿAllāmah* of our times, Bakr Abū Zayd.[6]
3. *Al-Duʿā wa Manzilatahu min al-ʿAqīdah al-Islāmiyah,* by Dr. Jīlan al-Arūsī.[7]
4. *Shurūṭ al-Duʿā wa Mawaniʿ al-Ijābah,* by Shaykh Saʿīd al-Qaḥṭānī.
5. *Al-Duʿā,* by ʿAbd Allāh al-Khudayrī.
6. *Kitāb al-Duʿā,* by Ḥusayn al-ʿAwāyishah.
7. *Al-Nubadh al-Mustaṭābah fī al-Daʿwāt al-Mustajābah*, by Salīm al-Hilālī.

Some sections of this book are paraphrased from the above works, and since I have mentioned this in the Introduction, I have not referenced this every time it occurs. Details of these works and others can be found in the Select Bibliography at the end of this book. Other works were also used, in particular the works of Ibn Qayyim al-Jawziyyah, the doctor of the soul and the master of spiritual diseases and their cures. Where this was done, the relevant work was referenced in the footnotes.

---

6 In reality, this book is in a class of its own – like all the other books by this amazing personality! Whereas other books follow a 'standard' pattern of talking about the various apsects related to *duʿā*, Shaykh Bakr takes a refreshing and novel approach, referencing hundreds of obscure works, and coming forward with details not found in these 'traditional-style' books, obviously conforming to his usual scholarly style. It is unfortunate that this Shaykh and Imām of *Ahl al-Sunnah* is not given much attention in the West, perhaps because of the fact that he himself does not like publicity, and rarely gives lectures or classes, concentrating instead on writing.

7 This is a master's dissertation presented to the College of *Daʿwah* (Department of *ʿAqīdah*) of the Islāmic University of Madīnah, in the year 1410 A.H. This is the best reference that this author has come across that discusses the concept of *duʿā* and its status in Islām.

I request the reader to notify me if he comes across any mistakes in this work, or has any other constructive advice that he wishes to give.[8] In the end, perfection is only with Allāh!

On a personal note: this book was written at a time when I myself was undergoing a great personal crisis. It was a time when I myself was turning to Allāh, making *duʿā* constantly and earnestly for a miracle to occur to save me from the situation that I was in. And it was while I was writing the final pages of this book, sitting in front of my computer, that a phone call from an absolutely unexpected source came, informing me that, indeed, a miracle had occurred; and for Allāh all matters are easy, for He only has to say, '*Kun*,' and it is! Verily, all praise is due to Allāh, Who hears the plea of the one in distress, Who responds to the *duʿā* of the one who has been wronged, and Who grants justice to all.

So I hope that the following pages do not contain mere facts; dry quotes that do not stir sentiment and feeling. Rather, I pray that some of the *emotion* and *spirit* that was present while this book was being written can be felt by the reader as he turns its pages, and that he can *feel* the texts of the Qur'ān and Sunnah speak directly to his heart as he reads its lines. I pray that this work will help the reader come closer to Allāh, by realising his own great poverty and helplessness, and by appreciating the Beneficence and Power of the *Raḥmān*, the *Raḥīm*.

Abu Ammaar Yasir Qadhi

Al-Madīnah al-Nabawiyyah - The City of the Prophet (ﷺ)
1st Dhul-Qaʿdah 1421 A.H.
(26th Jan. 2001 C.E.)

Second edition revised and updated:

15th Muharram, 1424 A.H. (18th Mar., 2003 C.E.)

---

8 Comments may be sent care of the publisher, or e-mailed directly to the author at: yqadhi@hotmail.com

CHAPTER I

The Basics

1. The Meaning of *Du'ā*

The word '*du'ā*' is the verbal noun (*maṣdar*) of the verb '*da'ā*', which signifies 'to call out, to summon.'[9]

The word '*du'ā*' is mentioned in the Qur'ān to signify a number of meanings, as the following verses show:

1. Worship.

وَلَا تَدْعُ مِن دُونِ ٱللَّهِ مَا لَا يَنفَعُكَ وَلَا يَضُرُّكَ

"And do not call besides Allāh that which will not harm you or benefit you..."[10]

2. The seeking of aid.

وَٱدْعُواْ شُهَدَآءَكُم مِّن دُونِ ٱللَّهِ

"And call upon your witnesses besides Allāh..."[11]

3. A request.

ٱدْعُونِىٓ أَسْتَجِبْ لَكُمْ

"And call upon Me, for I will answer your prayers..."[12]

---

9 Ibn Manẓūr, *Lisān al-Arab* , 14/258. Also see Hans-Wher, p. 282.

10 Sūrah *Yūnus*, 106.

11 Sūrah *al-Baqarah*, 23.

12 Sūrah *Ghāfir,* 60.

4. A call.

يَوْمَ يَدْعُوكُمْ

"The day that He will call you..."[13]

5. Praise.

قُلِ ٱدْعُوا۟ ٱللَّهَ أَوِ ٱدْعُوا۟ ٱلرَّحْمَٰنَ

"Say, 'Call upon Allāh, or call upon *al-Raḥmān*..."[14]

6. Speech.

دَعْوَىٰهُمْ فِيهَا سُبْحَٰنَكَ ٱللَّهُمَّ

"Their speech therein will be: 'Glory be to you, O Allāh!'"[15]

7. A question.

ٱدْعُ لَنَا رَبَّكَ يُبَيِّن لَّنَا مَا هِىَ

"Call on your Lord so that He can clarify to us what it is…"[16]

And other meanings besides these.

As for its Islamic meaning, various scholars have defined it in similar terms.

Al-Khaṭṭabī said: "The meaning of *duʿā* is the servant's asking his Lord for His Help, and asking His continued support. Its essence is that a person shows his neediness to Allāh, and frees himself from any power or ability to change (any matter by himself). This characteristic is the mark of servitude, and in it is the feeling of human submissiveness. *Duʿā also* carries the meaning of praising Allāh, and attributing to Him Generosity and Bounteousness."[17]

---

13 Sūrah *al-Isrā'*, 52.

14 Sūrah *al-Isrā',* 110.

15 Sūrah *Yūnus*, 10.

16 Sūrah *al-Baqarah*, 68.

17 *Sha'n ad-Duʿā*, p. 4.

Ibn al-Qayyim defined it as, "Asking what is of benefit to the person, and asking the removal of what is harming him, or (asking) the repelling of it (before it afflicts him)".[18]

Another scholar wrote: "The appeal to Allāh, all Glory be to Him, of a request, by asking Him with desire for all good that is with Him, and to be submissive to Him in asking what is desired and in obtaining what is hoped for."[19]

2. *Du'ā* is a Form of Worship

Allāh, all Glory and Praise be to Him, has said:

وَقَالَ رَبُّكُمُ ٱدْعُونِىٓ أَسْتَجِبْ لَكُمْ
إِنَّ ٱلَّذِينَ يَسْتَكْبِرُونَ عَنْ عِبَادَتِى سَيَدْخُلُونَ جَهَنَّمَ
دَاخِرِينَ ﴿٦٠﴾

> Verily, your Lord has said: "Call upon Me, and I will answer you!" Those who are arrogant to worship Allāh will enter Hell, humiliated![20]

In this verse, Allāh has commanded us to ask Him and petition Him, and counted those who do not ask Him among those who are too arrogant to worship Allāh. From this, it is understood that *du'ā* is among the acts of worship, and this meaning was explicitly stated by the Prophet (ﷺ). Nu'mān ibn Bashīr reports that the Prophet (ﷺ) said:

> "*Du'ā* is worship".

He (ﷺ) then recited the verse:

---

[18] *Badā'i al-Fawā'id*, 3/2.

[19] This definition is taken from *Kitāb al-Du'ā* by Dr. Muḥammad al-Sayed Ṭanṭāwī.

[20] Sūrah *Ghāfir*, 60.

وَقَالَ رَبُّكُمُ ٱدْعُونِىٓ أَسْتَجِبْ لَكُمْ
إِنَّ ٱلَّذِينَ يَسْتَكْبِرُونَ عَنْ عِبَادَتِى سَيَدْخُلُونَ جَهَنَّمَ
دَاخِرِينَ ﴿٦٠﴾

> "Verily, your Lord has said: "Call upon Me, and I will answer you!" Those who are (too) arrogant to worship Allāh will enter Hell, humiliated!"[21]

Therefore, *du῾ā* is a type of worship; rather, it is amongst the greatest acts of worship, and one of the best ways to bring a worshipper closer to Allāh, all Glory and Praise be to Him. In this verse, Allāh has equated *du῾ā* with worship, for He commanded His servants to make *du῾ā* to Him, and then stated that whoever is too arrogant to *worship* Him will enter the Fire of Hell. So from this it is understood that the worship referred to in this verse actually means *du῾ā*.

In another verse, Allāh calls *du῾ā* the '*dīn*' or the entire religion, for He says:

هُوَ ٱلْحَىُّ لَآ إِلَٰهَ إِلَّا هُوَ فَٱدْعُوهُ مُخْلِصِينَ لَهُ ٱلدِّينَ ۗ

> He is the *Ḥayy* (Ever-Living), there is no deity except Him. So make *du῾ā* to Him, to Him is the *dīn*.[22]

And there is no other act that has been equated or paralleled with the entire *dīn*, or connected to the entire concept of worship (*'ibādah*).

One of the benefits that are obtained by realising that *du῾ā* is a form of worship is that the manner and procedure of *du῾ā* must only be taken from the Qur'ān and Sunnah. Just as a person cannot use his mind or whims to decide how to pray or fast, so too must he restrain himself to the texts of the Qur'ān and Sunnah when it comes to the manner and etiquette of *du῾ā*.

---

[21] This ḥadīth is authentic, and is reported by Aḥmad and the four *Sunans*, and others, from Nu῾mān ibn Bashīr, as reported in *Ṣaḥīḥ al-Jāmi῾* # 3407.

[22] Sūrah *Ghāfir,* 65.

3. *Duʿā* and its Relationship to *ʿAqīdah*

Duʿā has a very strong relationship with one's *ʿaqīdah* (creed) and *tawḥīd*.[23] *Duʿā* is also one of the best ways that a person can increase his *īmān* (faith), and appreciate Allāh's Names and Attributes. It is a powerful reminder of man's inherent incapability, and Allāh's unlimited powers.

Duʿā increases a person's *īmān* (faith) due to many factors. It makes evident the fact that a person has absolutely no control over his destiny, nor does he have the power to benefit himself or avert any evil from him. It shows the neediness that a Muslim feels towards his Lord. It proves that the one making *duʿā* sincerely believes that Allāh hears his *duʿā*, and will respond to it. Such a person must also affirm Allāh's Infinite Mercy, Beneficence and Generosity. And the more a person increases in the realisation of his poverty towards the Mercy of his Lord, the more he will increase in his *īmān* as well. Likewise, the more a person appreciates and realizes the perfection of Allāh's Names and Attributes, so too will he increase in his *īmān*. These two factors – knowing one's need of Allāh in every matter, and knowing Allāh's Perfect Nature – are the essence of *īmān* and servitude to Allāh.

The one making *duʿā* openly affirms his *īmān* for Allāh, for it shows that he believes in Allāh, and that Allāh, and only Allāh, can listen and answer his prayers.

Another way in which the importance of *duʿā* can be demonstrated is by showing that *duʿā* is an implicit affirmation of *tawḥīd* in all of its aspects.[24]

---

[23] This topic will only be briefly touched upon in this book. The reader is referred to the master's dissertation by al-Arūsī on the topic.

[24] *Tawḥīd* is the Unification of Allāh in His Existence and Lordship (known as *Tawḥīd al-Rubūbiyyah*), in His Perfect Essence and Attributes (*Tawḥīd al-Asmā' wa l-Ṣifāt*), and in His right to be worshipped (*Tawḥīd al-Ulūhiyyah*). *Tawḥīd* is the *essence* of Islām, and the first and final call of all of Allāh's prophets. The reader is referred to Dr. Bilāl Philip's *Fundamentals of Tawḥeed* (al-Hidaayah Publishing & Distribution, United Kingdom, 1999), for further details.

When one makes a *duʿā* to Allāh, one is implicitly acknowledging that Allāh exists, and that He is the true Lord. The person so doing is stating by his actions that Allāh controls all matters, for only Allāh has the power and capability to respond to his *duʿā*. He is admitting that Allāh is the Nourisher, Sustainer, Creator and Master of the entire creation, and all of this is the essence of *Tawḥīd al-Rubūbiyyah*. Even when a non-Muslim makes a *duʿā* to Allāh (even if it is by another name), he affirms all of these concepts as well. It is because of this affirmation that it is possible that a non-Muslim's *duʿā* is answered as well, for the response of a *duʿā* relates to *Tawḥīd al-Rubūbiyyah*. Allāh mentions in numerous verses in the Qur'ān (some of which will be mentioned later) that disbelievers call out to Him at times of need, and yet, when He responds to their *duʿā*, they worship others besides Him. So the point is that Allāh does respond to the *duʿā* of the *ḳāfir* (unbeliever) as well as the Muslim, for both turn to Allāh recognising that only Allāh can grant them what they desire. However, the *duʿā* of the Muslim has a greater chance of being accepted, for he calls out *only* to Allāh, whereas the *ḳāfir* calls out to others besides Allāh, turning to Allāh only when he is in great distress. Also, the fact that Allāh responds to the *duʿā* of the *ḳāfir* does not in any way imply that He is pleased with him, or that he will be saved from the fire of Hell. Rather, it shows that Allāh is the *Rabb*, the true Lord of both the Muslim and *ḳāfir*, and it shows that He is *al-Raḥmān*, the Ever-Merciful, for He shows Mercy to the Muslim in this life and the Hereafter, and He shows some Mercy to the *ḳāfir* in this life. Were it not for this Mercy, the *ḳāfir* would not even be blessed with a morsel of food or a sip of water. And this general mercy entails that Allāh responds occasionally to the *duʿā* of a *ḳāfir*, especially when it emanates from a heart that has turned sincerely and desperately towards Allāh.

Duʿā also necessitates that only Allāh deserves to be worshipped (*Tawḥīd al-Ulūhiyyah*), for if only Allāh has complete control over creation, and if only He can respond to the call of the one in distress, then only He deserves our complete submission and worship.

Duʿā also obligates that Allāh has the most Perfect Names and Attributes (*Tawḥīd al-Asmā' wa l-Ṣifāt*). For only He can hear the whispering plea of the servant, no matter where the servant is, and only He can understand the situation that the servant is in. His knowledge is far more complete than the knowledge of the servant himself concerning the plight that he is in. Likewise, only Allāh has the complete power and ultimate authority in granting what the servant desires.

So *duʿā* is a powerful indication of *tawḥīd* in all of its three aspects.

4. *Duʿā* to other than Allāh is *Shirk*

From what has preceded, it is clear that *duʿā* can only be directed towards Allāh alone.

قُلْ إِنَّمَآ أَدْعُواْ رَبِّى وَلَآ أُشْرِكُ بِهِۦٓ أَحَدًا ﴿٢٠﴾

> Say (O Muḥammad): "I make *duʿā* only to my Lord (Allāh alone), and I associate none as partners along with Him."[25]

To make *duʿā* to other than Allāh is pure *shirk* (associating partners with Allāh), which is the one sin that Allāh will not forgive.

This is due to the fact that the one that makes a *duʿā* to other than Allāh is in fact attributing to a created object characteristics and attributes that only Allāh has. So, the person who makes a *duʿā* to a saint, or rock, or idol, believes that that object can hear him, and has eternal life, and is capable of responding to his invocation, and has knowledge of his situation, and can see the state that he is in, and has mercy upon him, and has the power to grant him what he wishes. Yet, the perfection of all of these attributes is only with Allāh. It is only Allāh Who can hear everything, in fact, Allāh knows our very thoughts even if we do not vocalise them. It is only Allāh Who knows our situation perfectly, and has a Divine Mercy for us, and is All-Powerful in responding to our requests. Allāh describes all other objects to which *duʿā* is made in the following verse:

---

25 Sūrah *al-Jinn*, 20

إِن تَدْعُوهُمْ لَا يَسْمَعُوا دُعَاءَكُمْ وَلَوْ سَمِعُوا مَا اسْتَجَابُوا لَكُمْ ۖ
وَيَوْمَ الْقِيَامَةِ يَكْفُرُونَ بِشِرْكِكُمْ ۚ وَلَا يُنَبِّئُكَ مِثْلُ خَبِيرٍ

If you invoke (or call upon) them, they hear not your call, and even if they were to hear (you), they could not grant your (request) to you. And on the Day of Resurrection, they will disown your worshipping them. And none can inform you (O Muḥammad) like Him Who is the All-Knower (of each and everything)[26]

So the object that is called upon besides Allāh, whether it is an idol or a dead saint, cannot hear such calls in the first place. They do not have the perfect Attribute that *al-Samīʿ* (The Hearer of Everything) has, and even if they are alive and have a sense of hearing, this sense is extremely limited, for they can only hear within a very small distance, if the voice is loud enough. Can such restricted hearing be compared in any way to the attributes of *al-Samīʿ*? Allāh then states that, even if they could hear such calls, they would not be able to respond to them. Thus because these objects simply do not have the power or capability to respond to any requests. Allāh describes these worshipped objects as:

يَدْعُوا مِن دُونِ اللَّهِ مَا لَا يَضُرُّهُ
وَمَا لَا يَنفَعُهُ ۚ ذَٰلِكَ هُوَ الضَّلَالُ الْبَعِيدُ ﴿١٢﴾ يَدْعُوا لَمَن
ضَرُّهُ أَقْرَبُ مِن نَّفْعِهِ ۚ لَبِئْسَ الْمَوْلَىٰ وَلَبِئْسَ الْعَشِيرُ ﴿١٣﴾

He calls besides Allāh that which hurts him not nor profits him. That is a straying far away. He calls unto him whose harm is nearer than this profit: certainly, an evil *mawla* (patron) and certainly an evil friend! [27]

---

[26] Sūrah *al-Fāṭir*, 14

[27] Sūrah *al-Ḥajj*, 12-13

So the person calling an object besides Allāh is in reality calling something that can neither benefit him nor harm him in this world. Although these objects can, in and of themselves cause no harm, by calling them instead of Allāh, a person brings harm upon himself by committing *shirk*, so what an evil and foolish act it is. As Allāh says:

وَمَنْ أَضَلُّ مِمَّن يَدْعُواْ مِن دُونِ ٱللَّهِ مَن
لَّا يَسْتَجِيبُ لَهُۥٓ إِلَىٰ يَوْمِ ٱلْقِيَٰمَةِ وَهُمْ عَن دُعَآئِهِمْ غَٰفِلُونَ ﴿٥﴾

And who is more astray than one who makes a du'ā to other than Allāh - who will not answer him until the Day of Resurrection, and who are (even) unaware of their du'ās to them? [28]

The object that is called besides Allāh does not even know it is being called, and if *du'ā* were made to them until the Day of Judgement, nothing would occur!

In fact, look at the example that Allāh gave of the one who calls to other than Allāh:

قُلْ أَنَدْعُواْ مِن دُونِ ٱللَّهِ
مَا لَا يَنفَعُنَا وَلَا يَضُرُّنَا وَنُرَدُّ عَلَىٰٓ أَعْقَابِنَا بَعْدَ إِذْ هَدَىٰنَا ٱللَّهُ
كَٱلَّذِى ٱسْتَهْوَتْهُ ٱلشَّيَٰطِينُ فِى ٱلْأَرْضِ حَيْرَانَ لَهُۥٓ أَصْحَٰبٌ
يَدْعُونَهُۥٓ إِلَى ٱلْهُدَى ٱئْتِنَا ۗ قُلْ إِنَّ هُدَى ٱللَّهِ هُوَ ٱلْهُدَىٰ ۖ
وَأُمِرْنَا لِنُسْلِمَ لِرَبِّ ٱلْعَٰلَمِينَ ﴿٧١﴾

Say (O Muḥammad (ﷺ)): "Shall we invoke others besides Allāh (false deities), that can do us neither good nor harm, and shall we turn on our heels after Allāh has guided us? Like one whom the devils have made to go astray, confused (wandering) through the earth, his companions calling him to guidance (saying): 'Come to us.'" Say: "Verily, Allāh's Guidance

[28] Sūrah *al-Aḥqāf*, 5

> is the only guidance, and we have been commanded to submit (ourselves) to the Lord of the Worlds."[29]

So from all this it is apparent that anyone who makes a *duʿā* to other than Allāh has committed a form of major *shirk*, rather, the greatest form of *shirk*!

وَمَن يَدْعُ مَعَ ٱللَّهِ إِلَـٰهًا ءَاخَرَ لَا بُرْهَـٰنَ لَهُۥ بِهِۦ
فَإِنَّمَا حِسَابُهُۥ عِندَ رَبِّهِۦٓ ۚ إِنَّهُۥ لَا يُفْلِحُ ٱلْكَـٰفِرُونَ ﴿١١٧﴾

> And whoever makes a *duʿā* to (or worships) other than Allāh, any other god, of whom he has no proof, then his reckoning is only with his Lord. Surely, the disbelivers will not be successful.[30]

It is irrelevant what excuses, or distorted logic, those that make *duʿā* to others alongside Allāh use to try to justify this *shirk*, for the reality of an act is not affected by invented names given to it. So you find some of them claiming that they are only calling out to 'holy' people, whereas others use the concept of intercession (*shafāʿah*) to justify this *shirk*. Yet others pervert the correct understanding of *tabarruk* (seeking blessings from an object), while others use the concept of *tawassul* (seeking a means of nearness to Allāh). No matter what means a person seeks to use, the fact should be clear to everyone that to call upon a dead person, or an angel, or a prophet, or a rock or stone, or a deity other than Allāh, is the *essence* of *shirk*, concerning which there is no difference of opinion amongst Muslims. This type of *shirk* is the worst type, for it is directing the greatest act of worship to other than Allāh. A person who commits this type of *shirk* has removed himself from the fold of Islām, and this act of his is no different from prostrating to an idol.[31]

Despite the clarity of this type of *shirk*, it is appalling to note that such acts are rampant amongst many Muslim societies and cul-

---

[29] Sūrah *al-Anʿām*, 71

[30] Sūrah al-*Mu'minūn*, 117

[31] Abū Zayd, p. 248.

tures. It is possible to hear a person who believes that he is Muslim, and might even be praying or fasting, call out, 'O ʿAbd al-Qādir al-Jīlanī! Save me!' And here is another one that makes a *duʿā*, 'O Badawī! O Tījānī! O Rifāʿī![32] Guide me! Help me! Give me my sustenance! Take care of my needs!' And yet a third might say, 'O Muḥammad, (ﷺ)! Grant me a righteous child!' So they call out to 'pious' saints, believing that these saints have the power to respond to their *duʿās*, or that they have a right over Allāh that Allāh answers their prayers.

Another manifestation of this evil is the culture of grave-worship that is predominant in certain Muslim countries. The erecting of beautiful structures over the graves of 'holy' people, and travelling distances to visit these graves, is forbidden in Islām for the very reason that such glorification leads to *shirk*. It is even prohibited to pray (perfrom ṣalāt) in front of a grave, even though the ṣalāt is to Allāh, so what is the case of the one who actually makes a *duʿā* to the dead?

Similarly, others use these dead 'saints' as intercessors between them and Allāh, thinking that, by using these people as intermediaries, their *duʿās* will have a stronger chance of being accepted by Allāh. This act of theirs is based on their own ignorance, for the Arabs at the time of the Prophet (ﷺ) would worship their idols with the exact same excuse – that they were only trying to come closer to Allāh – and yet, despite this excuse, Allāh considered them to be committing *shirk*. The reason for this being that the pure concept of *tawḥīd* in Islām does not allow for *any* intermediaries between man and Allāh when it comes to the worship of Allāh. Worship is a right that is due *only* to Allāh, and it is *shirk* to divert any act of worship to other than Allāh.

To conclude, *duʿā* is one of the greatest acts of worship, and therefore to make a *duʿā* to other than Allāh is the *essence* of *shirk*. And

32 These are all names of Sūfi 'saints.' Although it is possible that some of these personalities might have been pious servants of Allāh, there is no doubt that what their followers are doing is major *shirk*.

there is no difference in making *du'ā* to a prophet, or an angel, or a pious person, or to a grave, a star, a rock, or a stone; all of these are created objects, and cannot compare in any way to Allāh. Likewise, there is no difference if a person makes *du'ā* to them or uses them as intermediaries between him and Allāh; both of these acts are manifestations of *shirk*.[33]

[33] For further details of *shirk*, its dangers, types and categories, see the author's *Explanation of Shaykh Muḥammad ibn 'Abdul Wahhāb's Kashf al-Shubuhāt - A Critical Study of Shirk* (Al-Hidaayah Publishing & Distribution, Birmingham, UK, 2003 CE).

CHAPTER II

The Types of *Duʿās*

Duʿā can be categorised in a variety of ways, depending on the perspective that one is using. Some of the more useful categorisations are as follows:

1. With Respect to the Actuality of *Duʿā*

When one examines the texts of the Qur'ān and sunnah, one finds that there are two types of *duʿās* that are mentioned.

The first type, which is the one that most people are familiar with, is known as *duʿā al-mas'alah*, or the '*duʿā* of asking'. This is when a person asks to be given something that is of benefit to him, or asks that some harm be removed from him. So the worshipper asks Allāh to fulfil a need; for example, he says, "O Allāh! Grant me good in this world, and good in the Hereafter!" So this is an example of *duʿā al-mas'alah*.

The second type of *duʿā* is known as *duʿā al-ʿibādah*, or the '*duʿā* of worship'. This is a very broad concept, for every single act of worship includes in it this type of *duʿā*. Every praise that a person pronounces, every prayer that he performs, is done with an intrinsic plea and cry that emanates from the heart of every believer: "O Allāh! I am doing this act of worship because you are All-Mighty and Powerful! You are the only one that deserves all types of praise! O Allāh! Accept this act from me!" Therefore, when a person says, '*Alḥamdulillah*' or '*Subḥān Allāh*', this can be taken to be examples of *duʿā al-ʿibādah*. When a person prays the ṣalāt, or gives zakāt, or fasts, all of these are examples of *duʿā al-ʿibādah*.

These two types of *duʿās* are inherently related to one another. Every *duʿā al-mas'alah* intrinsically contains a *duʿā al-ʿibādah*, and every *duʿā al-ʿibādah* necessitates a *duʿā al-mas'alah*. To clarify this expression, two examples are given.

When the Muslim prays, "O Allāh! Bless me with pious offspring", then this is a clear example of a *duʿā al-mas'alah*, as he is asking for some benefit. However, this simple *duʿā* implies, without him saying anything, that Allāh is the One Who hears his prayer, and responds to it, and He is the One that gives sustenance, and blesses people with offspring. It implies that Allāh is the Ever-Living, the Giver of life, the Ever-Merciful who responds to His servants. This simple *duʿā* necessitates that the person who makes it attributes to Allāh many beautiful and perfect attributes. Thus, this *duʿā al-mas'alah* intrinsically contains *duʿā al-ʿibādah* at the same time.

As a second example, a person says, '*Lā ḥawla wa lā quwwata illa billāh*' or, 'There is no change or power except with the (help and will) of Allāh.' At face value, this expression, is a *duʿā al-ʿibādah*, as nothing is actually being asked from Allāh. However, this expression necessitates that a person make *duʿā al-mas'alah* to Allāh. When a person affirms that there is no power, nor is it possible to change anything, except with the Will and Permission of Allāh, then this automatically necessitates that he ask Allāh, and only Allāh, whenever he wishes to achieve something. So, this *duʿā al-ʿibādah* necessitates *duʿā al-mas'alah*.

So whenever the word '*duʿā*' occurs in the Qur'ān and Sunnah, it has one of three possibilities: it either refers to both types of *duʿā*, or it refers to *duʿā al-mas'alah*, or it refers to *duʿā al-ʿibādah*.

An example in which the word '*duʿā*' refers to both types of *duʿā* is:

قُلْ مَا يَعْبَؤُا بِكُمْ رَبِّي
لَوْلَا دُعَآؤُكُمْ فَقَدْ كَذَّبْتُمْ فَسَوْفَ يَكُونُ لِزَامًا ﴿٧٧﴾

> Say (O Muḥammad): My Lord only pays attention to you because of your *duʿā* to Him. But now you have indeed rejected (Him), so the (torment) will be yours permanently.[34]

This verse includes *duʿā al-mas'alah* and *duʿā al-ʿibādah*; in other words, the reason that Allāh pays attention to us is because of our worship (*duʿā al-ʿibādah*) and asking (*duʿā al-mas'alah*) that we do of Him.

An example in which the word '*duʿā*' primarily refers to *duʿā al-mas'alah* is:

أَمَّن يُجِيبُ ٱلْمُضْطَرَّ إِذَا دَعَاهُ

> Or who is there that responds to the call (*duʿā*) of the one in distress (besides Allāh)?[35]

An example in which it primarily refers to *duʿā al-ʿibādah* is:

يَٰٓأَيُّهَا ٱلنَّاسُ ضُرِبَ مَثَلٌ فَٱسْتَمِعُوا۟ لَهُۥٓ ۚ إِنَّ ٱلَّذِينَ
تَدْعُونَ مِن دُونِ ٱللَّهِ لَن يَخْلُقُوا۟ ذُبَابًا وَلَوِ ٱجْتَمَعُوا۟ لَهُۥ ۖ

> O Mankind! An example has been set forth, so listen to it. Those that you call (i.e. worship) besides Allāh will never be able to create a fly, even if they all united to do it".[36]

However, even though the direct references in the last two verses are only to *one* type of *duʿā*, indirectly both types are included, as they are inherently related to one another.

2. With Respect to the One Being Asked

Duʿā is, by its very nature, a call or request to another being. Therefore, it is possible to categorise *duʿā* with respect to the one being asked, for it is possible that the one that is being asked is Allāh, and it is possible that it is a false deity. It is also possible that

---

34 Sūrah *al-Furqān*, 77.

35 Sūrah *al-Naml*, 62.

36 Sūrah *al-Ḥajj*, 73.

the person making *duʿā* combines *duʿā al-mas'alah* and *duʿā al-ʿibādah* to the same deity at all times, or he differentiates between them.

So this leads to four categories of people, as follows:

The first category are those people who worship other than Allāh, and call out to these others at all times. These people do not acknowledge Allāh as the Lord or One that deserves worship. Examples of this category are the Hindus, Buddhists, and the followers of other religions who do not believe in Allāh in the first place. So these people direct their *duʿā al-ʿibādah* and *duʿā al-mas'alah* to other than Allāh.

The second category are those who believe in Allāh, and worship Him, yet never ask anything of Him. Instead, basing their idea on perverted logic, they use intermediaries in order to approach Allāh, and ask these intermediaries to bless them with what they need. The extreme Sūfi groups are notorious for this type of act, for they usually ask dead 'saints' and prophets to bless them with what they need. Therefore, their *duʿā al-ʿibādah* (in the broad sense) is to Allāh, but their *duʿā al-mas'alah* is to other than Allāh.

The third category are those people who believe in Allāh, and worship Him, but only turn to Him at times of severity. When they are in extremely desperate situations, they combine their *duʿā al-ʿibādah* and *duʿā al-mas'alah* to Allāh, but at times of ease, they call out to other than Allāh. And this was the religion of the *Jāhilīyyah* Arabs at the time of the Prophet(ﷺ).[37]

The last category are the true Muslims, those that always combine *duʿā al-ʿibādah* and *duʿā al-mas'alah*, and direct it to Allāh, and only to Allāh. So they direct their worship, prayer, and charity, to Allāh, and they turn to Him only for all of their needs.

---

[37] For a more detailed discussion of these categories, see *An Explanation of Muḥammad ibn ʿAbdul Wahhāb's Four Principles of Shirk*, by the author (Al-Hidaayah Publishing & Distribution, Birmingham, UK, 2003 CE).

3. With Respect to the One Making *Du'ā*

When one looks at the different categories of people that make *du'ā*, it is possible to classify them into four categories.[38] This is because *du'ā*, as has been mentioned, is of two types, *du'ā al-'ibādah* and *du'ā al-mas'alah*. Therefore, it is possible to have four logical combinations of these categories with regards to the one making *du'ā*, for he can either combine both types of *du'ā*, or practice only one type, or leave both types. (Note that this categorisation contains some overlap with the preceding one, but at the same time is unique, as it deals with the one *asking*, and not the one *that is asked*).

The first category of people are those who combine both types of *du'ā*, and this is the way of the true Muslim. So he worships Allāh, realising that this worship is the purpose of his creation and being, and he seeks Allāh's help in this worship, realising that without this help he will not be able to achieve this goal. Therefore, he has combined *du'ā al-'ibādah* with *du'ā al-mas'alah*.

Allāh combined these two types of *du'ās* in numerous verses in the Qur'ān, the simplest of them being the oft-recited verse:

إِيَّاكَ نَعْبُدُ وَإِيَّاكَ نَسْتَعِينُ ﴿٥﴾

> You (alone) do we worship, and You alone do we seek help from.[39]

So this verse clearly shows the important relationship between *du'ā al-'ibādah*, and *du'ā al-mas'alah*, and the wise person is he who understands and acts upon both of these types of *du'ā* in his life.

The second category of people are those that have left both types of *du'ā*, so they neither worship Allāh, nor seek His help or aid in any matter. So in this category fall the people that worship false deities, believing these deities to be worthy of their *du'ā al-'ibādah* and *du'ā al-mas'alah*. They never turn to Allāh, and thus have lost this world and the Hereafter.

---

[38] Al-Arūsi, pp. 153-155.

[39] Sūrah *al-Fātiḥah*, 5.

Also, those that have rejected religion entirely, such as the communists, atheists and agnostics, fall into this category as well. To such people, the only way to achieve any goal is through physical means, for in their rejection of a god they have implicitly worshipped creation. And these are the worst of mankind.

The third category are those people that practice *duʿā al-ʿibādah*, but ignore *duʿā al-mas'alah*. Such thinking can only come from an ignorant person, or one who is deviated in his beliefs.

As for the ignorant Muslim – and unfortunately how common they are in our times – then he forgets that the real way and sure path to achieve his goal is by making *duʿā* to Allāh. He becomes so caught up in this world that, although he might pray and fast and give zakāt, he forgets the *spiritual* aspect of Islām, and the beauty of the Names and Attributes of Allāh. To such a person, Islām becomes a series of mundane acts, devoid of any meaning, performed at regular intervals. Such a person needs to re-evaluate his concept of Islām, and even of life, in order that he can correct his misunderstanding. He must ponder over the meanings of the Names and Attributes of Allāh, and realise the ultimate Power and Knowledge of the Creator, and only then will he be able to see the error of his ways. He must realise that every act he does, whether it is related to this world or the Hereafter, must be done with the help and aid of Allāh, for if Allāh does not help him in achieving what he desires, he will never be able to achieve it.

As for the person who actually *believes* that it is incorrect to use *duʿā al-mas'alah*, and instead restricts himself to *duʿā al-ʿibādah*, then such a person without a doubt has committed a grave mistake. These people are only found in deviated sects – sects that have perverted the meanings of the Qur'ān and Sunnah in order to justify their positions. Examples of this are the extreme Sūfis, for many of them believe that it is actually a *sin* to ask Allāh for anything! Basing this belief on a few fabricated *aḥādīth*,[40] they claim that a person

---

[40] See the last chapter of this work for an example of such an ḥadīth.

must always be content with what Allāh decrees for him, and therefore should not pray for a change in his situation! The falseness of this logic is in their understanding of 'contentment,' for to be content with Allāh means that one should not curse the Divine Decree, or be angry at Allāh for what has occurred. It does *not* mean that one must be happy and satisfied at every incident that occurs to one, particularly if it is related to a sin or an evil pertaining to one's religion. In addition, we find that all Allāh's prophets, without exception, made *duʿā* to Allāh for all matters. Therefore, this understanding of the extreme *Sūfīs* is not in accordance with the understanding of the prophets.

The fourth, and final, category are those people that ignore *duʿā al-ʿibādah*, and only practice *duʿā al-mas'alah*. Such people believe in Allāh, but follow their own selfish desires, and strive in order to satisfy their every whim. So they leave worship of Allāh, but they realise that Allāh is the Controller of all affairs, and, therefore, ask Him for their selfish needs.

The primary example of this is Iblīs, *Ṣhayṭān* himself, may Allāh's eternal curse be upon him. For when he was expelled from Paradise due to his arrogance, he actually made a *duʿā* to Allāh - *duʿā al-mas'alah* – to allow him to live until the Day of Judgement. And Allāh responded to his *duʿā* and granted him his wish, even though Iblīs knew full well that this time that he was granted would only be used to mislead others, out of his spite and jealousy. So Iblīs left *duʿā al-ʿibādah* out of arrogance, but was forced to use *duʿā al-mas'alah* out of greed.

Likewise, all those who have preferred the life of this world over the Hereafter have fallen into the same mistake as Iblīs.

Allāh states in the Qur'ān:

فَمِنَ ٱلنَّاسِ مَن
يَقُولُ رَبَّنَآ ءَاتِنَا فِى ٱلدُّنْيَا وَمَا لَهُۥ فِى ٱلْـَٔاخِرَةِ مِنْ
خَلَـٰقٍ ﴿٢٠٠﴾ وَمِنْهُم مَّن يَقُولُ رَبَّنَآ ءَاتِنَا فِى ٱلدُّنْيَا

حَسَنَةً وَفِي ٱلْأَخِرَةِ حَسَنَةً وَقِنَا عَذَابَ ٱلنَّارِ ﴿٢٠١﴾
أُوْلَٰٓئِكَ لَهُمْ نَصِيبٌ مِّمَّا كَسَبُواْۚ وَٱللَّهُ سَرِيعُ ٱلْحِسَابِ ﴿٢٠٢﴾

> And there are those amongst mankind who say, 'O Allāh! Give us in this life,' and they will have no share of the Hereafter. And there are those who say, 'O Allāh! Give us good in this life, and good in the Hereafter, and save us from the Fire of Hell!' These shall have a share of what they earned, and Allāh is swift in Reckoning.[41]

So these are the four categories of people when it comes to practicing both categories of *duʿā*.

4. With Respect to What is Asked

The actual *duʿā* itself can be categorised in many different ways, depending on which perspective one looks from.

So, it is possible to divide what is asked for into two categories: matters pertaining to religion, and matters pertaining to the world. Examples of the first type are to ask for increased faith, or an increase in good deeds, or forgiveness for one's sins. Examples of the second category are to ask for an increase in money, or to be cured from a disease, or to be granted more children.

The true Muslim asks Allāh from both of these categories, realising that the good pertaining to this world is in reality a means of attaining the good in the Hereafter. So, an increase in wealth, children, and health is in fact a means of coming closer to Allāh by obeying His commandments and sacrificing in His way. On the other hand, ignorant and deviated Muslims will only ask Allāh for one of these two categories, ignoring the other.

Another way to categorise what is asked for is by examining the benefit or harm it causes. So, it is possible to state that the entire *duʿā* of all of creation centres around four pillars:

---

[41] Sūrah *al-Baqarah*, 201-202.

Firstly: good that exists. For example, one might be in a state of good health, or have great wealth. So *duʿā* is made that this state lasts, and is not taken away.

Secondly: good that is desired. For example, a person does not have good health, but wishes for it. This is asked for by means of *duʿā*.

Thirdly: evil that exists. For example, a person might be sick, or suffer from poverty. So *duʿā* is made that this situation be changed.

Fourthly: evil that does not exist. For example, a person might fear a certain disease, or another trial. So *duʿā* is made that this evil never occurs, and is averted.

All of these four types of *duʿā* are combined in the comprehensive *duʿā* that is found in the last verses of Sūrah *Āl-ʿImrān*:

رَبَّنَا فَٱغْفِرْ لَنَا ذُنُوبَنَا وَكَفِّرْ عَنَّا
سَيِّـَٔاتِنَا وَتَوَفَّنَا مَعَ ٱلْأَبْرَارِ ﴿١٩٣﴾ رَبَّنَا وَءَاتِنَا مَا وَعَدتَّنَا
عَلَىٰ رُسُلِكَ وَلَا تُخْزِنَا يَوْمَ ٱلْقِيَـٰمَةِ ۗ إِنَّكَ لَا تُخْلِفُ ٱلْمِيعَادَ ﴿١٩٤﴾

> Our Lord! Forgive us our sins, and remit us from our evil deeds, and cause us to die in a state of righteousness. Our Lord! Grant us what you promised us through Your messengers, and do not disgrace us on the Day of Judgement, for You never break Your promise.[42]

So the phrase, 'Forgive us our sins, and remit us from our evil deeds' is a *duʿā* that an existing evil be removed. And the phrase, 'and cause us to die in a state of righteousness', is a *duʿā* asking that an existing good, that of the presence of *īmān,* continue and not be taken away until death. And the phrase, 'Grant us what you promised us through Your messengers', is a *duʿā* for a good that does not yet exist to be given. Lastly, the phrase, 'do not disgrace us on the Day of Judgement', is a *duʿā* to avert an evil that does not exist.

---

[42] Sūrah *Āl-ʿImrān,* 193-194.

CHAPTER III

The Excellence and Benefits of *Duʿā*

Duʿā is the most noble act in the sight of Allāh, all Glory and Praise be to Him. This is recognised in the ḥadīth narrated by Abū Hurayrah in which the Prophet (ﷺ) said:

> "There is nothing that is more noble in the sight of Allāh than *duʿā*".[43]

This is due to the fact that *duʿā* is a means of showing one's poverty and incapability to Allāh. It is a manner of humiliating one's self to Allāh and acknowledging the power and capabilities of Allāh, all Glory and Praise be to Him. This has already been mentioned in the ḥadīth we quoted wherein *duʿā* is a part of worship.

Some of the benefits of *duʿā* are as follows:[44]

1. *Duʿā* is the Most Noble of all Acts in the Sight of Allāh

This is based on the above ḥadīth: "There is nothing that is more noble in the sight of Allāh than *duʿā*".[45] Al-Shawkānī[46] commented

---

[43] Authentic, narrated by Aḥmad, al-Tirmidhī, al-Ḥākim, and others, all of them from Abū Hurayrah, as has been mentioned in *Ṣaḥīḥ al-Jāmiʿ* # 5392.

[44] See: *al-Duʿā*, al-Ḥamad, pp. 16-19.

[45] Authentic, narrated by Aḥmad, al-Tirmidhī, al-Ḥākim, and others, all of them from Abū Hurayrah, as has been mentioned in *Ṣaḥīḥ al-Jāmiʿ* # 5392.

[46] *Tuḥfat al-Dhākirīn*, p. 30.

on this ḥadīth by stating: "It has been said that this is the case because of the fact that it shows the Power of Allāh, and the incapability of the one making *duʿā*. But it is more correct to say that since *duʿā* is worship, and, as confirmed in another ḥadīth, the essence of worship, it is the most noble act because of this position. This because mankind has only been created to worship Allāh, as Allāh states,

وَمَا خَلَقْتُ ٱلْجِنَّ وَٱلْإِنسَ إِلَّا لِيَعْبُدُونِ ﴿٥٦﴾

"And I have not created *jinn* and man except to worship Me".[47]

2. *Duʿā* is the Best Act of Worship

Duʿā is the most beloved and greatest act of worship. It is a direct link between man and his Lord, and it is a sign of the relationship between them. The Prophet (ﷺ), said:

> The best form of worship is *duʿā*.[48]

3. *Duʿā* is the Essence of Worship

The verses quoted above are clear enough proof of this, as is the ḥadīth of the Prophet (ﷺ) in which he said:

> *Duʿā* is worship.[49]

4. *Duʿā* is a Sign of One's *Īmān*

When a person makes *duʿā* to Allāh, this is a clear indication that he believes in Allāh, and in the proper understanding of *tawḥīd*. For it automatically implies that he believes that Allāh exists and is the true Lord (*Tawḥīd al-Rubūbiyyah*), and that He is the One that deserves to be asked and worshipped (*Tawḥīd al-Ulūhiyyah*), and

---

[47] Sūrah *al-Dhāriyāt,* 56.

[48] Reported by al-Ḥākim (1/491), who considered it authentic, and al-Dhahabī agreed with him, as did al-Albānī (see *al-Ṣaḥīḥah*, # 1579).

[49] The *takhrīj* (referencing) of this *ḥadīth* has already been given.

that He is the One that has Perfect Attributes and Names, for He is capable of responding to the *duʿā* of His slave (*Tawḥīd al-Asmā' wa l-Ṣifāt*). This is why *duʿā* is one of the greatest acts of worship, and, when directed to other than Allāh, one of the clearest acts of *shirk*.

5. To Make *Duʿā* is to Obey Allāh

Allāh states:

وَٱدْعُوهُ مُخْلِصِينَ لَهُ ٱلدِّينَ

"And Call upon Him, making the religion Sincerely to Him".[50]

He also states:

وَقَالَ رَبُّكُمُ ٱدْعُونِىٓ أَسْتَجِبْ لَكُمْ

"And your Lord has said: Make *duʿā* to Me, I will respond to You".[51]

Therefore by making *duʿā*, mankind is in fact obeying what he has been commanded to do by Allāh. The person who makes *duʿā* will be rewarded by Allāh even if his request is not responded to, simply because he has obeyed Allāh's command!

6. Allāh is Close to the One Making *Duʿā*

As Allāh states in the Qur'ān:

وَإِذَا سَأَلَكَ
عِبَادِى عَنِّى فَإِنِّى قَرِيبٌ ۖ أُجِيبُ دَعْوَةَ ٱلدَّاعِ إِذَا دَعَانِ ۖ

"And when My servants ask you concerning Me, then (answer them), I am indeed near to them. I respond to the supplications of the supplicant when he calls on Me!"[52]

So Allāh is close to His servants, and He responds to their *duʿā*

---

[50] Sūrah *al-Aʿrāf*, 29.

[51] Sūrah *Ghāfir*, 60.

[52] Sūrah *al-Baqarah*, 186.

when they call upon Him. The fact that Allāh mentions *duʿā* immediately after stating that He is close to them shows that this is one of the ways in which a person can come closer to Allāh, and one of the ways in which Allāh will come closer to him.

7. *Duʿā* is the Only Cause of Allāh's Concern for Us

Were it not for the fact that mankind makes *duʿā* to Allāh, Allāh would not care about creation. This fact, in and of itself, is sufficient to make a person realise the importance of *duʿā*. Allāh states in the Qur'ān:

قُلْ مَا يَعْبَؤُا بِكُمْ رَبِّي
لَوْلَا دُعَآؤُكُمْ ۖ فَقَدْ كَذَّبْتُمْ فَسَوْفَ يَكُونُ لِزَامًا ﴿٧٧﴾

> Say (O Muḥammad): My Lord only pays attention to you (Ar. *Yaʿbaʾu*) because of your *duʿā* to Him. But now you have indeed rejected (Him), so the (torment) will be yours permanently.[53]

One of the authorities of the *salaf* (the early generation of the Muslims) said: "It has reached me that the meaning of this verse is: I have not created you because I have a need for you, I have only created you so that you may ask Me, so I will forgive you and give you what you ask".[54]

Al-Shawkānī writes in commentary of this verse: "Allāh has made it clear in this verse that He is not in need of anyone's worship, and that He has only commanded them so that they can benefit themselves. It is said, 'I did not *abʿa* (the Arabic word used in the verse) someone' meaning, 'I did not care about him, nor does he hold any status with me', … so the meaning of the verse is, 'Were it not for the fact that you make *duʿā* to Him, He would not care about you.'"[55]

Al-Saʿdī writes: "Allāh has informed us that He neither cares,

---

[53] Sūrah *al-Furqān*, 77.

[54] *Tafsīr al-Qurṭubī*, 13/83.

[55] *Fatḥ al-Qadīr*, 3/121.

nor concerns Himself except with these people (the believers), and that, were it not for your *duʿās* to Him – the *duʿā* of worship and the *duʿā* of asking – then He would not care about you nor love you".[56]

So only those people who make *duʿā* to Allāh, the *duʿā al-mas'alah* and the *duʿā al-ʿibādah*, are those whom Allāh is concerned with.

8. *Duʿā* is An Indication of Allāh's Generosity

Of Allāh's Names is *al-Karīm*, or the Ever-Generous. The concept of *duʿā* proves the extreme and infinite Generosity of Allāh, as every single created being asks Allāh, day and night, morning and evening, for all of their needs, and Allāh gives, and gives, and gives.

يَسْـَٔلُهُۥ مَن فِى ٱلسَّمَٰوَٰتِ وَٱلْأَرْضِ ۚ كُلَّ يَوْمٍ هُوَ فِى شَأْنٍ ﴿٢٩﴾

> All that is in the Heavens and Earth begs of Him (its needs); Everyday He has a matter to bring forth.[57]

This concept is also proven in the following ḥadīth, in which the Prophet (ﷺ) said:

> When one of you wishes for something, then let him increase (his wishes), for verily he is asking his Lord, the Most Exalted and High.[58]

And in another wording:

> When one of you asks something (from Allāh), then let him be plentiful (in what he asks for), for indeed he is asking his Lord.[59]

---

[56] *Taysīr al-Karīm al-Mannān*, p. 537. There are other interpretations of this verse as well, but these do not contradict the interpretation that has gone before. For further details, see *Aḍwā al-Bayān*, 4/181.

[57] Sūrah *al-Raḥmān*, 29.

[58] Reported by ʿAbd ibn Ḥumayd in his *Muntakhab* (1/193); authenticated by al-Albānī in *al-Ṣaḥīḥah*, # 1266.

[59] Reported by Ibn Ḥibbān (# 2403); see *al-Ṣaḥīḥah*, # 1325.

9. *Duʿā* is a Sign of Humility

When a person makes *duʿā*, he demonstrates his own humility and meekness to the Creator, and frees himself from arrogance. Hence why Allāh has stated:

وَقَالَ رَبُّكُمُ ٱدْعُونِىٓ أَسْتَجِبْ لَكُمْ
إِنَّ ٱلَّذِينَ يَسْتَكْبِرُونَ عَنْ عِبَادَتِى سَيَدْخُلُونَ جَهَنَّمَ
دَاخِرِينَ ﴿٦٠﴾

> "And your Lord has said: Make *duʿā* to Me, I will respond to You. For whoever is (too) haughty (and arrogant) to worship Me will enter the Fire of Hell, in a state of humiliation".[60]

Al-Shawkānī said, commenting on this verse: "This noble verse proves that *duʿā* is an act of worship, because He commanded His servants to make *duʿā* to Him, and then said, '....whoever is too haughty to worship Me'. From this, we derive that *duʿā* is worship, and to leave making *duʿā* to our Lord is arrogance, and, in fact, the most disgusting type of arrogance. How is it possible that a slave can feel arrogant in making *duʿā* to the One that created him, and gave him sustenance, and made him out of nothing – the One that created the entire creation, and gave it sustenance, and gave it life, and will give it death, and then reward or punish it? In fact, there is no doubt that such arrogance is a type of madness, and an indication of sheer ungratefulness!"[61]

10. *Duʿā* Repels Allāh's Anger

Abū Hurayrah narrated that the Prophet (ﷺ) said:

> Verily, the person who does not ask Allāh, Allāh gets angry at him.[62]

---

[60] Sūrah *Ghāfir*, 60.

[61] *Tuḥfat al-Dhākirīn*, p. 28.

[62] Authentic, narrated by al-Tirmidhī from Abū Hurayrah, as is mentioned in *Ṣaḥīḥ al-Jāmiʿ*, 2418.

This because, by leaving *du'ā*, a person in fact abandons the most noble act of worship. In addition, if he were to leave *du'ā* out of arrogance, or a feeling of self-sufficiency, this would, in reality, be a type of disbelief in Allāh, and a deification of one's self.

Concerning this ḥadīth, one of the poets versified:

Allāh gets angry if you stop asking Him
And the son of Adam, when he is asked, gets angry!

And one of the most famous scholars of the second century, Imām Sufyan ath-Thawrī, would start his *du'ā* by praising Allāh as follows: "O You whose most beloved servant is he who asks Him the most; and O You whose most hated servant is he who does not ask Him; and no one else is such, O Lord!"[63]

This relates to the fact the Allāh loves to be asked. 'Ubādah ibn Ṣāmit reports that the Prophet (ﷺ) said:

> "There is no Muslim on the face of the earth that asks Allāh for anything except that Allāh gives it to him, or averts from him a similar evil, as long as he does not ask for something evil or for breaking the ties of kinship".[64]

So this once again shows the importance of *du'ā*, as it is obligatory for a person to avoid Allāh's anger. Since leaving *du'ā* entails Allāh's anger, this is proof enough that making *du'ā* is obligatory.

11. *Du'ā* is a Cause of Being Saved from the Fire

Since *du'ā* is the highest form of worship, if a person leaves *du'ā*, then he has left worshipping Allāh. Therefore, he will enter the fire of Hell.

'Ā'ishah asked the Prophet (ﷺ) about a person who used to do good, but did not accept Islām. She said: "O Messenger of Allāh!

---

[63] Reported in *Tafsīr Ibn Kathīr*, 4/85.

[64] Authentic, narrated by al-Tirmidhī from 'Ubādah ibn Ṣāmit, as is mentioned in *Ṣaḥīḥ al-Jāmi'* # 5637. Shaykh al-Albānī said of it in *Ṣaḥīḥ al-Tirmidhī*, # 2827: "It is *ḥasan ṣaḥīḥ* (authentic)."

Ibn Jud'ān used to, in the days of *Jāhilīyyah*, take care of his relatives, and feed the poor. Will (his actions) be of any benefit to him?" So the Prophet (ﷺ): responded:

> No, O 'Ā'ishah! For never did he say: O Allāh! Forgive me my sins on the Day of Judgement.[65]

So in this ḥadīth, the Prophet (ﷺ) informed 'Ā'ishah that Ibn Jud'ān would not benefit from any of his good deeds, and would enter the Fire of Hell, purely and simply because he never made *du'ā* to Allāh to forgive him. The ḥadīth implies that Ibn Jud'ān did not accept Islām, but since acceptance of Islām necessitates asking Allāh for forgiveness, the Prophet (ﷺ) equated not accepting Islām with leaving *du'ā*.

12. Leaving *Du'ā* is a Sign of Laziness

The Prophet (ﷺ) said:

> The most incapable (or lazy) person is he who does not make *du'ā*, and the most miserly is he who does not give *salām*."[66]

How true are these Prophetic words of wisdom! For what energy does it take a person to make *du'ā* to Allāh? And what greater sign of laziness and incapability is there than the one who leaves this act that does not take up any of his time or effort?

13. *Du'ā* is the Only Act that Repels Predestination

The Prophet (ﷺ) stated:

> Nothing repels predestination (*qadr*) except *du'ā*.[67]

In other words, it is possible that a certain misfortune has been decreed for a person, yet, because of the sincerity and quality of his

---

[65] Reported by Muslim.

[66] Reported by Ibn Ḥibbān (# 1939) who considered it authentic, and al-Albānī agreed with him in his *al-Ṣaḥīḥah*, # 154.

[67] Reported by al-Tirmidhī (# 139), who declared it *ḥasan gharīb*, Ibn Mājah (# 90) and al-Būṣayrī said (1/45) that al-'Irāqī considered it to be *ḥasan*, and others. Al-Albānī agreed with al-'Irāqī in his *Ṣaḥīḥah*, # 154.

duʿā, Allāh will repel that misfortune from him, and change this decree. So every Muslim should seek refuge in Allāh from future calamities and misfortunes that might befall him, for that is the only way that he can avoid them.

14. *Duʿā* is the Only Act that Changes Predestination

Not only does *duʿā* repel a future misfortune that might befall a person, it also changes and removes a current calamity and misfortune. The Prophet (ﷺ) stated:

> Caution will not be of any benefit against predestination, but *duʿā* benefits (matters) that have occurred and that are (yet) to occur. And indeed, *duʿā* meets with a calamity, and fights it until the Day of Judgement.[68]

So no matter how cautious a person is, he will not be able to save himself from Allāh's decree. The only way that he can repel a calamity that has befallen him, or will befall him, is by resorting to *duʿā*. The Prophet (ﷺ) stated that it is as if the *duʿā* rises up and fights the calamity, defending the person who made the *duʿā* from this calamity until the Day of Judgement.

In another ḥadīth, the Prophet (ﷺ) said,

> Whoever the door of *duʿā* has been opened for, then all the doors of mercy have been opened for him. And nothing is more pleasing to Allāh, that He be asked of the things that are granted, than good health. *Duʿā* is of benefit to (matters) that have occurred, and that are yet to occur. So I advise you, O servants of Allāh, to make *duʿā*![69]

---

[68] Reported by al-Ṭabarānī in his *al-Awsaṭ* (# 2519), and al-Ḥākim (1/492) who declared that it was authentic; although al-Dhahabī disagreed with him due to the presence of a weak narrator. However, the ḥadīth has supporting evidence, since it was reported with another slightly weak chain by Aḥmad (5/234) and al-Ṭabarānī in his *al-Kabīr* (20/103). So the *ḥadīth* is *ḥasan* with these two chains, and this is the opinion of al-Albānī in his checking of *Mishkāt al-Maṣābīḥ*, # 2234.

[69] Reported by al-Tirmidhī (#3548) who pointed out that it has some weakness in its chain. However, it has supporting evidence, due to which al-Albānī considered it to be *ḥasan* in his *Ṣaḥīḥ al-Jāmiʿ* # 3409.

So no person should give up hope of Allāh's Mercy. No matter what misfortune has befallen him, he should raise his hands to Allāh, and sincerely pray that this misfortune be lifted and removed.

Ibn al-Qayyim mentioned that there are three possibilities with regards to *duʿā* and Divine Decree. Firstly, it is possible that the *duʿā* is stronger than the Decree and, thus, repels it permanently. Secondly, it is possible that the *duʿā* is weaker than the Decree, so the Decree occurs, but the *duʿā* softens it a little bit. Thirdly, that they are of equal strength, so each prevents the other from acting.[70]

The topic of *duʿā* and its relationship with predestination will be discussed in greater detail in a later chapter.

15. *Duʿā* is a Sign of Wisdom

When a person realises that everything that occurs is by the Will and Power of Allāh, then he also realise that the best way to achieve any goal is to ask Allāh. After all, the wise man is he who makes the best plan to arrive at his destination, and uses the optimum means to achieve his goal.

So what wiser man is there than he who realises that the goals of all of his desires lie with Allāh, and that the means of achieving these goals also lie with Allāh? Therefore, he takes *duʿā* as his primary means of achieving the goal. And *duʿā* never harms a person, even if it is not responded to, so what reason is there for a person to ignore or reject it?

16. *Duʿā* is Beloved by Allāh

The evidences that show *duʿā* is an act of worship automatically imply that it is beloved by Allāh. There is also a ḥadīth narrated to this effect: "Ask Allāh from His Bounty, for verily Allāh loves to be asked".[71]

---

[70] *Al-Dā' wa al-Dawā'*, p. 42.

[71] Reported by al-Tirmidhī (# 3571), who pointed out that it has some weakness in its chain, and al-Albānī agreed with him. See *al-Ḍaʿīfah*, # 492.

17. *Duʿā* is a Characteristic of the Believer

The Qur'ān is replete with verses in which the angels, prophets and believers make *duʿā* to Allāh. These verses show that *duʿā* is of the characteristics of true believers. In certain verses, Allāh describes some of His favoured servants as being frequent in *duʿā*:

إِنَّهُمْ كَانُوا يُسَٰرِعُونَ فِي ٱلْخَيْرَٰتِ
وَيَدْعُونَنَا رَغَبًا وَرَهَبًا ۖ وَكَانُوا لَنَا خَٰشِعِينَ ﴿٩٠﴾

> "Verily, they used to hasten to do good deeds, and they used to make *duʿā* to Us with hope and fear, and used to humble themselves before Us."[72]

18. The Reward of *Duʿā* is Guaranteed

Jābir ibn ʿAbdillāh stated that the Prophet (ﷺ) said:

> "There is no person who asks Allāh for anything except that Allāh gives it to him, or keeps away from him a similar evil, as long as he does not ask for something evil or for breaking the ties of kinship". At this, a person said to the Prophet (ﷺ): "In that case, we will ask for plenty!" The Prophet (ﷺ) responded: "Allāh (is even) more plentiful !"[73]

In this ḥadīth, there is clear proof of the fact that Allāh has taken upon Himself a promise to respond to the *duʿā* of every person who asks Him, with the condition that the person who is asking Allāh fulfils the conditions of *duʿā*. In this case, Allāh will either give him what he asks for, or avert from him an evil of an equivalent nature to the good that he was asking for, as long as he does not ask for an evil.

So what excuse does a person have in not making *duʿā* to Allāh! No matter what the outcome of his *duʿā* is, it will only be for his

---

72 Sūrah *al-Anbiyā'*, 90.

73 Authentic, narrated by al-Tirmidhī from ʿUbādah ibn Ṣāmit, as is mentioned in *Ṣaḥīḥ al-Jāmiʿ* # 5637. And Shaykh al-Albānī said of it in *Ṣaḥīḥ al-Tirmidhī*, # 2827, "It is *ḥasan ṣaḥīḥ* (authentic)."

benefit. Ibn Ḥajr stated: “Every single person that makes *duʿā* will be responded to, but the actual responses are different. Sometimes, the exact matter that was prayed for is given, and sometimes, something equivalent to it is given”.[74]

19. *Duʿā* is a Cause of Victory

Duʿā brings down patience and fortitude, and is a cause of victory over the enemies. This is why one of the *duʿās* that has been guaranteed an answer is the *duʿā* made during the battle between Muslims and non-Muslims. We find that on more than one occasion Allāh mentions the believers making *duʿā* at the time of battle, as, for example, the army of Dāwūd:

وَلَمَّا بَرَزُوا۟ لِجَالُوتَ وَجُنُودِهِۦ قَالُوا۟ رَبَّنَآ أَفْرِغْ
عَلَيْنَا صَبْرًا وَثَبِّتْ أَقْدَامَنَا وَٱنصُرْنَا عَلَى ٱلْقَوْمِ
ٱلْكَـٰفِرِينَ ﴿٢٥٠﴾ فَهَزَمُوهُم بِإِذْنِ ٱللَّهِ

> And when they (Ṭālūt and Dāwūd) advanced to meet Jālūt (Goliath), they prayed: ‘Our Lord! Pour forth on us patience, and make us victorious over the disbelieving people.’ So they defeated them by Allāh’s permission...[75]

20. *Duʿā* is a Sign of Brotherhood

One of the *duʿās* that has been guaranteed a response is the *duʿā* that a Muslim makes for his Muslim brother in his absence. This is because such a *duʿā* is a clear sign of love and solidarity between Muslims. The fact that a person remembers another Muslim in his absence, and raises his hands to Allāh to make a special *duʿā* for him, clearly proves that he wants only good for him. It demonstrates the concern and care that he has for his fellow Muslims. Hence why the Qur’ān describes the believers as having concern for others, and making *duʿā* for their brethren in faith:

---

[74] *Fatḥ al-Bārī*, 11/95.

[75] Sūrah *al-Baqarah*, 250-251.

وَٱلَّذِينَ جَآءُو مِنۢ بَعۡدِهِمۡ يَقُولُونَ رَبَّنَا ٱغۡفِرۡ لَنَا
وَلِإِخۡوَٰنِنَا ٱلَّذِينَ سَبَقُونَا بِٱلۡإِيمَٰنِ وَلَا تَجۡعَلۡ فِي قُلُوبِنَا
غِلّٗا لِّلَّذِينَ ءَامَنُواْ رَبَّنَآ إِنَّكَ رَءُوفٞ رَّحِيمٌ ١٠

> "And those (Muslims) that come after them say, 'O Our Lord! Forgive us and our brethren who preceded us in Faith, and do not put in our hearts any hatred to those who have believed. Our Lord! You are indeed full of kindness, Most Merciful'".[76]

21. *Duʿā* is the Weapon of the Weak and Wronged

How great is the Mercy of Allāh, Who has given the weakest of the weak a weapon with which he can fight the greatest tyrant and oppressor! For *duʿā* is a weapon that everyone can afford to possess, and no one needs to be taught how to use it. The *duʿā* of the oppressed, and the one who has been wronged, is of a surety answered (as shall be discussed below).

This is why we find the prophets making *duʿā* to Allāh when they have been wronged. Look at the story of Nūḥ, who, when his people rejected him, called out to Allāh to destroy them! Because of his *duʿā* the entire world was flooded with water, and only those whom Allāh saved on the ark lived. Ponder over the stories of Ṣāliḥ, and Hūd, and the other prophets, and look at the end of those that rejected them. Consider the fate of the Pharaoh and those that believed in him, when Mūsa made a *duʿā* against them, the very Nile that they used to depend on for life was used to kill them!

So the *duʿā* is the weapon of the believer, by which he can fight against any and every tyrant and oppressor![77]

---

[76] Sūrah al-*Ḥashr,* 10.

[77] Although the *duʿā is* the weapon of the believer, the ḥadīth narrated to this effect is fabricated. It states: "The *duʿā* is the weapon of the believer, and the pillar of the religion, and the light of the heavens and earth." See the last chapter.

22. *Du'ā* is a Cure for All Diseases

Diseases are of two types: physical, and spiritual. Physical diseases are the sicknesses that man faces from time to time, such as fever and other aches and pains of the body. Spiritual diseases, or diseases of the soul, can also be divided into two categories: diseases of doubt and diseases of desires. All the problems relating to the soul stem from these two types of disease.

The diseases of desires are those impermissible urges and cravings that afflict a person that he does not have the power to fight or overcome. So the one that steals only does so because he is too weak to control his desire for money, and does not have the *īmān* necessary to limit himself to permissible methods of earning money. Likewise, the one who fornicates only does so due to a weakness in his faith that causes him to leave permissible methods of satisfying his desires and to follow impermissible avenues.

The diseases of doubts are those diseases that occur due to misconceptions or misunderstandings. Such misconceptions could be intentional or unintentional. So, for example, when some ignorant Muslims make *du'ā* to other than Allāh, it is due to the fact that they have not understood the concept of *du'ā*, and not appreciated Allāh's Names and Attributes. Therefore, they turn to others, ascribing them with Attributes only Allāh deserves.

Du'ā is the cure for all of these diseases. As for diseases of the body, then it is clear that a person prays to Allāh to cure him of any physical affliction or ailment that he is suffering from. As for diseases of desires, the way that a person removes them is by turning to Allāh, praying that Allāh grants him the *īmān* that is necessary for avoiding the sins that he is doing. By realising that only Allāh can grant him such an increase, he is automatically showing his trust and hope in Allāh, and in the process increasing his *īmān*! As for diseases of doubt, the way for a person to cure them is by sincerely praying to Allāh to grant him guidance, and to bless him with proper *īmān*, and an understanding of the Qur'ān and Sunnah. It has been authentically narrated that the Prophet (ﷺ) himself would pray to Allāh to guide him to the truth concerning any matters in which there was a difference of opinion. So if this were the case with the Prophet (ﷺ), then for us such a *du'ā* is even more imperative.

Ibn al-Qayyim says: "*Du'ā* is of the most beneficial cures, and it is the enemy of all diseases. It fights them, and cures them, and prevents their occurrence, and causes them to be raised up or reduced after its occurrence. It is the weapon of the believer".[78]

23. *Du'ā* Makes a Person More Optimistic

When a person makes *du'ā*, he finds in this *du'ā* a way out of the problems he is facing. No matter how great the problem is, he realises that there is an exit from this problem through *du'ā*. So his spirits are lifted, and he is optimistic about his situation. *Du'ā* gives him hope, and increases his trust in Allāh's mercy. It opens up a door that shows him the escape from the cage of problems that he is in, and it lights up the path that grants him an exit from his darkness.

24. *Du'ā* Opens Up a Dialogue With the Creator

What is intended by this is the fact that the person who makes *du'ā* sincerely opens up a new 'relationship' with Allāh that did not exist before he started his *du'ā*. He calls upon Allāh, sincerely, with his full heart, concentrating on his *du'ā*, believing that Allāh is hearing him, hoping Allāh's response, and fearing its delay. He calls upon Allāh with His most beautiful Names and Attributes, perhaps realising for the first time the true meaning and application of these Names and Attributes. His *īmān* increases, as his hopes and fears increase, and his love of Allāh also increases. At the same time, he remembers his sins, for sins are like closed doors that prevent the *du'ā* from being responded to, and he fears that, because of these sins, his *du'ā* will be rejected. So he repents to Allāh, and

---

78 *Al-Dā' wa al-Dawā'*, p. 41.

changes his life, striving to please Allāh, realising that only Allāh can change his situation, and thus, in the process, he develops a new relationship with Allāh.

Ibn al-Qayyim, the 'doctor of the heart', writes:

> It is possible that a person has a need for something... so he earnestly prays and requests Allāh for it, until the sweetness of asking and imploring Allāh is opened for him. So he enjoys being humbled before Him, and trying to draw closer to Him, using His Names and Attributes, and his heart becomes void of everything besides Him, and he cuts off any relationship or hope for good from anyone else – all of which would never have occurred had it not been for his need.... So it is possible that what good has come about because of this state of his is even greater, and more pleasing to him, than the actual need (that was the cause of such a state), to such an extent that he wishes to continue in this state, and prefers it over the actual fulfilment of his need. So his happiness due to this state is greater than the happiness he would achieve had his need actually been fulfilled. Some of those that have recognized (the signs of Allāh) have stated: "Sometimes, I have a certain need (that I wish to ask) Allāh, so I ask Him earnestly. Then, I find that the door of dialogue opens up for me, and I recognise Allāh more (i.e. become more aware of Him), and feel humbled before Him, due to which I prefer that the answer to my prayer be delayed, so that this state may continue!" [79]

It is possible then that a believer so enjoys this new relationship that he actually fears the response of his *duʿā*, and wishes that Allāh prolong it so that he can enjoy his servitude to Allāh!

25. *Duʿā* is One of the Easiest Acts of Worship

After reading all of these great benefits of *duʿā*, one might presume that it is one of the most difficult acts of worship, for surely an act with so many rewards and benefits cannot be an effortless act!

---

[79] *Madārij al-Sālikīn*, 2/229.

In fact, quite the contrary is true. *Duʿā* is one of the easiest acts of worship, for how much energy does it require? And how much time does it take up?

Duʿā is not confined to a certain place, or a certain time, or a certain routine or mode. Rather, all persons, whether male or female, old or young, rich or poor, scholar or worshipper, can make *duʿā*, at all times, and in all places. All that is needed is an attentive heart, and a humble soul.

So here is yet another blessing of *duʿā*: that it is so simple and uncomplicated, and yet replete with so many blessings and distinctions.

There are many more benefits to *duʿā*, but the ones mentioned will suffice for this discussion.

CHAPTER IV

The Pre-Conditions of *Duʿā*

We have already discussed the fact that *duʿā* is a type of worship, so it is essential to discuss the pre-conditions that are necessary if one wishes one's *duʿā* to be answered. Just like a person's ṣalāt will not be accepted until he performs the necessary pre-requisites, such as *wuḍū*, facing the qiblah, and covering the body, likewise a person's *duʿā* will likely not be accepted until these pre-requisites are met.[780]

Ibn al-Qayyim writes, hinting at these factors:

> *Duʿā* and the seeking of protection from Allāh are like weapons, but the sharpness of a weapon is not sufficient for it to cause effect, for the person that handles it also plays a role. So whenever the weapon is a perfect one, having no blemish in it, and the forearm is strong, and there are no preventing factors, then it will cause an effect on the enemy. But if any of these three factors are missing, then the effect will also be lessened. So, if the *duʿā* in and of itself is not correct, or the person making the *duʿā* has not combined between his heart and tongue in the *duʿā*, or if there is a preventing factor, then the desired effect will not occur.[81]

---

80 However, it is possible that a person's *duʿā* is accepted if some of these conditions are not met. The response of a *duʿā* depends on the Will of Allāh, and He responds to whom He pleases. Therefore, it is possible that the *duʿā* of a disbeliever who does not meet any of these condition is responded to, and it is possible that a Muslim who fulfills all of these conditions is not responded to. However, without a doubt, the person who strives to fulfill and put into practice all of these factors will have a much greater chance of having his *duʿā* answered. For these conditions, see al-Ḥamad, pps. 26-36, and the other source books. For an excellent discussion of the concept of pre-conditions and etiquette as it relates to *duʿā*, see al-Arūsī, pp. 163-234.

81 *Al-Dāʿ wa al-Dawāʿ*, p. 58.

Some of the pre-conditions needed for *duʿā* are as follows:

1. The Realisation that Only Allāh Responds to *Duʿā*

This is the essence of *tawḥīd*. A person must believe fully that only Allāh is capable of hearing his prayer, and only Allāh has the power to grant him what he desires. This is the essence of *tawḥīd al-ʿi'tiqādī*, or the '*tawḥīd* of one's belief.'[82] The Qur'ān mentions this fact in many verses. Allāh specifically states:

أَمَّن يُجِيبُ ٱلْمُضْطَرَّ إِذَا دَعَاهُ
وَيَكْشِفُ ٱلسُّوٓءَ وَيَجْعَلُكُمْ خُلَفَآءَ ٱلْأَرْضِ ۗ أَءِلَٰهٌ
مَّعَ ٱللَّهِ ۚ قَلِيلًا مَّا تَذَكَّرُونَ ﴿٦٢﴾

> "Who (else is there) that responds to the call of the one in distress when he calls out, and He removes evil (from him), and makes you inheritors of the earth? Is there any other god besides Allāh? Little is it that you remember!"[83]

This is why *duʿā* is the greatest form of worship, and, if directed to other than Allāh, the greatest form of *shirk* as well.

2. Sincerity in *Duʿā* to Allāh Alone

After a person realises that only Allāh can respond to his *duʿā*, the logical consequence is that he prays only to Allāh. This is the essence of *tawḥīd al-ʿamalī*, or the '*tawḥīd* of one's actions.'

---

[82] *Tawḥīd* can be divided into two categories (*Tawḥīd al-ʿI'tiqādī* and *Tawḥīd al-ʿAmalī*), or into three categories, if one splits *Tawḥīd al-ʿI'tiqādī* into two other categories (*Tawḥīd al-Rubūbiyyah* and *Tawḥīd al-Asmā' wa l-Ṣifāt* – in this categorisation scheme *Tawḥīd al-ʿAmalī* is then named *Tawḥīd al-Ulūhiyyah*). Both the bipartite and tripartite divisions of *tawḥīd* have been found in the books of the *salaf*, and there is no contradition between them.

[83] Sūrah *al-Naml,* 62.

The proof for this condition is found in many Qur'ānic verses and *aḥādīth*. Some of these verses are:

وَأَنَّ ٱلْمَسَٰجِدَ لِلَّهِ فَلَا تَدْعُوا۟ مَعَ ٱللَّهِ أَحَدًا ﴿١٨﴾

> "And Verily the mosques are for Allāh alone, so do not call upon anyone besides Him!"[84]

أَغَيْرَ ٱللَّهِ تَدْعُونَ إِن كُنتُمْ صَٰدِقِينَ ﴿٤٠﴾

> "Will you call upon other than Allāh if you are truthful?"[85]

إِنَّ ٱلَّذِينَ تَدْعُونَ مِن دُونِ ٱللَّهِ عِبَادٌ أَمْثَالُكُمْ

> "Those whom you call upon besides Allāh are slaves like yourselves"[86]

وَٱلَّذِينَ تَدْعُونَ مِن دُونِهِۦ لَا يَسْتَطِيعُونَ نَصْرَكُمْ وَلَآ أَنفُسَهُمْ يَنصُرُونَ ﴿١٩٧﴾

> "And those who you ask besides Him can neither come to your aid, nor can they help themselves!"[87]

The meaning of the phrase, '...besides Allāh...' includes everything that is worshipped besides the Creator, from lifeless objects like idols or the sun to trees, animals, men, a pious person, a prophet, an angel, or any other object besides.

Another proof is the advice that the Prophet (ﷺ) gave to Ibn ʿAbbās one day, when he (ﷺ) said:

> "O slave! Guard (the duties of) Allāh, and He will guard you! Guard (the duties of) Allāh, and you will find Him in front of

84 Sūrah *al-Jinn*, 18.

85 Sūrah *al-Anʿām*, 40.

86 Sūrah *al-Aʿrāf,* 194.

87 Sūrah *al-Aʿrāf,* 197.

you! And when you ask, ask only from Allāh, and when you seek any help, seek help only from Allāh!"[88]

3. To Perform *Tawassul* Properly

Tawassul is the seeking of Allāh's help and response through the performance of certain acts. In other words, the person making *du'ā* uses *tawassul* to increase the chances of his *du'ā* being accepted. *Tawassul* is performed by mentioning Allāh's Names and Attributes, or by mentioning a good deed that a person has done, or by asking a living, pious person to make *du'ā* on his behalf, or by showing his own humility and faults in front of Allāh.

Due to the great misunderstandings that exist regarding *tawassul*, this topic calls for more discussion, so we will elaborate further on this in a separate section.

4. Lack of Hastiness

To be hasty in one's prayer is a cause of rejection of the *du'ā*. Abū Hurayrah narrated that the Prophet (ﷺ) said:

> "The *du'ā* of any worshipper will continue to be responded to, as long as he does not ask for a sin or breaking the ties of kinship, and as long as he is not hasty".

It was asked, "O Messenger of Allāh? And what does it mean to be hasty?" He (ﷺ) responded:

> "A worshipper says, 'I have prayed and prayed, and I don't see that it will be accepted', so he gives up hope of being answered, and leaves *du'ā*".[89]

To 'give up' means to turn away and break off from something, and the meaning intended here is that a person leaves *du'ā*. This same meaning is given in the verse:

---

[88] Authentic, narrated by Abū Dāwūd, Aḥmad, al-Tirmidhī, al-Ḥākim from Ibn 'Abbās, and authenticated by al-Albānī in *Ṣaḥīḥ al-Jāmi'* #7957.

[89] Narrated by Muslim from Abū Hurayrah, as mentioned in *Ṣaḥīḥ al-Jāmi'* # 7705.

﴿لَا يَسْتَكْبِرُونَ عَنْ عِبَادَتِهِۦ وَلَا يَسْتَحْسِرُونَ ١٩﴾

"They are not too proud to worship Him, nor do they weary",[90]

meaning that they do not stop worshipping Him.

This shows that the *du'ā* should be continuous, and that a person should avoid giving up *du'ā* just because it has not been responded to. There is another ḥadīth which also proves this point, for Abū Hurayrah narrated that the Prophet (ﷺ) said:

> "You will be responded to as long as you are not hasty, meaning that (a person) says, 'I have prayed and prayed, and my prayer has not been answered!'"[91]

Yet another proof of this is the verse,

﴿وَيَدْعُ ٱلْإِنسَٰنُ بِٱلشَّرِّ دُعَآءَهُۥ بِٱلْخَيْرِ ۖ وَكَانَ ٱلْإِنسَٰنُ عَجُولًا ١١﴾

> "And man invokes (Allāh) for evil as he invokes (Allāh) for good, yet man is ever hasty!"[92]

Ibn al-Qayyim mentions: "And of the diseases that afflict *du'ā* and prevent its response is that a person is hasty in expecting a response, and the response is delayed, so he gives up hope, and leaves *du'ā*. His example is like that of a person who planted a seed, or a seedling, then guarded it, and took care of it, and watered it, but when it delayed in (giving its fruit) and reaching perfection, he left it and did not take care of it anymore!"[93]

This does not mean, however, that a person should not pray that his *du'ā* be answered quickly, for it has been authentically narrated that the Prophet (ﷺ) prayed for rain and said:

> "...quickly, and not delayed...".[94]

---

[90] Sūrah *al-Anbiyā',* 19.

[91] Narrated by al-Bukhārī, Muslim, Abū Dāwūd and others, from Abū Hurayrah, as is mentioned in *Ṣaḥīḥ al-Jāmi'* # 8085.

[92] Sūrah *al-Isrā'*, verse 11.

[93] *Al-Jawāb al-Kāfī*, p. 10.

[94] Authentic, narrated by Ibn Mājah, al-Ṭahāwī, al-Ḥākim and others, from Ka'b ibn Murrah, as mentioned in *Irwā' al-Ghalīl* 2/145.

The hastiness that is prohibited is that a person leaves *duʿā*, thinking that he will not be responded to. There is no harm in asking Allāh to respond to the *duʿā* quickly, so understand this difference!

5. *Duʿā* for Things that are Good

In order for the *duʿā* to be accepted by Allāh, all Glory and Praise be to Him, it is essential that it must be for something pure and good. The ḥadīth quoted earlier stated that, "The *duʿā* of any worshipper will continue to be responded to, as long as he does not ask for a sin or breaking the ties of kinship", and this clearly shows this aspect. The reason that the sin of breaking ties of kinship is mentioned explicitly is due to its grave nature of that sin, but the same rule applies to all other sins.

6. To Have Good Intentions

It is imperative that a person making *duʿā* have the best of intentions for whatever he is asking. So, if someone asks for an increase in wealth, he should intend with that that he spend more on his relatives and the poor, and increase in reward in this manner. Likewise, if someone asks that Allāh bless him with a pious spouse, his intention should be so that he can avoid falling into prohibited acts, and begin a pious family.

The proofs for this are obvious, for it is not possible for a Muslim to ask Allāh for something in order that he do evil with it.

This principle is alluded to in the *duʿā* that the Prophet (ﷺ) taught us to say when visiting the sick. ʿAbdullāh ibn ʿAmr narrates that the Prophet (ﷺ), said:

> When a person comes to visit the sick, then let him say: O Allāh! Cure your servant so-and-so, for he will then inflict a wound on an enemy, or walk for your sake to the prayer.[95]

So the purpose for which the cure is asked is so that the sick person may aid the religion once he is cured.

---

[95] Reported by Abū Dāwūd (# 3107). See *Ṣaḥīḥ al-Jāmiʿ*, # 466.

7. The Presence of an Attentive Heart

The whole point of *du'ā* is that a person call out with a sincere heart to his Creator. This sincerity cannot be achieved if one calls out heedlessly, without earnestness. The Prophet (ﷺ) said,

> "Make *du'ā* to Allāh in a state that you are certain that your *du'ā* will be responded to, and know that Allāh does not respond to a *du'ā* that originates from a negligent, inattentive heart".[96]

This shows that the *du'ā* must be made with a mindful heart, such that one knows exactly what one is asking for, and remembers who he is asking, for he is asking the Lord of Honour. It does not befit, therefore, a servant to ask his Lord in a neglectful manner, such that he is not even aware of what he is saying, or using memorised sentences that he repeats over and over again without understanding these phrases and appreciating their meanings.

There is another ḥadīth that also helps clarify this point. Imām Aḥmad reports from 'Abdullāh ibn 'Umar that the Prophet (ﷺ) said:

> "Hearts are like vessels, some have greater capacity than others. Therefore, O people, when you ask from Allāh, all Glory and Praise be to Him, ask from Him in a state in which you are certain that your prayers will be answered, for verily Allāh does not accept from His slave any *du'ā* that is made from a neglectful heart".[97]

Al-Ḥāfiẓ al-Nawawī stated: "Know that the purpose of *du'ā* is that one have an attentive heart (towards Allāh), as we have already mentioned, and the proofs for this are more than can be mentioned, and the knowledge of it is so apparent that it need not be discussed!"[98]

---

96 Authentic, narrated by al-Tirmidhī and al-Ḥākim from Abū Hurayrah, and authenticated by al-Albānī in *Ṣaḥīḥ al-Jāmi'* # 245.

97 Reported by Aḥmad, from Ibn 'Umar. Al-Haythamī said in *Majma' al-Zawā'id* (10/148), "Its chain is authentic," and al-Mundhirī said the same in *al-Targhīb* 2/492.

98 *Al-Adhkār*, p. 356.

8. Purity of One's Sustenance

Allāh, all Glory and Praise be to Him, says:

فَمِنَ ٱلنَّاسِ مَن يَقُولُ رَبَّنَآ

ءَاتِنَا فِى ٱلدُّنْيَا وَمَا لَهُۥ فِى ٱلْـَٔاخِرَةِ مِنْ خَلَـٰقٍ ﴿٢٠٠﴾

"For, verily there are those amongst men who say, 'O Our Lord! Grant us in this world,' and they have no share of the Hereafter".[99]

Abū Hurayrah narrated that the Prophet (ﷺ) said:

> "O People! Allāh is *al-Ṭayyib* (Pure), and He only accepts that which is pure! Allāh has commanded the Believers what He has commanded the Messengers, for He said,
>
> "O Messengers! Eat from the pure foods, and do right".
>
> Furthermore He said:
>
> "O you who believe! Eat from the pure and good foods We have given you".
>
> Then the Prophet (ﷺ) mentioned a traveller on a long journey, who is dishevelled and dusty, and he stretches forth his hands to the sky, saying, "O my Lord! O my Lord!" – while his food is unlawful, his drink is unlawful, his clothing is unlawful, and he is nourished unlawfully; how can he be answered?[100]

Therefore, among the necessary conditions for any *duʿā* to be accepted is the purity and lawfulness of one's food.

Saʿd ibn Abī Waqqās, one of the Prophet's (ﷺ) famous Companions, was once asked: "Why is it that your prayers are responded to, amongst all of the other Companions?" He replied: "I do not raise to my mouth a morsel except that I know where it came from and where it came out of".[101]

---

[99] Sūrah *al-Baqarah*, 200.

[100] Reported by Aḥmad, Muslim, and al-Tirmidhī from Abū Hurayrah, as mentioned in *Ṣaḥīḥ al-Jāmiʿ* # 2744.

[101] *Sharḥ al-Arbaʿīn*, Ibn Rajab, p. 275.

Additionally do not forget your consciousness of Allāh (*taqwa*), for it is the essence of all matters. This *taqwa* makes a person realise that Allāh is watching him at all times. Therefore, he will be careful with regard to what he eats and drinks, and from where he earns his money. Allāh, all Glory and Praise be to Him, says:

إِنَّمَا يَتَقَبَّلُ ٱللَّهُ مِنَ ٱلْمُتَّقِينَ ﴿٢٧﴾

> "Allāh only accepts (deeds) from those who fear him (*muttaqīn*)".[102]

So only the one that has *taqwa* of Allāh has a good chance of receiving a response to his *duʿā*, and part of that *taqwa* is that a person earns all his income from permissible means.

9. Prayer upon the Prophet (ﷺ)

The proof of this is the Prophet's (ﷺ) statement in which he said:

> "Every *duʿā* is covered until (the person) prays upon the Prophet (ﷺ)".[103]

The *duʿā* is 'covered,' meaning that it is not raised up to Allāh until the person making the *duʿā* accompanies it with the prayer upon the Prophet (ﷺ).

However, it seems that this is not a necessary condition, since the Prophet (ﷺ) himself did not practice this continually. There are numerous narrations from the Prophet (ﷺ) concerning specific *duʿās* which he made, and which he (ﷺ) commanded his Companions to make, which do not contain the prayer upon him (ﷺ).

---

[102] Sūrah *al-Mā'idah*, 27.

[103] Authentic, narrated by al-Nasā'ī from ʿAbdullāh ibn Bisr, and Ibn Ḥibbān from Muʿādh, and al-Daylamī from Anas and others, and it is authenticated in *Ṣaḥīḥ al-Jāmiʿ* # 4523.

For example, he (ﷺ) said:

> "O Allāh! I seek refuge in you from leprosy, madness and evil diseases."[104]

This narration shows that it is not a necessary condition to pray upon the Prophet (ﷺ) during every *duʿā*, but rather that it is recommended to do so.

A further indication of its commendability is the narration of the Prophet (ﷺ) in which he said:

> "A messenger came to me from my Lord and said, 'There is no worshipper who prays upon you once, except that Allāh will pray upon him ten times!"

A person stood up and said, "O Messenger of Allāh! Should I make half of my prayers upon you?" He (ﷺ) replied:

> "If you wish".

He then asked, "Should I make two-thirds of my prayers upon you?" He (ﷺ) replied:

> "If you wish".

He then asked, "Should I not make all of my prayers upon you?" He (ﷺ) replied:

> "In that case, Allāh would suffice you in your needs of this world and the Hereafter!"[105]

10. That the *Duʿā* Does not Interfere with Something More Important

Without a doubt, *duʿā* is one of the most important acts of worship. However, acts of worship can be divided into two categories: those that have a specific time, and those that can be done at any

---

[104] Authentic, narrated by Abū Dāwūd and al-Nasā'ī from Anas ibn Mālik, and authenticated in *Ṣaḥīḥ al-Jāmiʿ* # 1281.

[105] Authentic, reported by al-Tirmidhī from Ubayy ibn Kʿab, and authenticated by al-Albānī in *Ṣaḥīḥ al-Jāmiʿ* # 57.

time. *Du'ā* is of the second category, in that there is no specific time of the day in which it is restricted. However, prayer (*ṣalāt*) is of the first category. Therefore, it is not correct to engage in an act of worship that can be done at any time (for example, *du'ā*), at the expense of an act of worship that has a specific time (for example, *ṣalāt*). So, when one hears the call to prayer, one must respond to it, and pray the *ṣalāt* in the mosque, along with other believers. One cannot use the excuse that one is making *du'ā* at home, and therefore cannot respond to the call.

Likewise, if a person is making *du'ā*, and his parents call him for any assistance, then responding to his parents takes precedence over *du'ā*.

There is sufficient proof for this principle in the story of Jurayj, a monk who used to worship Allāh all day and night. The Prophet (ﷺ) narrates:

> There was a person from the Children of Isrā'īl by the name of Jurayj, who would pray in his monastery. His mother came to him and called him (to come out). So he asked himself: 'Should I respond or continue to pray?' And he chose the prayer. This happened three times, all the time he would choose the prayer over responding to his mother. So she said (in anger), 'O Allāh! Do not let him die until he sees the faces of prostitutes!'
>
> It so happened that a prostitute asked the townspeople, 'Do you wish that I tempt him?' They responded, 'Yes!' So she went to the monastery, and presented herself to him, but he refused. She then went away, and presented herself to a shepherd, who fell to her advances, and she gave birth to a child. (She was asked who the father was), so she replied, 'Jurayj!' At this, the townspeople gathered their axes and sticks and went to his monastery. They found him praying, but this did not stop them from tearing down his monastery and beating him. He said, 'Woe to you! What are you doing?' They responded, 'Woe to you, O Jurayj! We thought you were better than that. You have caused this girl to become pregnant.'
>
> At that, Jurayj asked that the baby be brought. He purified himself, and made a *du'ā* to Allāh. Then he poked the baby,

> and said, 'O child! Who is your father?' The child answered, 'The shepherd!' When the townspeople saw this (miracle) they said, 'Allow us to build your temple with gold and silver!' Jurajy replied, 'No, with mud (the way it was)', so they rebuilt it for him.[106]

This ḥadīth has many benefits in it, but the point that is being made is the fact that Jurayj did not respond to his mother, but rather continued in his prayer. Therefore, his mother became angry, and made a *duʿā* against him. As shall be discussed shortly, the *duʿā* of a parent against his or her offspring is responded to.

So, Jurayj preferred his prayer over responding to his mother. Yet, it was proper that he should have shortened his prayer, and responded to his mother; he could have prayed at any time, but he could not delay his mother's request. (As a side point, this ḥadīth also shows that the scholar is greater in status than the worshipper, as Jurayj did what he did because he did not have knowledge. Had he been a scholar, and known the importance of responding to one's parents, he would have obliged his mother.)

Likewise, when any obligatory act must be responded to, then *duʿā* must be postponed for another time.

---

[106] Reported by al-Bukhārī (# 3436), Muslim (# 2550), and others.

CHAPTER V

THE ETIQUETTE OF *DU῾Ā*

There are a number of manners and etiquette procedures that accompany the performance of *du῾ā* . This so that the *du῾ā* is accepted.

The difference between this section and the preceding one is that such etiquette occurs *while* a person is making a *du῾ā*, whereas the acts mentioned in the previous section must occur *before* a person makes *du῾ā*.

1. Praising Allāh before the *Du῾ā*, and Praying upon the Prophet (ﷺ)

This because the person who is making the *du῾ā* is asking for forgiveness, mercy and sustenance from his Creator, so it behoves the worshipper to start his *du῾ā* with the praise and glorification of Allāh, all Glory and Praise be to Him, such that this praise is befitting His status.

Faḍalah ibn ῾Ubayd narrates that the Prophet (ﷺ) was once sitting in the mosque, when a person entered and prayed two *rak̲a῾ats*. After he finished, he said, "O Allāh, forgive me and have mercy on me!" The Prophet (ﷺ) said:

> "You have been hasty, O worshipper! When you finish your prayer, then sit down and praise Allāh with the praise that He is worthy of, and pray upon me, then state your *du῾ā*."

After that, another man prayed, and then praised Allāh and prayed upon the Prophet (ﷺ). The Prophet (ﷺ) said to him:

> "O worshipper! Make your *du῾ā*, and it will be answered!"[107]

---

[107] Authentic, narrated by al-Tirmidhī and al-Nasā'ī from Faḍalah ibn ῾Ubayd, and authenticated by al-Albānī in *Ṣaḥīḥ al-Jāmi῾* # 3988.

This same narration has also come in a different wording from Faḍalah, in which he said: the Prophet (ﷺ) heard a man making a *du*ʿ*ā* in his ṣalāt, and he did not pray upon the Prophet (ﷺ). The Prophet (ﷺ) said:

> "He has been hasty".

He (ﷺ) then called him, and said to him, or to someone else:

> "When one of you has prayed, then let him begin with praising Allāh and glorifying Him, then let him pray upon the Prophet (ﷺ). After that, he may make any *du*ʿ*ā* that he wishes".[108]

The Prophet (ﷺ) described the initial person's prayer as hasty since he had preceded the prayer over the means.

ʿAbdullāh ibn Masʿūd narrated that the Prophet (ﷺ) said:

> "There is no one who is more *Aghyar*[109] than Allāh, and that is why He has prohibited all indecencies, open and secret. And there is no one who loves to be praised more than Allāh, and that is why He has praised Himself".[110]

Allāh, all Glory and Praise be to Him, wants us to praise Him so that we ourselves may benefit from this praise, since Allāh is not in need of anything, and we can never reach a position to benefit or harm Him. From this, the error of those who say, "If Allāh Himself loves to be praised, then how can we not love it?", can be seen.

Allāh, all Glory and Praise be to Him, has praised Himself in the Qur'ān on numerous occasions. For example He said:

---

[108] Authentic, narrated by Aḥmad, Abū Dāwūd, al-Tirmidhī, and others, from Faḍalah ibn ʿUbayd, and authenticated by al-Albānī in *Ṣaḥīḥ al-Jāmi*ʿ # 648.

[109] The word *aghyar* suggests a protective jealousy over something, and protecting it from all evil and harm. For example, it can be said that a man has *ghiyarah* over his wife.

[110] Narrated by al-Bukhārī, Muslim, and Aḥmad from Ibn Masʿūd, as mentioned in *Ṣaḥīḥ al-Jāmi*ʿ # 7165.

ٱلْحَمْدُ لِلَّهِ رَبِّ ٱلْعَٰلَمِينَ ﴿٢﴾
ٱلرَّحْمَٰنِ ٱلرَّحِيمِ ﴿٣﴾ مَٰلِكِ يَوْمِ ٱلدِّينِ ﴿٤﴾

"All praise is due to Allāh, the Lord of the Worlds. The Ever-Merciful, the Bestower of Mercy. The Master of the Day of Judgement".[111]

وَهُوَ ٱلْغَفُورُ ٱلْوَدُودُ ﴿١٤﴾ ذُو ٱلْعَرْشِ ٱلْمَجِيدُ ﴿١٥﴾ فَعَّالٌ لِّمَا يُرِيدُ ﴿١٦﴾

"He is Oft-Forgiving, full of Love. Owner of the Throne, the Glorious. He does what He intends."[112]

Du῾ā with Allāh's Greatest Name:

One of the best ways to praise Allāh is by using His Greatest Name.

Buraydah narrated that the Prophet (ﷺ) heard a person say: "O Allāh! I ask you, by virtue of the fact that I testify that You are Allāh, there is no deity except You, the One, whom all the Creation turns to for help, who does not beget and is not begotten, and there is none equivalent to Him!"

He (ﷺ) said:

> "This person has asked Allāh by His Greatest Name, which if He is asked with, He gives, and if He is petitioned with (i.e., a *du῾ā*), He answers".[113]

Imām al-Ṭibi said, explaining this ḥadīth:

> This ḥadīth shows that Allāh has a Great Name (*al-Ism al-A῾ẓam)*, and if He is called by this name, He responds, as is mentioned in the ḥadīth. Other *aḥādīth* have also mentioned

---

[111] Sūrah *al-Fātiḥah*, 1-3.

[112] Sūrah *al-Burūj,* 14-16.

[113] Authentic, narrated by Abū Dāwūd (*Ṣaḥīḥ al-Sunan* # 1341), al-Tirmidhī (*Ṣaḥīḥ al-Sunan* # 2763) and others, from Buraydah al-Aslamī.

examples of the *Ism al-Aʿẓam*, and in those narrations, there are names not mentioned in this ḥadīth, except that the Name 'Allāh' occurs in all of these narrations. By this, it can be inferred that this Name (i.e. Allāh) is the *Ism al-Aʿẓam*.[114]

Yet another point that can be inferred from the ḥadīth is the permissibility of *tawassul* with one's belief (*īmān*), since the wording of the ḥadīth says, '...I ask You, by virtue of the fact that...,' meaning, '...due to the fact that I bear witness that You are Allāh, answer my request...' Belief (*īmān*) comes under pious actions. Another proof of this position is the ḥadīth of the people trapped in the cave, who prayed to Allāh to release them by doing *tawassul* with their pious deeds. Allāh responded to their prayer, and removed the rock blocking their exit. This story will be discussed in greater detail in the chapter concerning *tawassul*.

2. Raising One's Hands

Amongst the etiquette of *duʿā* that is known by all Muslims, young or old, is that of raising one's hands while making *duʿā*. In fact, the raising of one's hands during *duʿā* has been narrated in so many different traditions that Shaykh al-Islām Ibn Taymiyah said: "As for the Prophet (ﷺ), raising his hands in *duʿā*, then this has been narrated in so many *aḥādīth* that they cannot be counted!"[115]

Of these *aḥādīth* is that of Abū Mūsa al-Ashʿarī, who narrated: "The Prophet (ﷺ) made a *duʿā*, and I saw him raise his hands, until I could see the whiteness of his armpits".[116]

And Ibn ʿUmar narrated: "The Prophet (ﷺ) raised his hands and said:

"O Allāh! I ask your protection for what Khālid has done!"[117]

---

[114] *Tuḥfat al-Aḥwadhī*, 9/446.

[115] Arūsi, p. 212.

[116] Narrated in al-Bukhārī (4323), from Abū Mūsa al-Ashʿarī.

[117] Narrated in al-Bukhārī (4339) from ʿAbdullāh ibn ʿUmar.

Anas also narrated that the Prophet (ﷺ) "...raised his hands until I saw the whiteness of his armpits".[118]

Furthermore Salmān al-Fārsī said that the Prophet (ﷺ) said:

> "Indeed, Allāh is Shy and Beneficent. He is Shy when His servant raises his hands to Him (in a *duʿā*) to return them empty, disappointed!"[119]

Subhān Allāh! The Lord of the Creation feels Shy when one of His servants lifts his hands up to Him to make *duʿā*! Verily, hearts are filled with love and awe at the Generosity and Beneficence of Allāh.

It is important that one's palms face upwards, and not the back of one's hands. Mālik ibn Yasār narrated that the Prophet (ﷺ) said,

> "If you ask Allāh, then ask him with the palms of your hands outwards, and not with the outward portion of the hands (i.e. with the palms facing down)".[120]

It is not befitting for a person to ask with his palms facing down, for this is a sign of arrogance, and an indication that he is not really in need of his request.

There are many reasons why raising one's hands in *duʿā* is beloved to Allāh. Of these reasons is that it is an indication of Allāh's complete power and right to be worshipped. It proves – by actions and not words – that Allāh is worthy of being asked, and that He is the one Who Hears and Knows everything, for He knows the situation of His servant better than the servant himself. It is a sign that the One being asked is Ever-Merciful (*al-Rahīm*), Loving to His

---

[118] Narrated in al-Bukhārī (6341) without a complete chain of narrators, but its chain is given by Abū Nuʿaym in his *al-Mustakhraj*, as Ibn Ḥajr pointed out in *Fatḥ al-Bārī*.

[119] Narrated by Aḥmad, Abū Dāwūd (# 1488), al-Tirmidhī (# 3556), Ibn Mājah (# 3865) and others, from Salmān al-Fārsī, and authenticated by al-Albānī in *Ṣaḥīḥ al-Jāmiʿ*, # 1757.

[120] Authentic, narrated by Abū Dāwūd from Mālik ibn Yasār, and narrated by Ibn Majāh, al-Ṭabarānī, and al-Ḥākim from Ibn ʿAbbās, and authenticated by al-Albānī in *Ṣaḥīḥ al-Jāmiʿ* # 593.

servants (*al-Wadūd*), responding to His slave (*Samī' al-Du'ā*). It shows that Allāh is the Ever-Generous (*al-Karīm*), the Self-Sustaining (*al-Ghanī*), and that only He deserves to be asked, and only He is capable of responding. It demonstrates that man is poor and destitute for his Lord's blessings, for he has humbled himself in front of the One full of Honour, and raised his hands up to him, indicating his poverty.

In other words, it is a physical manifestation of all that this noble act of *du'ā* embodies.

There are three different types of motions that are narrated from the Companions. The first type is to point with one's forefinger, without necessarily lifting one's hands. This action is done when one asks for forgiveness, or makes a general *dhikr* (remembrance of Allāh), or while making a *du'ā* during the *khuṭbah (sermon)*, or during the *tashahhud* (that part of the prayer said in the final sitting position of each cycle of two *rak'āt*).

The second type is to raise one's hands to the level of one's shoulders, with the palms facing up. This is done for regular *du'ās* that one makes at any time.

The last type of action is only done in extremely severe circumstances, such as asking for rain after a drought, or seeking protection from an imminent enemy attack. In this case, the hands are stretched forth towards the sky, without joining the two palms together. When this is done, a person's armpits become exposed due to the severity of the stretching.

This is affirmed by the narration of Ibn 'Abbās, who said: "The asking (of any *du'ā* should be accompanied by) raising your hands to the level of your shoulder, or around that level. The seeking of forgiveness (*istighfār*) (should be accompanied by) pointing with one finger (i.e. the forefinger). Petitioning (is done by) stretching forth your hands totally (above the head, such that the armpits are exposed)".[121]

---

[121] Authentic, narrated by Abū Dāwūd # 1486, from Ibn 'Abbās, and Ibn Ḥajr in *Fatḥ al-Bārī* also said it was in the *Mustadrak* of al-Ḥākim, who did not give any comment on the authenticity of the ḥadīth.

The general rule is that when a person makes *duʿā*, he should raise his hands. However, there is one case in which the Prophet (ﷺ) did not raise his hands, and that was during the Friday *khuṭbah*. So for the *duʿā* during the *khuṭbah*, it is not Sunnah for the Imām or the people to raise the hands, except if the person giving the *khuṭbah* makes a special prayer for rain (*istisqā*), for it is Sunnah to raise one's hands for this particular *duʿā*.

Also, it is not Sunnah to raise one's hands for the general *duʿās* of the day, such as the *duʿās* for entering a mosque and house, and for exiting them.

As for the exact manner in which the hands should be raised, then note that they should be raised to the level of the shoulders, and placed together. One can either turn one's palms towards the sky (in which case the back of one's hands will face the earth), or turn the palms to face one's own face, in which case the back of the hands will face away from him.[122]

As for wiping one's hands on the face after one has made *duʿā*, then this is discussed in a later section.

3. Facing the Qiblah

The qiblah is a blessed direction to face, and through it Allāh has caused the Muslims to unite all over the world. By facing the qiblah, a Muslim turns himself in the direction of the very first place of worship ever built on earth – the Kaʿbah.

It has been authentically narrated that the Prophet (ﷺ) would face the qiblah when making *duʿā*. ʿAbdullāh ibn Zayd narrated: "The Prophet (ﷺ) left (Madīnah) to this prayer place, seeking rain. So he made a *duʿā*, and asked for rain, then he faced the qiblah and turned his cloak inside-out".[123] Imām al-Bukhārī put this ḥadīth in

---

[122] Abū Zayd, p. 26, 116. This is based on a weak ḥadīth.

[123] Reported by al-Bukhārī (# 6343), Muslim (# 894) and others. The turning of the cloak is a unique Sunnah that is performed at the end of the rain-prayer, and signifies optimism and hope that the situation will change from drought to rainfall.

a Chapter entitled, "Making *duʿā* facing the Qiblah," showing that it forms the etiquette of *duʿā*.

It has also been narrated that when the Quraysh tormented the Prophet (ﷺ), he '...faced the Kaʿbah and made a *duʿā* against them.'[124]

So a person is encouraged to turn towards the qiblah when he wishes to make a *duʿā*.

4. Performing *Wuḍū*

Of the etiquettes of *duʿā* is that a person be in a state of *wuḍū* (ritual purity) while making *duʿā*. This is confirmed in the ḥadīth of Abū Mūsa al-Ashʿarī in which he stated that the Prophet (ﷺ), after the Battle of Ḥunayn, called for water, performed *wuḍū*, then raised his hands and said:

> "O Allāh! Forgive ʿUbayd ibn ʿĀmir!"

Abū Mūsa said, "I could see the whiteness of his armpits".[125]

5. To Cry

One of the ways in which sincerity is shown in *duʿā* is through crying. This brings about a feeling of humility in front of Allāh, and shows the importance of one's request. It displays the great need that the servant has from his Lord, and that he can never be without His help and aid.

Once, the Prophet (ﷺ) recited some verses from the Qur'ān, including the Prophet Ibrāhīm's statement:

رَبِّ إِنَّهُنَّ أَضْلَلْنَ كَثِيرًا مِّنَ ٱلنَّاسِۖ
فَمَن تَبِعَنِي فَإِنَّهُۥ مِنِّيۖ وَمَنْ عَصَانِي فَإِنَّكَ غَفُورٌ رَّحِيمٌ ﴿٣٦﴾

> O My Lord! These (idols) have caused many people to go astray, so whoever follows me is of me, and whoever disobeys me, then (even then) you are the Most Forgiving, Most Merciful.[126]

---

[124] Reported by al-Bukhārī (# 3960) and others.

[125] Reported by al-Bukhārī (# 4323) and Muslim (# 2498).

[126] Sūrah *Ibrāhīm*, 36.

And the Prophet ʿĪsa's statement:

إِن تُعَذِّبْهُمْ فَإِنَّهُمْ عِبَادُكَ وَإِن تَغْفِرْ لَهُمْ فَإِنَّكَ أَنتَ ٱلْعَزِيزُ ٱلْحَكِيمُ

If You punish them, then they are Your servants. And if You forgive them, then You are the One of Honour, the All-Wise.[127]

After reciting these verses, the Prophet (ﷺ) said:

"O Allāh! My *ummah*! My *ummah*!",

and he started crying. Allāh said to the angel Jibrīl, "O Jibrīl, go to Muḥammad – and your Lord knows – and ask him what makes him cry?"

So Jibrīl went to the Prophet (ﷺ) and asked him. The Prophet (ﷺ), responded that he was crying out of concern for his followers, just like Ibrāhīm and ʿĪsa were concerned for their followers, and Allāh knew why he was crying , without having to ask Jibrīl.

So Allāh said, "O Jibrīl! Go to Muḥammad and say: 'We will please you regarding your followers, and will not cause you grief'".[128]

6. To Expect the Best from Allāh

Amongst the etiquette of *duʿā* is that the person making the *duʿā* expects the best from Allāh, and anticipates a response from Allāh, whether that response is quick in coming or not.

Allāh says:

وَإِذَا سَأَلَكَ
عِبَادِى عَنِّى فَإِنِّى قَرِيبٌ أُجِيبُ دَعْوَةَ ٱلدَّاعِ إِذَا دَعَانِ

"And when My servants ask you concerning Me, then (answer them), I am indeed near to them. I respond to the invocations of the supplicant when he calls on Me!"[129]

---

[127] Sūrah *al-Māʾidah*, 118.

[128] Reported by Muslim (# 202) and others.

[129] Sūrah *al-Baqarah*, 186.

Zakariyya said, as Allāh quoted him in the Qur'ān,

إِنَّكَ سَمِيعُ ٱلدُّعَآءِ ﴿٣٨﴾

"Verily, You are the One who hears all invocations!"[130]

And Allāh says:

فَٱسْتَجَابَ لَهُمْ رَبُّهُمْ أَنِّى لَآ أُضِيعُ عَمَلَ عَٰمِلٍ مِّنكُم مِّن ذَكَرٍ أَوْ أُنثَىٰ

"So their Lord accepted of them (their supplication and answered them), 'Never will I allow to be lost the work of any of you, be he male or female!",[131]

and He said,

وَقَالَ رَبُّكُمُ ٱدْعُونِىٓ أَسْتَجِبْ لَكُمْ
إِنَّ ٱلَّذِينَ يَسْتَكْبِرُونَ عَنْ عِبَادَتِى سَيَدْخُلُونَ جَهَنَّمَ
دَاخِرِينَ ﴿٦٠﴾

Verily, your Lord has said: "Call upon Me, and I will answer you!" Those who are arrogant to worship Me will enter Hell, humiliated![132]

Ṣāliḥ said to his people:

فَٱسْتَغْفِرُوهُ ثُمَّ تُوبُوٓا۟ إِلَيْهِ إِنَّ رَبِّى قَرِيبٌ مُّجِيبٌ

"So ask Him for forgiveness, and turn to Him in repentance. Verily, my Lord is Ever-Near, Responsive",[133]

and Allāh also said,

وَلَقَدْ نَادَىٰنَا نُوحٌ فَلَنِعْمَ ٱلْمُجِيبُونَ ﴿٧٥﴾

"And indeed, Noah called upon Us, and We are the best of those who answer."[134]

---

[130] Sūrah *Āl-ʿImrān,* 38.

[131] Sūrah *Āl-ʿImrān*, 195.

[132] Sūrah *Ghāfir,* 60.

[133] Sūrah *Hūd*, 61.

[134] Sūrah *Ṣāffāt*, 75.

Therefore, Allāh is close to His worshippers, and He is present with them in His knowledge, aid and protection. The Prophet (ﷺ) has commanded us to leave the response to our *duʿās* to Allāh, and to expect that Allāh will answer our *duʿās*, for he (ﷺ) said:

> "Make *duʿā* to Allāh in a state that you are certain that your *duʿā* will be responded to."[135]

This ḥadīth means that we should firmly believe that Allāh is not going to leave our *duʿā* unanswered, for He is the Most Beneficent. Therefore, whenever a worshipper asks Allāh with sincerity, hoping for Allāh's mercy, and fulfilling the etiquette and manners of *duʿā*, he should be certain that his *duʿā* will be responded to.

The ḥadīth concerning Allāh's 'Shyness' has already been mentioned;

> "Indeed, Allāh is Shy and Beneficent. He is Shy when His servant raises his hands to Him (in a *duʿā*) to return them empty!"[136]

In other words, Allāh wants to respond to the worshipper when he has not even requested something, so how is the situation after the worshipper has asked his Creator? For Allāh is Shy at allowing the hands of His servant to return empty after he has raised them to Him. Allāh treats us with the utmost Beneficence and Generosity.

Abū Hurayrah narrates that the Prophet (ﷺ) said,

> "Allāh, all Glory and Praise be to Him, has said, 'Whatever My servant assumes of Me, that is how I will treat him, and I am with him when he remembers Me'".[137]

So if a person only expects good from Allāh, and is certain that Allāh will not destroy his hopes and desires, then Allāh will fulfil

---

[135] Authentic, narrated by al-Tirmidhī and al-Ḥākim from Abū Hurayrah, and authenticated by al-Albānī in *Ṣaḥīḥ al-Jāmiʿ* # 245.

[136] Authentic, narrated by Aḥmad, Abū Dāwūd, al-Tirmidhī and others, from Salmān al-Fārsī, and authenticated by al-Albānī in *Ṣaḥīḥ al-Jāmiʿ* # 1757.

[137] Reported by Muslim, from Abū Hurayrah, as mentioned in *Ṣaḥīḥ al-Jāmiʿ* # 8138.

his expectations. On the other hand, if he is not certain of the response of Allāh, and he feels that he will not be responded to, then he will be treated the way that he feels. Al-Shawkānī commented on this ḥadīth as follows:

> In this ḥadīth, Allāh encourages His servants to expect the best from Him, since He will treat them according to their expectations. So whoever expects good from Him will be showered with His Good, and will be shown His Beautiful Generosity... But he who is not like that will not be treated in this manner. And this is the meaning of the fact that He is with him when he remembers Him. So it is obligatory on the slave to always assume the best of Allāh. And he should help himself to achieve this state by always recalling the texts (of the Qur'ān and Sunnah) that show the great Mercy of Allāh.

This is why the true Muslim always expects the best from Allāh. The Prophet (ﷺ) states:

> "Let not any of you die except that he assumes the best from Allāh".[138]

Since a person does not know when he will die, the implication of the ḥadīth is that a Muslim must always have good thoughts and assume the best about his Creator, such that, when death does overtake him, he is still intent upon this feeling.

Ibn al-Qayyim said,

> Whoever reflects upon this issue deeply will realise that having the best expectations from Allāh is equivalent to having good deeds, and doing good with one's soul. For only when a person expects the best from Allāh will he perform good deeds, since he will expect that Allāh will reward him for his deeds and accept them. Therefore, the reason that he performed these good deeds was because of his good expectations of Allāh; so the more a person betters his expectations from Allāh, the more good deeds he does!"[139]

---

[138] Reported by Muslim (# 2877) and others.

[139] *Al-Jawāb al-Kāfī*, p. 23.

In other words, having the best expectations necessitates doing good deeds. Therefore, the one who continues to sin, and does not do any good deeds, does not truly have the best expectation of Allāh. Rather, such a person has a shallow understanding of this concept, and follows his desires!

7. To Pray with Humility and Fear

This state is one that has been commanded by the Qur'ān:

ٱدْعُوا۟ رَبَّكُمْ تَضَرُّعًا وَخُفْيَةً ۚ إِنَّهُۥ لَا يُحِبُّ ٱلْمُعْتَدِينَ ﴿٥٥﴾

> Call upon your Lord with humility, and in secret. Verily, He does not like the aggressors.[140]

Likewise, Allāh has described the Prophet Zakariyya and his wife as:

إِنَّهُمْ كَانُوا۟ يُسَٰرِعُونَ فِى ٱلْخَيْرَٰتِ
وَيَدْعُونَنَا رَغَبًا وَرَهَبًا ۖ وَكَانُوا۟ لَنَا خَٰشِعِينَ ﴿٩٠﴾

> Verily, they used to hasten to do good deeds, and they used to make *du'ā* to Us with hope and fear, and used to humble themselves before Us.[141]

So it is important that the servant show humility to the Creator, and humble himself before Him while making *du'ā*. For is it not befitting that a slave appear in front of his Creator and Master in a state of humility, realising the status of his Lord, and fearing his own shortcomings in his duty towards Him?

8. To Complain Only to Allāh

Part of the completeness of a person's *tawḥīd* is that he does not complain to anyone else, in order to gain their sympathy and pity. Rather, the true Muslim submits all of his affairs to Allāh, and com-

---

[140] Sūrah *al-A'rāf,* 55.

[141] Sūrah *al-Anbiyā',* 90.

plains of his pitiful state to his Creator, without expecting any compassion from anyone else.

The prophets of Allāh, whenever they were in severe situations and extenuating circumstances, would turn to Allāh, and show their need of Allāh's help.

When Zakariyya grew old, and was not blessed with any progeny, he cried out:

رَبِّ لَا تَذَرْنِي فَرْدًا وَأَنتَ خَيْرُ ٱلْوَٰرِثِينَ

> O My Lord! Do not leave me alone (without progeny), and you are the best of inheritors.[142]

When Ibrāhīm left his wife and child in the middle of the desert, without any support or help, he prayed to Allāh, describing their pitiful situation:

رَّبَّنَآ إِنِّيٓ أَسْكَنتُ مِن ذُرِّيَّتِي بِوَادٍ غَيْرِ ذِي زَرْعٍ عِندَ بَيْتِكَ
ٱلْمُحَرَّمِ رَبَّنَا لِيُقِيمُوا۟ ٱلصَّلَوٰةَ فَٱجْعَلْ أَفْـِٔدَةً مِّنَ ٱلنَّاسِ
تَهْوِيٓ إِلَيْهِمْ وَٱرْزُقْهُم مِّنَ ٱلثَّمَرَٰتِ لَعَلَّهُمْ يَشْكُرُونَ ﴿٣٧﴾

> O My Lord! I have left my family to live in a valley that has no fruits, close to your Sacred House, so that they may establish the prayer. Our Lord! Therefore cause a group of people to love them, and provide them with fruits so that they may give thanks.[143]

When Ayyūb was tried and tested by Allāh, and his family and wealth were taken away from him, to such an extent that even his body suffered a terrible disease, he cried out:

أَنِّي مَسَّنِيَ ٱلضُّرُّ وَأَنتَ أَرْحَمُ ٱلرَّٰحِمِينَ

> O My Lord! Verily, some harm has afflicted me, and You are the Most Merciful of all those who are merciful.[144]

---

[142] Sūrah *al-Anbiyā'*, 89

[143] Sūrah *Ibrāhīm*, 37.

[144] Sūrah *al-Anbiyā'*, 83.

When Mūsa fled Egypt to avoid Pharaoh, and was all alone in the Valley of Midian, with no helper or aid, he prayed:

رَبِّ إِنِّي لِمَآ أَنزَلْتَ إِلَيَّ مِنْ خَيْرٍ فَقِيرٌ

O My Lord! Verily, I am needy to whatever good that You send down to me.[145]

And when Ya῾qūb did not know the fate of his favourite son Yūsuf, and his oldest son stayed behind in Egypt, while Yūsuf's brother Ben Yamīn was also taken captive, all he could cry out was:

إِنَّمَآ أَشْكُوا۟ بَثِّى وَحُزْنِىٓ إِلَى ٱللَّهِ

Verily, I only complain of my grief and sorrow to Allāh![146]

So it is important that one turn only to Allāh, and complain of one's situation only to him. For what value is there in turning to another created being, who cannot benefit or harm himself without Allāh's help, much less benefit or harm others? And why would one seek to gain the pity of he who himself should be pitied due to his helplessness and incapability?

9. To Pray Quietly

While making a *du῾ā*, a person should not pray loudly, so that others can hear him. The proper way to make *du῾ā* is in a subdued voice, as Allāh mentions:

ٱدْعُوا۟ رَبَّكُمْ تَضَرُّعًا وَخُفْيَةً ۚ إِنَّهُۥ لَا يُحِبُّ ٱلْمُعْتَدِينَ ﴿٥٥﴾

Call upon your Lord with humility, and in secret. Verily, He does not like the aggressors.[147]

That is why Allāh praised the *du῾ā* of Zakariyya when He described it as:

[145] Sūrah *al-Qaṣaṣ*, 24.

[146] Sūrah *Yūsuf*, 86.

[147] Sūrah *al-A῾rāf*, 55.

إِذْ نَادَىٰ رَبَّهُۥ نِدَآءً خَفِيًّا ۝٣

When he made a *du'ā* to his Lord in secret (or privately).[148]

This principle is also mentioned in a ḥadīth. Once, the Companions were travelling, and loudly engaging in *dhikr* (remembrance of Allāh). The Prophet (ﷺ), said:

> "O people! Be gentle on yourselves, for you are not calling someone who is deaf or absent. Rather, you are calling the One Who hears everything, Ever-Close".[149]

Shaykh al-Islām Ibn Taymiyyah delved into the wisdom of making *du'ā* silently, and mentioned a number of benefits to this:[150]

Firstly, it is a sign of strong *īman*, as the person demonstrates that he firmly believes that Allāh can hear even the quietest of prayers and thoughts.

Secondly, it is a sign of respect and manners in front of Allāh. For, just as it is considered improper for the servant to raise his voice in front of his master, or the peasant in front of the king, even so it is improper that a slave raise his voice loudly in front of the Creator – and to Allāh belongs the highest parable and example. Since Allāh can hear the most silent of prayers, it is not befitting that a person make *du'ā* in a loud voice.

Thirdly, it is a means of achieving humility and humbleness, which is the essence of worship. The one who is humble does not ask except meekly, whereas the one who is arrogant asks loudly. So softening the voice aids one in achieving this desired humility in *du'ā*.

Fourthly, it is a means of achieving sincerity, since others will not notice him.

Fifthly, it aids the heart in concentrating on the *du'ā*, since rais-

---

[148] Sūrah *Maryam*, 3.

[149] Reported by al-Bukhārī (# 6384).

[150] Paraphrased from *Majmū' al-Fatāwa*, v. 15, pp. 14-20.

ing one's voice loudly distracts one from one's thoughts. So, to make a *duʿā* quietly will help the person keep his thoughts together, and not be distracted from the state that he is in.

Sixthly, it shows the closeness that the true believer feels to his Creator. So it is a means of strengthening the relationship that the believer should have with Allāh, as it allows him to feel that Allāh is closer than any other object to him. Hence why Allāh praised Zakariyya when He described his *duʿā* as being 'secret'.

Seventhly, it aids a person in continuing the *duʿā* and not breaking off. This because it is easier on the tongue and body, for it does not wear out or tire a person, in contrast to one who makes a *duʿā* loudly.

Eighthly, it causes less distraction, for raising one's voice brings about the attention of others, and this leads to a person becoming conscious of his surroundings. However, if he lowers his voice, then he will be able to cut himself off from his environment and not be distracted by it.

Lastly, it prevents a person from being the target of envy and jealousy. For indeed, men and *jinn* are full of evil souls that envy others, and there is no greater cause for enmity than to see a person turn to Allāh in private conversation, engrossed in His remembrance. So if a person makes *duʿā* silently, he protects himself from this evil.

The Companions of the Prophet (ﷺ) understood the importance of saying a duʿā silently. Ibn ʿAbbās stated: "A silent duʿā is seventy times better than a loud one!"[151] And it has even been narrated that Ibn Masʿūd once forced a group of people out of the masjid (mosque), because they were raising their voices loudly while remembering Allāh. In this respect he said, "I don't think except that you are innovators!"[152] And al-Ḥassan al-Baṣrī said, "We used to be amongst a group of people (i.e., the Companions) who would never do any act in public if they could do so in private. And those Mus-

---

[151] Narrated by Ibn al-Mubārak in his *al-Zuhd* (# 40).

[152] Abū Zayd, p. 91.

lims would strive in making their *du'ā*, and not a sound would be heard from them! For they used to whisper to their Lord."[153]

10. Acknowledging One's Sins

Part of the etiquette of *du'ā* is to acknowledge one's shortcomings and sins in front of one's Creator. This is also a means of properly worshipping Allāh.

Abū Hurayrah said:

> "The best *du'ā* is for a person to say: O Allāh! You are my Lord, and I am your servant. I have wronged myself, and acknowledge my sins. O my Lord! Forgive me my sins, for You, and only You, are my Lord, and none forgives sins except You!"[154]

And 'Alī ibn Abī Ṭālib reported that the Prophet (ﷺ) said,

> "Verily, Allāh likes a worshipper who says: 'There is no one worthy of worship except You. I have wronged myself, so forgive my sins, for none forgives sins except You.' Allāh says, 'My servant knows that he has a Lord who forgives and punishes!'"[155]

That is why the best *du'ā* in which a person can ask for forgiveness contains a pure and sincere acknowledgment of one's deficiencies and sins. The Prophet (ﷺ) said:

> The *sayyid al-istighfār* (the best *du'ā* to ask for forgiveness) is that a person says: O Allāh! You are my Lord, there is no one worthy of worship except You. You created me, and I am your slave. And I am (following) Your covenant and Promise as much as I can. I seek Your refuge in the evil that I have done. I acknowledge Your favours upon me, and I acknowledge my sins. So forgive me, since no one forgives sins except You![156]

---

[153] Reported by at-Ṭabarī in his *Tafsīr* (5/514).

[154] Authentic as a statement of Abū Hurayrah, reported by Aḥmad, 1/515.

[155] Authentic, narrated by Aḥmad, Abū Dāwūd, al-Tirmidhī and others, from 'Alī ibn Abī Ṭālib, and authenticated by al-Albānī in *al-Ṣaḥīḥah* # 1653.

[156] Reported by al-Bukhārī (# 6306) and others.

So when one raises one's hands to Allāh, expecting a response from Him, one should also ponder over one's own relationship with Allāh, and the shortcomings that one possesses. In this way the person should recall his many sins, and feel his own humility – that is he should remember that he is asking One whom he has disobeyed, and sinned against, and not fulfilled his rights upon Him. Let him taste his impudence when he asks Allāh for more and more, without fulfilling the basic deeds that are obligatory upon him.

11. To Implore Allāh Earnestly

Of the etiquette of *du'ā* is that a person implore Allāh, and beseech Him. This sense of urgency is demonstrated in the Sunnah of the Prophet (ﷺ). 'Ā'ishah reported that when the Prophet (ﷺ) was afflicted with magic, he made *du'ā*, then he made *du'ā*, then he made *du'ā*.[157] This incident demonstrates a sense of urgency and insistence that is needed while making *du'ā*.

Additionally, we find this same characteristic in many of the *du'ās* that the Prophet (ﷺ) used to make. For example, he (ﷺ), would pray:

> O Allāh! Forgive me all (my sins) that I have already done, and will do (in the future), and what I have done in private, and what I have done in public, and all (sins) that you know from me.[158]

Now, it was possible to just say, 'Forgive all my sins', and the meaning would have been the same. However, in this beautiful prophetic *du'ā*, there is a strong sense of urgency – of imploring Allāh, and beseeching Him, of pleaing to Him, and insisting on this forgiveness. All of this is not conveyed in the simple phrase, 'Forgive my sins'.

---

[157] Reported by Muslim (# 2189) and others.

[158] Reported by Muslim (# 771) and others.

12. To be Determined in One's Request

Anas ibn Mālik narrates that the Prophet (ﷺ) said:

> "When one of you makes a *du'ā*, then let him be firm and determined in his *du'ā*, and let him not say, 'O Allāh! If You will, then please forgive me', for there is no one who can force Allāh to do anything".[159]

Therefore, what is desired is that a person be firm in his *du'ā*, asking from Allāh in a determined manner. If, on the other hand, a person says, "O Allāh! Grant me my *du'ā* if you wish", this goes against the firmness and resolution that is desired, for it is as if he is saying, "O Allāh! If You answer my *du'ā*, then I thank You, otherwise I do not ask You of it". This shows a degree of arrogance towards Allāh, all Glory and Praise be to Him, and implies a sense of self-sufficiency on the part of the person making the *du'ā*. A person is always in need of Allāh's help and aid, and as such should always ask of Allāh in a manner that shows his poverty for Allāh's support.

It should be pointed out that it is allowed to use this phrase when the person does not know if the matter he is asking for is for his good or not. So, it is permissible to pray: 'O Allāh! If you know that such-and-such a matter (related to this world) is good for me, then grant it to me'. What is prohibited is to use this phrase in matters that one needs without a doubt, such as Allāh's Forgiveness, or Mercy, or Blessings, etc.

13. To Use the Proper Names and Attributes of Allāh

To Allāh belong the Most Beautiful Names and Perfect Attributes. One of the purposes of these Names and Attributes is so that believers can increase in their Love for Allāh when they contemplate the meanings of these Names and Attributes. One of the best ways to truly understand and comprehend the meaning of these Names and Attributes is to use the appropriate one when making *du'ā*.

---

[159] Narrated by al-Bukhārī (# 6339), Muslim (# 2678), Aḥmad and others.

So, when one is asking for forgiveness, one should use the Names that are appropriate to the concept of forgiveness, such as *al-Tawwāb* (the One who continually accepts Repentance), *al-Ghaffār* (the One who continually Forgives), *al-Raḥīm* (the Ever-Merciful), and so forth. And when one is asking for sustenance, one should use Allāh's Name *al-Razzāq* (the One who Provides), and *al-Ghanī* (the One who Gives and is not in need of anything). Whatever a person is asking for, there will be an appropriate Divine Name or Attribute that he can use.

14. To Repeat the *Duʿā* Three Times

This is a recommended action while making a *duʿā*, for it shows a sense of urgency in obtaining what is asked for. The act of repeating a *duʿā* thrice is narrated in many *aḥādīth* from the Prophet (ﷺ), as, for example, the one reported by Ibn Masʿūd, who said: "When the Prophet (ﷺ) finished his prayer, he (ﷺ) raised his voice, and prayed against them (the leaders of the Quraysh who had persecuted him). And whenever he made a *duʿā*, he would repeat it thrice, and whenever he asked (from Allāh), he would do so thrice. So he (ﷺ) then said:

> "O Allāh! Upon you is (the retaliation) of the Quraysh!
> O Allāh! Upon you is (the retaliation) of the Quraysh!
> O Allāh! Upon you is (the retaliation) of the Quraysh!"[160]

Anas ibn Mālik also reported that the Prophet (ﷺ) said:

> "Whoever asks for Paradise three times, Paradise says: 'O Allāh! Enter him into Paradise!' And whoever seeks refuge from the Hellfire three times, the Hellfire says: 'O Allāh! Save him from the Hellfire!'[161]

---

[160] Reported by, among others, al-Bukhārī (420), Muslim (1794) (and the wording is his), from Ibn Masʿūd.

[161] Authentic, narrated by al-Tirmidhī, al-Nasā'ī and al-Ḥākim, from Anas, and authenticated in *Ṣaḥīḥ al-Jāmiʿ* # 6275.

15. To Pray with Concise *Duʿās*

'Concise' *duʿās* are those which are brief, yet contain many meanings, and ask for general benefits, and seek refuge in general evils. The Prophet (ﷺ) used to pray frequently with concise *duʿās*, and he was the one who had been given the most eloquent and concise of words. It was as if he (ﷺ) were asking for all the good possible of both worlds, and seeking refuge in all evils, in the briefest and most eloquent of phrases, so that the people who heard him (ﷺ) could memorise his *duʿās* easily, and understand what he said.

The Prophet (ﷺ) used to avoid prolonged, useless speech, for ʿĀ'ishah narrates that the Prophet (ﷺ) "...used to love concise *duʿās*, and he would leave all (*duʿās*) besides those".[162]

Al-Khaṭṭābī states: "So let him (i.e. the worshipper) choose for his *duʿā* the appropriate words, and let him praise his Lord using the best praises, and the noblest of them, and the most comprehensive in meaning. For (*duʿā*) is a secret conversation between the slave and the Master of all masters, whom no one resembles, nor does He have an equal!"[163]

Many such *duʿās* have been preserved for us in the books of ḥadīth. For example, Farwah ibn Nawfal reported that he asked ʿĀ'ishah for a *duʿā* that the Prophet (ﷺ) used to pray with. She answered: "He (ﷺ) used to say:

> "O Allāh! I seek refuge in you from the evil of what I have done, and the evil that I have not done!"[164]

This *duʿā* is a general, comprehensive one which seeks refuge in Allāh from all evil, whether a person has done that evil or not.

Another comprehensive *duʿā* that the Prophet (ﷺ) used is:

---

[162] Authentic, narrated by Abū Dāwūd, Aḥmad, Ibn Ḥibbān and others, from ʿĀ'ishah, and authenticated in *Ṣaḥīḥ al-Jāmiʿ* # 4949

[163] *Sha'n al-Duʿā*, p. 15.

[164] Narrated by Muslim from Abū Dharr, and Abū Dāwūd and al-Nasā'ī from ʿĀ'ishah, as mentioned in *Ṣaḥīḥ al-Jāmiʿ* # 1293.

> "O Allāh! Forgive my sins and my ignorance, and my transgressions in my affairs, and all that You know of me. O Allāh! Forgive me my sins done seriously or jokingly, purposely or unintentionally, and all else that is with me! O Allāh, forgive me what I have done, and what I have yet to do, and what I have done in secret, and what I have done openely, and all that you know of me. You are the First, and you are the Last, and You are capable of all things!"[165]

And from such concise prayers is the *du'ā* of the Prophet (ﷺ):

> "O Allāh, Our Lord! Grant us the good in this world, and the good in the Hereafter, and save us from the punishment of Hell!"[166]

Therefore, remember the value of your time, and do not cease to make *du'ā* to Allāh on all occasions and as often as you can. And how many are the words that spring forth from our mouths, that will not benefit us at all, or even be used against us on the Day of Judgement (we seek refuge in Allāh from that!). Yet, how easy these simple *du'ās* are, and how concise and brief, and how full of blessings and mercy! For is it not possible that a person says one of these concise *du'ās*, thinking it a small and trivial request, and yet the angels of mercy take it, and the doors of Heaven are opened for it, and the Compassionate Lord responds to it, so that on the Day of Judgement, the Scales weigh heavy because of it?

And how true the Arabic proverb: the best speech is that which is concise yet clear in meaning.

16. To Use the *Du'ās* of The Qur'ān and Sunnah

Of the etiquettes of *du'ā* is that one uses the *du'ās* found in the Qur'ān and Sunnah as much as possible. These *du'ās* are blessed *du'ās*, and are far better than any *du'ās* that we can make.

---

[165] Reported by al-Bukhārī and Muslim, from Abū Mūsa al-Ash'arī, as mentioned in *Ṣaḥīḥ al-Jāmi'* # 1264.

[166] Reported by al-Bukhārī and Muslim, as mentioned in *Ṣaḥīḥ al-Jāmi'* # 1306.

There are many evidences that such *du'ās* have more of a chance of being responded to.

Regarding the last verse of *Sūrah al-Baqarah*,

رَبَّنَا لَا تُؤَاخِذْنَآ إِن نَّسِينَآ أَوْ أَخْطَأْنَا رَبَّنَا وَلَا تَحْمِلْ عَلَيْنَآ إِصْرًا كَمَا حَمَلْتَهُۥ عَلَى ٱلَّذِينَ مِن قَبْلِنَا رَبَّنَا وَلَا تُحَمِّلْنَا مَا لَا طَاقَةَ لَنَا بِهِۦ وَٱعْفُ عَنَّا وَٱغْفِرْ لَنَا وَٱرْحَمْنَآ

> "O Our Lord! Do not punish us if we forget, or fall into error. O Our Lord! Do not place a burden on us, as you have placed upon those before us! Pardon us, forgive us, and have mercy on us…"

the Prophet (ﷺ) said, "Allāh has said: Yes, I have done so."[167]

In another beautiful ḥadīth, the Prophet (ﷺ) informs us that the *du'ā* in Sūrah al-Fātiḥah is responded to by Allāh:

> Allāh has said: I have divided the *ṣalāt* between My servant and Me in two halves, and My servant will have what he asks for. So when the servant says, '*Alḥamdu lillāhi Rabb il-'Ālamīn*', Allāh responds, 'My servant has praised Me!' And when he says, '*Al-Raḥmān al-Raḥīm*' Allāh responds, 'My servant has glorified Me'. And when he says, '*Mālik yawm al-Dīn*', Allāh responds, 'My servant has exalted Me'. And when he says, '*Iyyāk̲a na'budu wa iyyāk̲a nasta'īn*', Allāh says, 'This is between My servant and I, and My servant shall have what he desires'. And when he says, '*Ihdina al-Ṣirāṭ al-Mustaqīm…*' Allāh says, 'This is for My servant, and he will get what he desires'.[168]

Abū Hurayrah narrated that the Prophet (ﷺ) said:

> "The closest any worshipper can be to his Lord is while he is in prostration, so increase your *du'ās* in it"[169]

---

[167] Reported by Muslim and others. See *Tafseer Ibn Katheer*, 1/368.

[168] Reported by Muslim (# 395) and others.

[169] Reported by Muslim, Abū Dāwūd, al-Nasā'i and others, from Abū Hurayrah, as mentioned in *Ṣaḥīḥ al-Jāmi'* # 1175.

One also finds evidence for this in the Prophet's (ﷺ) actions. Ibn 'Abbās reported, "The Prophet (ﷺ) would teach us the following *du'ā* just as he would teach us a Sūrah of the Qur'ān: 'O Allāh, I seek refuge in You from the punishment of Hell, and I seek refuge in You from the punishment of the grave, and I seek refuge in You from the trials of the Anti-Christ (*al-Dajjāl*), and I seek refuge in You from the trials of life and death.'"[170]

In another narration, Jābir ibn 'Abdillāh said, "The Prophet (ﷺ) would teach us the *du'ā* of *istikhārah*[171] just as he would teach us a Sūrah of the Qur'ān."[172]

Thus, the Prophet (ﷺ) would be eager to teach the Companions precise *du'ās* that they should pray with, and these *du'ās*, in turn, were taught by the Companions to those after them, and eventually preserved in the books of the Sunnah.

The blessings of the *du'ās* of the Qur'ān and Sunnah are too numerous to mention. Perhaps the greatest blessing of these *du'ās* is that they encourage one's optimism that the *du'ā* will be responded to. The fact that Allāh Himself informs us of a particular *du'ā*, and encourages us to use it, is one of the greatest means of inspiring us to be confident, and instilling us with hope that our *du'ās* will be answered. Another blessing is that one finds that the *du'ās* of the Qur'ān and Sunnah are the most beautiful and eloquent *du'ās* – and how can this not be so, when such *du'ās* are the speech of Allāh and the speech of His Messenger (ﷺ)? These *du'ās* are also poignant, concise and comprehensive. In fact, there is hardly any need that any person has of the needs of this world or the Hereafter except that he will find a specific *du'ā* that caters to his situation in the texts of the Qur'ān and Sunnah.

---

[170]Reported by Muslim, # 590, and others.

[171]A *du'ā* that is prayed when one is uncertain as to which course of action one should take in any particular situation.

[172]Reported by al-Bukhārī, # 1162, and others.

Shaykh al-Islām Ibn Taymiyyah writes, "So people should make the *du'ās* that are found in the Qur'ān and Sunnah, for there is no doubt in the excellence and blessings of these *du'ās.* These *du'ās* are of the Straight Path – the Path of those whom Allāh has favoured, of the prophets, the sincere, the martyrs, and the righteous, and what a great company they are!"[173]

Of course, this does not mean that one is obligated to stick to the *du'ās* of the Qur'ān and Sunnah. Any *du'ā* is permissible to make (as long as the *du'ā* is regarding something permissible). However, there is no doubt that the speech of Allāh, and the speech of the Messenger of Allāh (ﷺ), is a blessed speech, and, therefore, the *du'ās* narrated in them are more worthy than other *du'ās.*[174]

One important reminder must be mentioned here: one who uses such *du'ās* should be aware of the meanings of them. If one merely reads such *du'ās* without understanding what he is reading, then he has contradicted most of the etiquettes of *du'ā*, for how can he sincerely and humbly petition Allāh when he does not even know what he is asking for?!

17. To Start *Du'ā* with One's Self

It is desirable that the person making the *du'ā* should first ask of it for himself. This is so for a number of reasons. Firstly, a person should desire all good for himself, so it does not make sense to pray for others and forget one's self. Secondly, the fact that a person prays for himself shows that what he is praying for is an important goal

---

[173] *Majmū' al-Fatāwa*, 1/346.

[174] There are a number of good books on this topic. Of the classical books in this field are: *al-Adhkār* of al-Ḥāfiẓ an-Nawawī, *al-Kalim aṭ-Ṭayyib* of Shaykh al-Islām Ibn Taymiyyah, *al-Wābil al-Sayyib* of his student, Ibn al-Qayyim, and *Tuḥfat al-Dhākirīn* of al-Shawkānī. Some of these books have been translated into English. Perhaps one of the more useful books for laymen is the one by the modern author, Muḥammad al-Qahtānī, which has been translated into English under the title, "*Fortification of the Muslim Through Remembrance and Prayer*" (Dar al-Khayr, Jeddah, 1995).

and objective. In other words, this ensures that he desires for his brothers what he desires for himself. Thirdly, it increases him in his sincerity in this *duʿā*, for verily mankind is weak, so when he makes *duʿā* only for his brother, it is possible that it will not be as sincere as when he makes a *duʿā* for himself *and* his brother.

This principle is demonstrated in a number of Qur'ānic verses, such as:

رَبَّنَا ٱغْفِرْ لَنَا وَلِإِخْوَٰنِنَا ٱلَّذِينَ سَبَقُونَا بِٱلْإِيمَٰنِ

"O Allāh! Forgive us, and our brothers (in faith) who have preceded us!"[175]

قَالَ رَبِّ ٱغْفِرْ لِى وَلِأَخِى وَأَدْخِلْنَا فِى رَحْمَتِكَ ۖ

"And he (Mūsa) prayed: O my Lord! Forgive me and my brother, and enter us into your Mercy!"[176]

رَبَّنَا ٱغْفِرْ لِى وَلِوَٰلِدَىَّ وَلِلْمُؤْمِنِينَ يَوْمَ يَقُومُ ٱلْحِسَابُ ﴿٤١﴾

"O Our Lord! Forgive me, and my parents, and all of the believers the Day that the Account will be taken!"[177]

وَٱسْتَغْفِرْ لِذَنۢبِكَ وَلِلْمُؤْمِنِينَ وَٱلْمُؤْمِنَٰتِ ۗ

"And Seek forgiveness (O Muḥammad) for your sins, and for the believing men and women."[178]

Likewise, this principle is affirmed by the practice of the Prophet (ﷺ). Ubayy ibn Kaʿb reports that whenever the Prophet (ﷺ) remembered someone and prayed for him, he would begin with himself.[179]

---

175 Sūrah *al-Ḥashr*, 10.

176 Sūrah *al-Aʿrāf*, 151.

177 Sūrah *Ibrāhīm*, 41.

178 Sūrah *Muḥammad,* 19.

179 Authentic, narrated by Abū Dāwūd, al-Tirmidhī, al-Nasā'ī and others, from Ubayy ibn Kaʿb, and authenticated in *Ṣaḥīḥ al-Jāmiʿ* # 4723.

However, this was not the constant habit of the Prophet (ﷺ), for there are other narrations to show that sometimes he (ﷺ) would pray for another person without praying for himself. For example, when he was speaking about Hājar, Ismā'īl's mother , he (ﷺ) said:

> "May Allāh have mercy on the mother of Ismā'īl. Had she left Zam Zam (to flow, and not stopped it with some sand) it would have been a clear lake".[180]

He also said regarding Ḥassān ibn Thābit,

> "O Allāh! Help him with the Holy Spirit (the Angel Jibrīl)!",[181]

and for Ibn 'Abbās,

> "O Allāh! Grant him an understanding of the religion!"[182]

These, and other examples besides these, show the permissibility of making a *du'ā* without mentioning one's self, but in general it is recommended to do so.

18. To Pray for All Muslims

Part of the completeness of one's *īmān* is that a person loves for his brother what he loves for himself. Therefore, just as he desires that he be guided to the truth, and be forgiven for his sins, so too should he desire the same for his fellow Muslims.

The Prophet (ﷺ) is commanded in the Qur'ān to:

وَٱسْتَغْفِرْ لِذَنۢبِكَ وَلِلْمُؤْمِنِينَ وَٱلْمُؤْمِنَٰتِ

> ...seek forgiveness (from Allāh) for your sins, and the sins of the believing men and women.[183]

---

[180] Reported by al-Bukhārī, from Anas ibn Mālik, as reported in *Ṣaḥīḥ al-Jāmi'* # 8079.

[181] Reported by al-Bukhārī (453), Muslim (2485) and others, from Abū Hurayrah.

[182] Reported by al-Bukhārī (143), Muslim (2477) and others, from Ibn 'Abbās.

[183] Sūrah *Muḥammad*, 19.

Likewise, the Prophet Nūḥ prayed to Allāh:

رَّبِّ ٱغْفِرْ لِى وَلِوَٰلِدَىَّ وَلِمَن دَخَلَ بَيْتِىَ
مُؤْمِنًا وَلِلْمُؤْمِنِينَ وَٱلْمُؤْمِنَٰتِ

> "O My Lord! Forgive me, and my parents, and whoever entered my house as a believer, and all the believing men and women".[184]

And the Prophet (ﷺ) said:

> "Whoever seeks forgiveness for the believing men and women, then a good deed will be written for him for every single believing man and women (that he prayed for)".[185]

So it is encouraged for the Muslim to remember all of his brothers and sisters when he is making a *duʿā*, and to pray for the entire Muslim *ummah*. He should also pray against the enemies of Islām, against tyrants and non-Muslim rulers that fight and torture the Muslims. All of this is a sign of the person's own *īmān*, and is contained within the etiquette of *duʿā*.

Of particular importance is that a person prays for his own parents (if they are alive, or if they died as Muslims). Allāh specifically instructs the believers in this respect,

وَٱخْفِضْ لَهُمَا جَنَاحَ ٱلذُّلِّ مِنَ ٱلرَّحْمَةِ وَقُل رَّبِّ ٱرْحَمْهُمَا
كَمَا رَبَّيَانِى صَغِيرًا ﴿٢٤﴾

> And lower unto them the wings of humility and mercy, and say, 'O My Lord! Have mercy on them, even as they took care of me while I was young.'[186]

---

[184] Sūrah *Nūḥ*, 28.

[185] Reported by al-Ṭabarānī in his *al-Kabīr*, and al-Ḥaythamī said in *Majmaʿ al-Zawā'id*: "Its *isnād* (chain of transmission) is good." Al-Albānī reported this statement, but did not pronounce a verdict on the ḥadīth himself. See *Ṣaḥīḥ al-Jāmiʿ*, # 6026.

[186] Sūrah *al-Isrā'*, 24.

The *duʿā* of Nūḥ has already been given above, in which he prayed for his parents, as did Ibrāhīm:

رَبَّنَا ٱغْفِرْ لِى وَلِوَٰلِدَىَّ وَلِلْمُؤْمِنِينَ يَوْمَ يَقُومُ ٱلْحِسَابُ ﴿٤١﴾

O My Lord! Forgive me, and my parents, and all of the believers the Day that the Reckoning will occur![187]

19. To Say *'Āmīn'*

When a person is listening to another person make *duʿā*, it is recommended that he say, *'Āmīn'*, which means 'O Allāh! Accept (or: Respond to) this *duʿā*.'

It is stated that the phrase *'Āmīn'* is one of the specialities of this nation, and that no nation before Islam had been given it.[188] This is inferred from the ḥadīth in which the Prophet (ﷺ) said:

> The Jews do not envy you for any matter as much as they envy you for *Āmīn*, and for giving *salāms* to one another.[189]

The purpose of saying *'Āmīn'* is so that it might increase the chances that a person's *duʿā* be answered. It is like repeating the *duʿā* over again, except that instead of going into all the details of one's *duʿā*, it is all summarised in the one phrase, *'Āmīn,'* which means, as we mentioned, 'O Allāh! Respond (to the *duʿā*)!' So it is like another *duʿā* after the first one.

---

[187] Sūrah *Ibrāhīm,* 41.

[188] Another opinion is that Mūsa and Hārūn were taught this phrase, but the Jews were not informed of this; this opinion is due to the story that follows shortly. (See Abū Zayd, pps. 203-209, for a complete discussion of *'Āmīn'*.) However, this opinion clashes with the well-known fact that the Christians to this day use this phrase (as Amen) after their prayers, so further research needs to be done on this issue: did the Christians take it from the Muslims, or was this phrase given to nations before us as well?

[189] Reported by al-Bukhārī in his *al-Adab al-Mufrad* (# 759 of al-Albānī's *Ṣaḥīḥ* version) and others.

Of course, there are certain *du'ās* that should be done privately, not in a group, and there are others that are done in a group. Examples of the first type are most of the *du'ās* that a person does during the day and night. It is an innovation to have a group *du'ā* for, say, entering the house, or after finishing the *ṣalāt*. An example of the second type is the *du'ā* that is done in *qunūt*, where the imām makes a *du'ā*, and the congregation behind him says, *'Āmīn.'* Likewise, if the person giving the Friday sermon makes a *du'ā*, the congregation is encouraged to say *'Āmīn'* after his *du'ā*. Furthermore to say 'Āmīn' after reciting *Sūrah al-Fātiḥah* is encouraged, regardless of whether one is praying, or reciting it outside the prayer, and regardless of whether one is the Imām or the follower. At all such times, *Āmīn* should be stated with an audible voice.[190]

There is a difference of opinion whether one should say *'Āmīn'* after one's own *du'ā*, but it seems that the general rule of *'Āmīn'* does not differentiate between a person's own *du'ā* and when a person is listening to another's *du'ā*, so it is permissible for a person to say *'Āmīn'* after his own *du'ā*.[191]

When Mūsa prayed to Allāh to punish Pharaoh, it is said that Hārūn was behind him, saying, *'Āmīn!'* Yet, even though only Mūsa was actually saying the *du'ā*, Allāh said in the Qur'ān:

قَدْ أُجِيبَت دَّعْوَتُكُمَا

Your (both of you) prayers have been answered![192]

So Allāh referred to both of them making a *du'ā*, even though Hārūn was only saying *'Āmīn'* behind Mūsa's *du'ā*. And in this is proof that the one who says *'Āmīn'* to a *du'ā* is like the one who made the *du'ā*.

One last point regarding this phrase. Many people do not pronounce the *'Āmīn'* correctly. Some of the mistakes that are made include:

---

[190] Abū Zayd, p. 205.

[191] Abū Zayd, p. 206.

[192] Sūrah *Yūnus*, 89. See *Tafsīr Ibn Kathīr* 2/411 for further details.

1. Prolonging the *alif,* so that it becomes, 'Aaaaameen.' This first *alif* should not exceed two *ḥarakas* in length.[193]
2. Making the *alif* too short, so that it becomes, 'Ameen.' Again, the length of this *alif* should be two *ḥarakas*, not more or less.
3. Placing an assimilation on the *mīm*, such that it becomes, 'Āmmmīn.' The *meem* has a *kasrah,* (the Arabic vowel 'i') on it, and not a *shaddah.*

As for the last syllable, it is permissible to shorten it to two *harakahs* or prolong it up to six. So to say, 'Āmeeeeen,' with a prolonged elongation is allowed.

20. To Make *Duʿā* at all Times

In other words, *duʿā* should be done at times of ease and hardship. *Duʿā* is one of the greatest acts of worship, and as such it should be performed at all times. Many people have a bad habit of only praying when a calamity befalls them, or when they wish for a particular good to occur. This goes against the attitude of a believer, for it shows that he only remembers Allāh at times of need. The true believer always remembers Allāh. The Prophet (ﷺ) stated:

> "Whoever wishes that Allāh responds to his *duʿā* at time of hardship, then let him increase his *duʿā* at times of ease!"[194]

And it is stated in an Arabic proverb, "Whoever knocks continuously, will eventually be let in!"

So ponder over this point, and do not presume the Ever-Generous to be like the created, for the more that you ask a person, the more he will tire of you, but the more that you ask Allāh, the greater He will love you.

---

[193] A *ḥarakah* is a unit that is used by the reciters of the Qur'ān, and is defined to be the time it takes to open one finger from a closed fist – perhaps equivalent to half a second.

[194] Reported by al-Tirmidhī (# 3382), al-Ḥākim (1/544) and others. See *al-Ṣaḥīḥah*, # 593.

21. To Make *Du'ā* for all Matters

Another common mistake that many people fall into is that they only ask Allāh for matters that are of great importance to them. However, Allāh should be asked for every matter, large or small. This because everything occurs by Allāh's Will, so if Allāh does not Will it, it will not occur, no matter how trivial the matter may be.

This is why 'Ā'ishah, the beloved wife of the Prophet (ﷺ), said: "Ask Allāh for everything, even if it is only a shoe-lace, because if Allāh does not make it easy, then it will not be possible".[195]

22. To Make *Du'ā* Plentifully

What is meant here is that a person should ask everything that he desires (as long as what he is asking is permissible), for he is asking the Most Generous of all those who are generous, and the most Beneficent of all those who are beneficent. Can anything compare with the Generosity of *al-Karīm*? For Allāh is *al-Mannān* (the One Who Gives Continuously, without expecting anything in return), *al-Barr* (The Benefactor), *al-Wahhāb* (The Ever-Bestower), *al-Karīm* (The Ever-Generous), *al-Akram* (The Most Generous); in fact, all of His Names are an indication of His Perfection and Exaltedness. So when one asks such a deity, how can one not then ask abundantly? Do you not see when a beggar goes to one who is well known for his generosity, he asks more than when he goes to one that is not known to be such? Do you not see that such a beggar will not be satisfied with a little amount from a generous person, whereas he would be satisfied with this same amount from a miser? So then why is that you are miserly in your asking when you need your Creator far more than this beggar is in need of someone's generosity?

---

[195] Reported as a ḥadīth of the Prophet in al-Tirmidhī (4/292) and others, but it is not authentic as a *marfū'* tradition. It is, however, authentic as a statement from 'Ā'ishah; see *al-Ḍa'īfah*, # 1326, for further details.

This is why the Prophet (ﷺ) said:

> When one of you wishes for something, then let him increase (his wishes), for verily he is asking his Lord, the Most Exalted and High.[196]

And in another wording:

> When one of you asks something (from Allāh), then let him be plentiful (in what he asks for), for indeed he is asking his Lord.[197]

23. To Make *Duʿās* When One is in a Condition of Response

There are certain conditions during which a person's *duʿā* is more likely to be responded to. So, the wise person utilises these situations and conditions whenever he is capable of doing so.

The exact situations in which a *duʿā* is more likely to be answered are discussed in a later chapter.

24. To Make *Duʿās* at the Times of Response

There are certain times during which a *duʿā* is more likely to be answered, and it is from the etiquette of *duʿā* that one increases one's *duʿā* during these times.

The times that *duʿās* are more likely to be answered are discussed in a later chapter.

---

[196] Reported by ʿAbd ibn Ḥumayd in his *Muntakhab* (1/193); authenticated by al-Albānī in *al-Ṣaḥīḥah,* # 1266.

[197] Reported by Ibn Ḥibbān (# 2403); see *al-Ṣaḥīḥah,* # 1325.

CHAPTER VI

Discouraged Acts During *Du*ʿ*ā*

Just as *du*ʿ*ā* has some pre-conditions and etiquettes attached to it, so too does it have certain characteristics that go against the spirit of *du*ʿ*ā*, and contradict the proper etiquette one should employ while asking from one's Lord. Obviously, all acts that contradict any of the etiquette or pre-requisites of *du*ʿ*ā* are all discouraged. Some of these acts, such as calling upon others besides Allāh, are acts of *shirk* that take one outside the fold of Islām. Others, such as making improper *tawassul,* are innovations that damage a person's *īmān*.

Some of the more common acts that are discouraged are listed below.

1. Poetry in *Du*ʿ*ā*

What is meant by 'poetry' is excessive rhyming of words, and matching word patterns in each sentence, since this does not befit the humility that should accompany *du*ʿ*ā*. However, if such rhyming is not excessive, or comes naturally to the tongue, then it is allowed, as some of the Prophet's (ﷺ) *du*ʿ*ās* contained rhyming phrases. What is prohibited is excessive rhyming, or going out of one's way to ensure it, such that the *du*ʿ*ā* resembles poetry.

Imām al-Khaṭṭābī wrote: "Excessive rhyming is not liked during *du*ʿ*ā*, nor (is it liked) to exert one's self in order to achieve it".[197] Others stated, "Make *du*ʿ*ā* with a tongue that is humbled and in need, and not with a tongue that is eloquent and articulate".[198]

---

[197] *Sha'n al-Du*ʿ*ā*, p. 17.

[198] Al-Ḥamad, p. 39.

Ibn ʿAbbās, while giving his students advice, reported:

> Lecture to the people once a week, and if you wish then twice, and if you want to increase then (at most) thrice. And do not make the Qur'ān tiresome for the people. And make sure that, when you come across a group of people, you do not interrupt their conversation by your talk and they get tired of you, but rather listen, and when you are asked, speak, so that they listen to you willingly. And beware of poetry and rhyming in your *duʿā*, for verily I encountered the Prophet (ﷺ) and his Companions avoiding this.[199]

2. Transgression in *Duʿā*

Duʿā has certain limits, and if one goes beyond these limits, one is transgressing in making *duʿā*. Allāh says in the Qur'ān:

ٱدْعُوا۟ رَبَّكُمْ تَضَرُّعًا وَخُفْيَةً ۚ إِنَّهُۥ لَا يُحِبُّ ٱلْمُعْتَدِينَ ﴿٥٥﴾

> Make *duʿā* to your Lord in humility and in secret. Verily, He does not like the transgressors![200]

There are a number of ways a person can transgress in his *duʿā*, such as:

Asking for things that are prohibited: it is the height of transgression to demand from your Creator those things that He has prohibited for you, either in this life or in the life Hereafter. A person should realise his place and status in front of his Creator, and beware of exalting himself to where he thinks that he is above his fellow creations, and is allowed to do what they are prohibited from doing. As Allāh says in the Qur'ān concerning the Jews:

يَسْـَٔلُكَ أَهْلُ ٱلْكِتَـٰبِ أَن تُنَزِّلَ عَلَيْهِمْ كِتَـٰبًا مِّنَ ٱلسَّمَآءِ ۚ
فَقَدْ سَأَلُوا۟ مُوسَىٰٓ أَكْبَرَ مِن ذَٰلِكَ فَقَالُوٓا۟ أَرِنَا ٱللَّهَ جَهْرَةً

---

[199] Reported by al-Bukhārī (6337) from Ibn ʿAbbās.

[200] Sūrah *al-Aʿrāf*, 55.

> The People of the Scriptures ask you to cause a Book to descend upon them from the Heavens! Indeed, they asked Moses for an even greater (thing), for they said: 'Show us Allāh in public!'[201]

Exaggerating in du'ā: the following narration shows what is meant by exaggeration in *du'ā*.

One of the sons of Sa'd ibn Abī Waqqās was making a *du'ā*, and his father passed by him, and heard him asking: "O Allāh! I ask you Paradise, and its benefits, and its delights, and its this-and-that... and I seek refuge in Hell, and its chains, and its food, and its this-and-that...".

Sa'd then said:

> "O my son! I heard the Prophet (ﷺ) say:
>
> There will be a group that will transgress in their *du'ā*.[202]
>
> So beware that you be amongst them! Verily, if you are given Paradise, you will be given all that is good in it, and if you are saved from the Hellfire, you will be saved from all the evils in it. O Allāh! We seek Your refuge from being among the ignorant!"

In another narration, 'Abdullāh ibn al-Mughaffal passed by one of his sons while he was making a *du'ā*. His son prayed, "O Allāh! I ask you to give me the white palace on the right hand side as soon as I enter Paradise!"

Hearing this, his father said, "O my son! Ask Allāh to bless you with Paradise, and seek refuge from the Fire, for verily I heard the Prophet (ﷺ) say:

> There will be a group that will over-step the bounds with regards to purification and *du'ā*.[203]

---

[201] Sūrah *al-Nisā'*, 153.

[202] Reported by Aḥmad and Abū Dāwūd, from Sa'd ibn Abī Waqqāṣ, and authenticated in *Ṣaḥīḥ al-Jāmi'* # 3671.

[203] Reported by Abū Dāwūd (1/24), Aḥmad (4/78) and others. See *Ṣaḥīḥ Abī Dāwūd*, p. 21.

In other words, a person should avoid needless requests in his *du'ā*. This point has also been hinted at in an earlier section.

Du'ā for a matter that has already been decreed: another way to transgress in *du'ā* is to ask Allāh for something that has already been decreed. So, it is not proper to ask Allāh, 'O Allāh! Allow the Muslims to enter Paradise, and cause the disbelievers to enter the Fire,' because this matter has already been decreed by Allāh.

3. Not Expecting a Response

Although this topic has been discussed in the etiquette of *du'ā*, because of its importance it is reiterated here. Too many people expect that Allāh will not respond to their *du'ā*, and it is possible that the only reason that their *du'ā* is not responded to is because of this presumption of theirs!

It is part of one's *īmān* to expect the best from Allāh, and to be sure that Allāh will respond to your *du'ā*, as He is the Ever-Merciful, All-Powerful.

A Muslim should make *du'ā* in all situations and circumstances. Even if a situation seems hopeless, this is not an excuse to give up *du'ā*. If a person has been told, for example, that one of his relative's has a terminal disease, and will only live for a short period of time, then let him not despair, and think that there is nothing that he can do. Rather, this is all the more reason to turn to Allāh, full of hope and sincerity, and pray that Allāh cure this relative of the disease. The One that decreed the situation in the first place is the only One that can change that decree, so it is essential to turn to Him.

Ponder over this beautiful statement from Sufyān ibn 'Uyaynah, when he said, "Let none of you think that his *du'ā* will not be answered because of (the sins) that he knows of himself. Indeed, Allāh responded to the *du'ā* of the worst of the creation, Iblīs, may Allāh curse him, when he said:

قَالَ رَبِّ فَأَنظِرْنِيٓ إِلَىٰ يَوْمِ يُبْعَثُونَ ﴿٣٦﴾ قَالَ فَإِنَّكَ مِنَ ٱلْمُنظَرِينَ ﴿٣٧﴾

He (Iblīs) said, 'O My Lord! Give me respite until the Day of Judgement!' He replied, 'Then you are of those who have been reprieved'.[204, 205]

So if even Iblīs' *du'ā* can be accepted, then surely the *du'ā* of a sinner has more right than his!

4. To Pray for Matters of this World Only

The true Muslim asks Allāh to bless him in this world and in the Hereafter. To ask Allāh only for matters of this world is a sign of weakness in one's *īmān*, as the blessings of the Hereafter are the true blessings.

Allāh states in the Qur'ān:

فَمِنَ ٱلنَّاسِ مَن
يَقُولُ رَبَّنَآ ءَاتِنَا فِى ٱلدُّنْيَا وَمَا لَهُۥ فِى ٱلْءَاخِرَةِ مِنْ
خَلَٰقٍ ﴿٢٠٠﴾ وَمِنْهُم مَّن يَقُولُ رَبَّنَآ ءَاتِنَا فِى ٱلدُّنْيَا
حَسَنَةً وَفِى ٱلْءَاخِرَةِ حَسَنَةً وَقِنَا عَذَابَ ٱلنَّارِ ﴿٢٠١﴾
أُو۟لَٰٓئِكَ لَهُمْ نَصِيبٌ مِّمَّا كَسَبُوا۟ ۚ وَٱللَّهُ سَرِيعُ ٱلْحِسَابِ ﴿٢٠٢﴾

And there are those amongst mankind who say, 'O Allāh! Give us in this life,' and they will have no share of the Hereafter. And there are those who say, 'O Allāh! Give us good in this life, and good in the Hereafter, and save us from the Fire of Hell!' These shall have a share of what they earned, and Allāh is swift in Reckoning.[206]

---

[204] Sūrah *al-Ḥijr*, 36-37.

[205] Abū Zayd, p. 29.

[206] Sūrah *al-Baqarah*; 201-202.

5. Improper Names and Attributes of Allāh

Of the matters that contradict the etiquettes of *duʿā* is to use a Name or Attribute that is not mentioned in the Qur'ān or Sunnah. This because Allāh's Names and Attributes are only taken from the Qur'ān and Sunnah, and not from one's imagination.

Another mistake is to choose a Name or Attribute that does not fit with one's *duʿā*. So, for example, if the Muslims are making a *duʿā* against some tyrants, it is improper to say, "O *Raḥmān*! O *Raḥīm*! Inflict your severest punishment on such-and-such a nation, for they have wronged the Muslims..." Likewise, if a person is asking for forgiveness, he should not call out using Attributes such as, 'Severe in Punishment (*Shadīd al-ʿIqāb*)'. It is essential that the appropriate Name or Attribute be chosen when making a *duʿā*.

6. *Duʿā* to Expedite Punishment

Some people presume that they *must* be punished for their sins, and reason that the punishment of this world is lighter than the punishment of the Hereafter. Therefore, they pray to Allāh to expedite whatever punishment that is in store for them in the Hereafter to this world. The danger of such a line of reasoning is that the person ignores the great Mercy of Allāh, and forgets to ask forgiveness for his sins. Instead of asking that which is encouraged and better, he asks instead for something that he cannot bear.

Anas ibn Mālik narrated that the Prophet (ﷺ) once visited a (sick) person who had become so thin that he was almost like a new-born chick. The Prophet (ﷺ) asked him:

> Did you make any *duʿā* or ask (Allāh) for anything?

He said: "Yes, I used to say: 'Whatever punishments are in store for me in the Hereafter, give it to me in this world!'" The Prophet (ﷺ) responded:

> *Subhān Allāh*! (All Glory and Praise be to Allāh!) You will never be able to bear it! Why did you not say: O Allāh! Give us the

> good of this world, and the good in the Hereafter, and save us from the Hellfire!

Anas added: "So the Prophet (ﷺ) prayed for him, and he was cured".[207]

7. *Du'ā* Against Oneself and Family

It is possible that a person, in a state of severe anger, curses and makes *du'ā* against himself, his family and friends, or his wealth. This is definitely an act that does not befit a Muslim, and the Prophet (ﷺ) warned against this, for he (ﷺ) said:

> "Do not make *du'ā* against yourselves, and do not make *du'ā* against your children, and do not make *du'ā* against your servants, and do not make *du'ā* against your wealth, for it is possible that it might correspond to an hour during which all prayers are answered, and your *du'ā* will be answered."[208]

No one wishes to inflict Allāh's curse and anger upon his loved ones, so we should be careful what we say in a state of anger, so as not to cause pain and grief not only upon our loved ones, but also upon ourselves.

8. To Curse Someone

It is not the character of a Muslim to curse others. The Prophet (ﷺ) said:

> The Muslim is not (given to) harming others, or cursing them, or being vulgar, or obscene.[209]

Once, the Companions were whipping an individual that had been caught drinking wine. 'Umar, in his anger, cursed the man.

---

[207] Reported by Muslim (# 3009), Aḥmad (3/107) and al-Tirmidhī (# 3487).

[208] Reported by Muslim and Abū Dāwūd, as mentioned in *Ṣaḥīḥ al-Jāmi'* # 7267.

[209] Reported by al-Bukhārī in his *al-Adab al-Mufrad* and others. See *al-Ṣaḥīḥah*, # 320.

Hearing this, the Prophet (ﷺ) said:

> Don't say that! Don't help *Shayṭān* against him![210]

Subḥān Allāh! What character and nobility, even in such severe circumstances! The punishment for drinking intoxicants is that a person be whipped a certain number of times, yet, even while inflicting this punishment, it is not allowed to curse or harm him in any other manner. And if this is the case with a drunkard, then how much more so for a Muslim that has committed a much smaller sin, or mistake, or even no crime at all!

It is also prohibited to curse the dead, for the Prophet (ﷺ) said:

> Do not curse the dead, for they have already gone forth to what they have sent.[211]

In other words, a dead person has already met whatever is in store for him, so there is nothing to be gained by cursing them. This applies to all dead people, except those whom Allāh or the Prophet (ﷺ) cursed.

Cursing is even prohibited when it comes to inanimate objects, diseases or animals. The Prophet (ﷺ) said:

> The wind is of the helpers of Allāh. It brings His Mercy and His Punishment. So when you see it, do not curse it, and ask Allāh its good, and seek refuge in Him from its evil.[212]

In another ḥadīth, the Prophet (ﷺ) said:

> Do not curse the rooster, for it wakes up (people) for the prayer.[213]

And in yet another ḥadīth, the Prophet (ﷺ) entered upon Umm al-Sā'ib, and found her shivering. He asked her what her problem

---

[210] Reported by al-Bukhārī.

[211] Reported by al-Bukhārī.

[212] Reported by Abū Dāwūd (# 4250), al-Ḥākim and others. See *Ṣaḥīḥ al-Kalim al-Ṭayyib*, # 153.

[213] Reported by Abū Dāwūd (# 4254), and authenticated in *al-Mishkāt*, # 4139.

was, so she replied, "I have a fever, may Allāh not bless it!" The Prophet (ﷺ) then said:

> Do not curse the fever, for it rids the sins of the children of Adam like a furnace rids iron of its evil.[214]

It should be mentioned that, in certain severe cases, to curse someone in particular is allowed, as it has been narrated that the Prophet (ﷺ) cursed certain specific individuals because they had caused great harm to the Muslims. However, this matter should be left to the judgement of scholars, and not be the subject of discussion amongst laymen.

9. To Limit Mercy

Abū Hurayrah reported: "The Prophet (ﷺ) stood up for prayer, and we stood up with him. A Bedouin who was praying with us said, 'O Allāh! Have mercy on myself and Muḥammad, and do not have mercy on any besides us two!' After the Prophet (ﷺ) had finished his prayer, he smiled and said:

> Indeed, you have confined something very vast (meaning the Mercy of Allāh)![215]

It is not a part of faith to try to stop Allāh's Mercy from descending upon others, and neither is a person capable of doing this, for Allāh says:

وَرَحْمَتِي وَسِعَتْ كُلَّ شَيْءٍ

And My Mercy prevails over all things![216]

10. To Pray for Death

The life of a true believer is a blessing from Allāh that can never be substituted. No matter what situation a person is in, he will always be in a blessed situation. The Prophet (ﷺ) said:

---

[214] Reported by Muslim.

[215] Reported by al-Bukhārī, Abū Dāwūd and Aḥmad, as mentioned in *Ṣaḥīḥ al-Jāmi'* # 5129.

[216] Sūrah *al-A'rāf*, 156.

> Wonderous indeed are the affairs of a believer, for every affair of his is good! If some good befalls him, he thanks Allāh, and that is good for him. And if some evil befalls him, he is patient, and that is good for him![217]

Therefore, a believer should be patient when a misfortune befalls him, and not wish for death, unless he fears for his religion, or a severe trial and tribulation.

Anas ibn Mālik reported that the Prophet (ﷺ) said:

> None of you should wish for death due to any calamity that has befallen him. If he has no choice but to wish for death, then let him say, 'O Allāh! Grant me life as long as life is better for me, and take me away (in death) whenever death is better for me!'[218]

And Qays ibn Abī Hāzim reported that he visited Khabbāb ibn al-Arath after he had been cauterised seven times, and he said, "Were it not for the fact that the Prophet (ﷺ) forbade us to make *du'ā* for death, I would have made such a *du'ā*".[219]

The Prophet (ﷺ) clearly stated that the life of a believer only brings more good, for Abū Hurayrah reported him (ﷺ) as saying:

> None of you should wish for death, nor should he make *du'ā* for it before it comes to him. Verily, once one of you dies, his deeds are cut off, and the extension of a life of a believer can only be for the better![220]

This ḥadīth also shows the mercy that the Prophet (ﷺ) had for his nation, and his desire that they receive the most blessings and the utmost good.

Shaykh 'Abd al-Raḥmān al-Sa'dī commented on this ḥadīth as follows:

---

217 Reported by Muslim, and Aḥmad.

218 Reported by al-Bukhārī, Muslim and Aḥmad, as mentioned in *Ṣaḥīḥ al-Jāmi'* # 7611.

219 Reported by al-Bukhārī (6349).

220 Reported by Muslim and Aḥmad, as mentioned in *Ṣaḥīḥ al-Jāmi'* # 7612.

This is a clear prohibition for wishing for death due to any problem that has fallen on an individual, whether it is a sickness, or poverty, or fear, or any other matter. Wishing for death has many evil consequences, some of which are:

1) It shows that the person is angry and dissatisfied with the condition that he is in, even though he has been commanded to be patient (at all times), and to be conscious of his obligations.

2) It makes the person very weak, and brings about laziness and indolence, and causes despair. And the servant is obligated to fight these characteristics, and to lessen (their effects) as much as he can. So he should be of strong heart and character, and optimistic so that whatever has occurred to him can be removed. This (attitude) brings about two benefits. Firstly, the Divine Kindness for he who strived to implement what he was commanded to. Secondly, a blessed and fruitful effort (to alleviate his circumstances), and this is based on the strength of his character, and his optimism.

3) To wish for death is sheer ignorance and cowardice, since the person is not aware of what his fate will be after death. So it is possible that he will try to get out of his present situation only to be faced with one worse than it, of the punishment of the grave and its evil.

4) It cuts off all of the good deeds a person can do, and in fact is doing at the present time. So the rest of his life will have no value. Then how is it that he can wish for cutting off all of his good deeds, the smallest amount of which is better for him that the entire world and all that it contains? And of special mention out of these good deeds, is his being patient at the misfortune that has befallen him, for Allāh rewards those who are patient without measure.[221]

---

[221] Al-Ḥamad, p. 71.

11. *Duʿā* for Evil, and Hastiness in *Duʿā*

The ḥadīth to this effect was quoted earlier, in which Abū Hurayrah reported that the Prophet (ﷺ) said:

> "The *duʿā* of any worshipper will continue to be responded to, as long as he does not ask for a sin or breaking the ties of kinship, and as long as he is not hasty".

It was asked, "O Messenger of Allāh? And what does it mean to be hasty?" He (ﷺ) responded:

> "A worshipper says, 'I have prayed and prayed, and I don't see that it will be accepted,' so he gives up hope of being answered, and leaves *duʿā*".[222]

It is not proper for a Muslim to pray to Allāh for something that is evil. Neither is it proper to ask Allāh to cause some problem between family members or friends.

So, a person should not ask, "O Allāh! Increase the spread of fornication and interest!" or, "O Allāh! Cause so-and-so to mistreat his mother, and cut off relations with his brothers and sisters!", as this is asking Allāh for something that is evil, and evil is not attributed to Allāh.

Likewise, it is not proper for a Muslim to become hasty and impatient in waiting for a response, as this goes against the etiquette of *duʿā*.

12. To Look Upwards During the Prayer

The Prophet (ﷺ) prohibited a person from raising his eyes towards the skies while making a *duʿā* in ṣalāt, for he said:

> Surely, the people will stop raising their eyes towards the skies while they make *duʿā* during ṣalāt, or their sight will be snatched away from them![223]

---

[222] Narrated by Muslim from Abū Hurayrah, as mentioned in *Ṣaḥīḥ al-Jāmiʿ* # 7705.

[223] Reported by Muslim (1/321) and others.

The desired humility of *du'ā* will not be achieved when one raises one's head arrogantly towards the skies, rather, one should have a humble and lowly appearance.

13. To Imply that One will not Ask Anything Else

It is all too common to hear a person say, "O Allāh! Please grant me such-and-such, and I will not ask you anything else after this!" Such thinking has two major problems with it. Firstly, it implies that Allāh is not Generous, as such a condition is usually put to a person who is miserly: "I only ask this of you, and I will not ask you anything else!" Secondly, it implies that a person is self-sufficient and not in need of Allāh's response to his *du'ās*. This because he says, "I will not ask you anything else after this," as if he can live without Allāh's blessings! Verily, every breath that we take is because of Allāh's blessings, and no one can be free of Allāh's help even for the twinkling of an eye!

So make *du'ā*, and make plenty of *du'ā*, for Allāh's Generosity is more than all that you can possibly ask for.

14. To Experiment in One's *Du'ā*

This occurs when a person thinks to himself, 'Let me make a *du'ā* and see if Allāh responds to me or not'. Such thinking conflicts with the sincerity and humility that is needed for a *du'ā* to be answered.

15. To Have Evil Intentions

It is necessary that a person make a *du'ā* in order for some noble or permissible goal. If someone makes a *du'ā* with evil intentions, such as one who prays for money so that he can use it for evil purposes, such a *du'ā* is not allowed.

16. To Make Frequent Mistakes

It is all too common to hear people that do not speak Arabic properly making *duʿās* with grammatical errors in them. Such a person might even change the whole meaning of the *duʿā* without realising, or he might make *duʿā* against himself and the congregation! This is why it is preferable for a person of knowledge – one who speaks Arabic – to lead the congregation and give the *khuṭbah*.

17. To Rely on Others to Make *Duʿā*

There is a certain segment of society that never makes *duʿā*. If you were to ask one of them what his excuse is, he would respond that he is too sinful to have his *duʿās* accepted by Allāh, and that he makes sure that other people ask on his behalf. He might even ask you to make *duʿā* for him that he be guided!

This constitutes a very big mistake. While it is permissible to ask another person to make *duʿā* for one's self (as shall be discussed in a later section), it is improper to rely on that person totally, to the extent that one fails to perform *duʿā* oneself.

Instead, one should make *duʿā* to Allāh, and expect the best from Him, and hope for Allāh's Mercy. If Allāh responds to the *duʿā* of the *kāfir*, then surely the *duʿā* of a sinful Muslim has more right to be responded to!

18. To Cry Out Loud in Public

Although crying is covered in the etiquette of *duʿā*, a person must avoid excessive crying, or crying out loud, when he is in front of others. In some mosques, the entire congregation weeps and wails with a loud voice, such that it is possible to hear them from a long distance away. People flock to these mosques just because it is known that the congregation will cry. Such attitudes and habits are in contradiction to the Sunnah of the Prophet (ﷺ) and the practice of the pious predecessors. A person should try to control his crying in front of other people, for it is a private act of worship between him and his Creator. If, however, a person is overcome with emotion and cannot control himself, then he is excused, but it is a mistake to make it a continual habit in public.

19. To Make Excessively Long *Duʿās* in Congregation

Another common mistake that occurs in congregation is that the Imām prolongs the *duʿā* to an unnatural extent. He might stand up to an hour, invoking Allāh, while the people behind him become impatient and annoyed. The Imām must take into account that there are women and children, the sick and the weak, all behind him. He must be concerned for their needs as well. Hence why the Prophet (ﷺ) prohibited Muʿādh from reciting a long sūrah while he was Imām, and he stated that this would cause hardship upon the Muslims. Likewise, the *duʿā* that is done in congregation should be of a moderate length, and cater to the needs of the whole community.

20. To Mention Himself Only if He is the Imām

It is reported that the Prophet (ﷺ), said:

> Let no one be the Imām of a people, and then only mention himself in the *duʿā*, and leave them out. If he does so, then he has cheated them.[224]

Although this ḥadīth might not be authentic, the meaning of it is applicable, as the Imām is responsible for the welfare of the entire congregation. Therefore, when he makes a *duʿā*, such as in the *witr* or *qunūt* prayer, he should not say, "O Allāh, forgive me, and increase my knowledge!" but rather, "O Allāh! Forgive us, and increase our knowledge," and so forth. This only applies to the *duʿā* that is done out loud. As for the *duʿā* that one does silently, such as in *sujūd* (prostration) or at the end of the prayer, then the Imām is allowed to pray only for himself.

---

[224] Reported by al-Tirmidhī (# 357), Abū Dāwūd (# 90), and Aḥmad (5/250). Al-Tirmidhī said that it is *ḥasan*, but Aḥmad Shākir pointed out that it might have some weakness in it (2/190). Al-Albānī stated that it is weak (*Ḍaʿīf al-Jāmiʿ*, # 6334).

CHAPTER VII

THE RECOMMENDED TIMES FOR *DUʿĀ*

Of the great mercy of Allāh is that He has favoured certain times over others. Thus, He has distinguished these timings so that the worshipper can eagerly anticipate their arrival, and thus pray earnestly and sincerely. Had all timings been the same, the worshipper would not have had the enthusiasm and fervor that exists during more blessed times.

Therefore, it is important that the one who desires that his *duʿā* be answered utilise these times, and ensure that his *duʿā* be more frequent and sincere during them.

1. *Duʿā* in the Last Third of the Night

During this time, when most of creation is in a deep sleep, the true worshipper is awake, earnestly praying to his Creator, reflecting upon Allāh's creation, the heavens and earth. In fact, Allāh describes the true believers as those who:

وَبِالْأَسْحَارِ هُمْ يَسْتَغْفِرُونَ ﴿١٨﴾

"...and, in the hours of dawn, they seek forgiveness from their Lord..."[225]

Not only that, but Allāh Himself comes down to His servant, and opens for Him the doors of Mercy and Forgiveness. Abū Hurayrah narrated that the Prophet (ﷺ) said:

---

[225] Sūrah *al-Dhāriyāt*, 18.

> "Our Lord descends every night, during the last third of it, to the skies of this world, and asks: 'Who is making *du'ā* to Me, so that I can respond to him? Who is asking Me, so that I can give him? Who is asking for My forgiveness, so that I can forgive him?'"[226]

And 'Amr ibn 'Absah reported that the Prophet (ﷺ) said:

> "The closest any worshipper can be to his Lord is during the last part of the night, so if you can be amongst those who remember Allāh at that time, then do so."[227]

This is a huge incentive, then, for any person who truly desires to come closer to Allāh, all Glory and Praise be to Him, and wishes to have his sins forgiven, and his *du'ā* responded to, to wake up when everyone else is asleep, and remember Allāh privately, and all the while praying to Him.

Furthermore Abū Sa'id and Abū Hurayrah both reported that the Prophet (ﷺ) said:

> "Allāh waits until the first third of the night has passed, then He descends down to the skies of this world and says: 'Is there any that seeks forgiveness? Is there any who wishes to repent? Is there any who is asking? Is there any who is making a *du'ā*?' And this continues, until the break of dawn".[228]

In another wording:

> "Our Lord – all Glory and Praise be to Him – comes down in the last third of the night to the skies of this world, and He says: 'Who is there that is making a *du'ā*, so that I can respond to him? Who is there that is asking Me, so that I can give him? Who is there that is seeking my forgiveness, so that I can forgive him?"[229]

---

[226] Reported by al-Bukhārī and Muslim, from Abū Hurayrah, as reported in *Ṣaḥīḥ al-Jāmi'* # 8021.

[227] Authentic, narrated by al-Tirmidhī, al-Nasā'ī, and al-Ḥākim from 'Amr ibn 'Absah, and authenticated by al-Albānī in *Ṣaḥīḥ al-Jāmi'* # 1173.

[228] Authentic, narrated by Aḥmad and Muslim from Abū Hurayrah and Abū Sa'id al-Khudrī.

[229] Reported by al-Bukhārī (#1145), Muslim (# 758) and others.

Hence why Abū Bakr al-Tartūshī said, "And this chapter is closed by stating: He is not a wise man who has a need to Allāh, yet he sleeps away his need at night!"[230]

So if a person wishes that his *du'ā* be answered, this is the best time to ask.

2. An Hour of the Night

In addition to the ḥadīth pertaining to *du'ā* at the last third of the night, there are also *aḥādīth* informing us that there is a general time at night during which *du'ās* are responded to. The Prophet (ﷺ) said:

> There is at night an hour, no Muslim happens to be asking Allāh any matter of this world or the Hereafter, except that he will be given it, and this (occurs) every night.[231]

3. *Du'ā* When the *Adhān* is Called

This is based on the ḥadīth of the Prophet (ﷺ):

> "Two (*du'ās*) are never rejected, or rarely rejected: the *du'ā* during the call for prayer, and the *du'ā* during the calamity, when the two armies attack each other".[232]

In another ḥadīth,

> "When the prayer is called, the doors of the skies are opened, and the *du'ā* is answered".[233]

And in another one,

> "Seek the response to your *du'ās* when the armies meet, and the prayer is called, and when rain falls".[234]

---

[230] Al-Hilālī, p. 47.

[231] Reported by Muslim (# 757).

[232] Reported by Abū Dāwūd (# 2540), Ibn Mājah, and al-Ḥākim, from Sahl ibn Sa'd, and authenticated by al-Albānī in *Ṣaḥīḥ al-Jāmi'* # 3079.

[233] Reported by al-Ṭayālisī in his *Musnad* (# 2106); authenticated in *al-Ṣaḥīḥah*, # 1413.

[234] Reported by al-Shāfi'ī in his *al-Umm* (1/223); authenticated in *al-Ṣaḥīḥah*, # 1469.

4. *Du'ā* Between the *Adhān* and *Iqāmah*

This is one of the best times for the prayer to be accepted, and what a great blessing it is! Five times every day, while a worshipper is waiting to offer his prayers to Allāh, he is given the opportunity to ask from Him his needs of this world and the Hereafter.

Anas ibn Mālik narrates that the Prophet (ﷺ) said:

> "The *du'ā* said between the *adhān* and the *iqāmah* is not refused, therefore offer your *du'ās* (at this time)".[235]

5. *Du'ā* During the Ṣalāṭ

This time is also one during which *du'ās* are answered and accepted by Allāh, all Glory and Praise be to Him. Abū Hurayrah narrated that the Prophet (ﷺ) said:

> "People will have to stop from looking up at the sky while making *du'ā* during *ṣalāt,* or else Allāh will snatch their sight away."[236]

Other narrations forbid looking up at the sky during prayer in general, and this narration shows that the prohibition is even stronger while one is making *du'ā*. This because one has a natural tendency to look upwards while making a *du'ā*, and, thus, the Prophet (ﷺ) mentioned *du'ā* explicitly in this narration.

Some of the postures of the *ṣalāt* during which the performance of *du'ā* has been narrated include the following:

1. After the initial *takbīr*, when one is starting the ṣalāt.

2. Before the *rukū'* and after one has finished reciting the Qur'ān – but this is only during the *witr* or other *qunūt* prayers.

---

[235] Narrated by Aḥmad, Abū Dāwūd (# 521) and al-Tirmidhī (# 212) from Anas ibn Mālik. Al-Tirmidhī considered it to be *ḥasan ṣaḥīḥ*, and Aḥmad Shākir agreed with him (1/416). Also see *Ṣaḥīḥ al-Jāmi'* # 3408.

[236] Narrated by Muslim, Aḥmad, and al-Nasā'ī, from Abū Hurayrah, as mentioned in *Ṣaḥīḥ al-Jāmi'* # 5479.

3. After one has stood up from *rukū*ʿ. Abū Hurayrah narrates the Prophet (ﷺ) used to say, after standing up from *rukū*ʿ: "Allāh is Ever-Hearing to one who praises Him. Our Lord! To You belongs all praise, the weight of the Heavens, and the weight of the earth, and the weight of anything that You desire. O Allāh! cleanse me with ice and water, cleanse me of my sins and mistakes as a white garment is cleansed of dirt!"[237]

4. During the *rukū*ʿ itself, for the Prophet (ﷺ) used to say during it: "Glorified be You, O Allāh, our Lord, and be Praised! O Allāh, forgive me!"[238]

5. During the *sujūd*, and this was the posture during which the Prophet (ﷺ) made most of his *du*ʿ*ās*.

6. While sitting between the two *sajdahs*.

7. After the final *tashahhud*, and before the end of the prayer.

These postures are in addition to the *du*ʿ*ās* that he (ﷺ) used to do while actually reciting the Qur'ān. Ḥudhayfah narrated in this respect:

> "I prayed one night behind the Prophet (ﷺ), and he started reciting Sūrah *al-Baqarah*. I thought to myself, 'He will surely stop after a hundred verses.' However, (after he reached a hundred verses), he went on, so I said to myself, 'He will surely finish the Sūrah in this *rak*ʿ*ah*'. When he finished *al-Baqarah*, I thought, 'He will surely go into *rukū*ʿ now', but he started Sūrah *al-Nisā'*, and continued reciting it until he finished. Then he started reciting Sūrah *Āl-*ʿ*Imrān*, and he completed its recitation! He was reciting in a very gentle and unhurried man-

[237] Narrated by Muslim (476) from ʿAbdullāh ibn Abī Awfā.

[238] Reported by al-Bukhāri and Muslim.

ner. Whenever he read a verse in which Allāh was glorified, he would glorify Allāh, and whenever he read a verse which requested something (from Allāh), he would request it, and whenever he read a verse that sought refuge in Allāh, he would seek refuge in Allāh...."[239]

So when a person is reciting the Qur'ān in a voluntary prayer, they are encouraged to make *du'ā* whenever one occurs in the Qur'ān. This is only for voluntary prayer, as for the obligatory prayers, it is not encouraged.

6. *Du'ā* while Prostrating

This is the most noble posture that a worshipper can be in, for it is the epitome of humility and submissiveness. And how can it not be, when a person in prostration lowers his face – the most noble and sacred part of his body – to the dust, seeking the pleasure of his Lord? This is why this posture is the most beloved by Allāh, all Glory and Praise be to Him. Abū Hurayrah narrated that the Prophet (ﷺ) said:

> "The closest any worshipper can be to his Lord is while he is in prostration, so increase your *du'ās* in it".[240]

For this reason, the Prophet (ﷺ) was prohibited by Allāh from reciting the Qur'ān while in a state of *rukū'* or *sujūd*, and he (ﷺ), in turn, prohibited the Muslims from this also. Ibn 'Abbās narrated that once the Prophet (ﷺ) lifted the curtain from his house and looked into the mosque, and the people were lined in rows behind Abū Bakr (and this was during the illness from which he (ﷺ) died). He then said:

> "O people! There is nothing left of prophethood except a true dream, a Muslim sees it himself or someone else sees it for him (i.e. he sees the other person in a dream). And I have been

---

[239] Narrated by Muslim and al-Nasā'ī, from Hudhayfah ibn al-Yamān.

[240] Reported by Muslim, Abū Dāwūd, al-Nasā'ī and others, from Abū Hurayrah, as mentioned in *Ṣaḥīḥ al-Jāmi'* # 1175.

> prohibited from reciting the Qur'ān while in *rukū*ʿ or *sujūd*, so during *ruku*ʿ, glorify your Lord, and during *sujūd*, exert yourself in making *du*ʿ*ā*, for it is very likely that you will be responded to".[241]

Therefore, recitation of the Qur'ān during these two postures is discouraged, and instead the worshipper should praise and glorify Allāh. During *sujūd* he should increase his *du*ʿ*ās* to his Creator, as they are likely to be responded to.

7. While Reciting *al-Fātiḥah*

There are many blessings contained within Sūrah *al-Fātiḥah*, and of these is the fact that Allāh accepts the *du*ʿ*ā* that is present in the Sūrah. The person recites it sincerely, fully aware of its meanings. Abū Hurayrah narrated that the Prophet (ﷺ) said:

> Allāh has said: I have divided the *ṣalāt* between My servant and Me in two halves, and My servant will have what he asks for. So when the servant says, '*Alḥamdu lillāhi Rabb il-*ʿ*Ālamīn*', Allāh responds, 'My servant has praised Me!' And when he says, '*Al-Raḥmān al-Raḥīm*' Allāh responds, 'My servant has glorified Me'. And when he says, '*Mālik yawm al-Dīn*', Allāh responds, 'My servant has exalted Me'. And when he says, '*Iyyāka na*ʿ*budu wa iyyāka nasta*ʿ*īn*', Allāh says, 'This is between My servant and I, and My servant shall have what he desires'. And when he says, '*Ihdina al-Ṣirāṭ al-Mustaqīm*...' Allāh says, 'This is for My servant, and he will get what he desires'.[242]

So in this ḥadīth, there is a great incentive for us to recite Sūrah *al-Fātiḥah* in every prayer with great humility and reflection, so that it is possible that we are given what we ask.

---

[241] Narrated by Muslim, Abū Dāwūd, and Aḥmad as mentioned in *Ṣaḥīḥ al-Jāmi*ʿ # 2746.

[242] Reported by Muslim (# 395) and others.

8. After *al-Fātiḥah*

Likewise, after finishing the recitation of Sūrah *al-Fātiḥah* in ṣalāt, one is encouraged to say, *'Āmīn'* out loud, for the Prophet (ﷺ) said:

> When the Imām says '*Āmīn*' then recite it behind him (as well), because whoever's *Āmīn* coincides with the *Āmīn* of the angels will have all of his sins forgiven.[243]

9. *Duʿā* Before the End of Ṣalāt

After a person has finished his *tashahhud*, and before he actually says *salām*, he should supplicate with any *duʿā* that he likes, as this is one of the times of response.

Ibn Masʿūd narrates: I was once praying, and the Prophet (ﷺ), Abū Bakr, and ʿUmar (were all present). When I sat down (in the final *tashahhud*), I praised Allāh, then sent *salāms* on the Prophet (ﷺ), then started praying for myself. At this, the Prophet (ﷺ), said:

> Ask, and you shall be given it! Ask, and you shall be given it![244]

Another proof of this is the ḥadīth given in the following section.

10. *Duʿā* After the Ṣalāt

There are numerous narrations that show that this time period is one during which *duʿās* are answered. Abū Umāmah al-Bāhilī asked the Prophet (ﷺ), "O Messenger of Allāh! Which *duʿā* is the most likely to be responded to?" The Prophet (ﷺ), replied:

> In the last part of the night, and after the obligatory prayers".[245]

In fact, the Prophet (ﷺ) stressed this time period to those whom he loved, for he said to Muʿādh ibn Jabal:

---

[243] Reported by al-Bukhārī (# 780), Muslim (# 410) and others.

[244] Reported by al-Tirmidhī (# 593) who said that it is *ḥasan ṣaḥīḥ*, and it is as he said. Also see *al-Mishkāt*, # 931.

[245] Reported by al-Tirmidhī (# 3499) and others. Al-Tirmidhī considered it to be *ḥasan*, and al-Albānī agreed with him (see his foonote on *Mishkāt*, # 1231).

> O Mu'ādh! I swear by Allāh, I love you. Therefore, do not forget to say after each prayer, 'O Allāh help me to remember You, and to thank You, and to perfect my worship for You'.[246]

It should be mentioned that there is a difference of opinion amongst scholars over the exact meaning of '..after the obligatory prayers', and this stems from the Arabic word that is used to convey the meaning of 'after', for the word used is *dubur*. Some scholars, such as Shaykh al-Islām Ibn Taymiyyah, considered the meaning of this ḥadīth to apply to the time period *before* one says the final *salām* of the prayer, and after one has finished reciting the *tashahhud*. So, according to those that follow this opinion, the word *dubur* would translate as 'at the end', and not, 'after'. According to this opinion, the time period would be the same as that mentioned in the previous section.

However, other scholars understand this ḥadīth to mean the time period after the prayer finishes, and the word carries both meanings, as Ibn al-Qayyim mentioned.[247]

11. *Du'ā* when the Armies Meet

During this critical period, when the Muslim is facing the enemy in battle, at a place where life and death meet, the *du'ā* of a worshipper is accepted by Allāh. Proof for this has already been given, and that is the narration of Sahl ibn Sa'd, who confirmed that the Prophet (ﷺ) said:

> "Two (*du'ās*) are never rejected, or rarely rejected: the *du'ā* during the call for prayer, and the *du'ā* during the calamity, when the two armies attack each other".[248]

In another narration:

---

[246] Authentic, narrated by Abū Dāwūd, Aḥmad and al-Nasā'i, from Mu'ādh ibn Jabal, and authenticated by al-Albānī in *Ṣaḥīḥ al-Jāmi'* # 7969.

[247] See *Zād al-Ma'ād*, 1/305.

[248] Reported by Abū Dāwūd (# 2540), Ibn Mājah, and al-Ḥākim, from Sahl ibn Sa'd, and authenticated by al-Albānī in *Ṣaḥīḥ al-Jāmi'* # 3079.

"Seek the response to your *du'ās* when the armies meet, and when the prayer is called, and when rain falls".[249]

12. An Hour on Friday

There is a special hour on Friday, during which all prayers are accepted and answered by Allāh, all Glory and Praise be to Him. This is part of the blessings that Allāh has blessed this day with, over all the other days of the week.

Abū Hurayrah narrated that the Prophet (ﷺ) said:

> "On Friday, there is an hour during which, if any Muslim is standing in front of Allāh in ṣalāt, and asking Allāh for something good, he will be granted his request."

Then he made a sign with his hands, showing that it was a very short period of time.[250]

There are numerous opinions as to the exact hour of Friday during which this occurs, but two opinions are the strongest: when the Imām sits down between the two *khuṭbahs* until the end of the *khuṭbah*, and after the *'Aṣr* prayer until the *Maghrib* prayer. Ibn al-Qayyim preferred the second over the first one.[251] This because of the following ḥadīth:

> Friday has twelve hours (or parts to it). There is one hour during which if a Muslim asks Allāh anything, Allāh will give it to him, so find it during the last hour after *'Aṣr*.[252]

This is also the opinion of the vast majority of early scholars and also of the Prophet's (ﷺ) Companions – that this hour occurs after *'Aṣr* prayer, right before sunset.[253]

---

[249] Reported by al-Shāfi'ī in his *al-Umm* (1/223); authenticated in *al-Ṣaḥīḥah*, # 1469.

[250] Narrated by al-Bukhārī (935) from Abū Hurayrah.

[251] *Zād al-Ma'ād*, 1/378-396.

[252] Reported by Abū Dāwūd (# 926 of *Ṣaḥīḥ al-Sunan*) and al-Nasā'ī (# 1316 of *Ṣaḥīḥ al-Sunan*).

[253] See al-Hilālī's discussion of this point in his book, pp. 50-55.

13. When Waking up at Night

When a person wakes up in the middle of the night, only to go back to sleep again, if he remembers Allāh at this time, his *du*ʿ*ā* will be accepted.

The Prophet (ﷺ) stated:

> Whoever wakes up at night, and says, '*Lā ilāha illa Allāh Waḥdahu lā sharīka lah, lahu al-mulk wa lahu al-ḥamd wa huwa alā kulli shay'in Qadīr. Alḥamdu lillah, wa Subḥān Allāh, wa lā ilāha illa Allāh, wa Allāhu akbar, wa lā ḥawla wa lā quwwata illa bi Allāh*', and then says, 'O Allāh, forgive me!' or makes a *du*ʿ*ā*, then he will be responded to. And if he performs *wuḍū* and prays, then his prayer will be accepted.[254]

14. After Performing *Wuḍū*

The Prophet (ﷺ) said:

> There is no one amongst you that makes *wuḍū*, and does so perfectly, and then says, 'I testify that there is no deity worthy of worship except Allāh. He is alone, having no partners. And I bear witness and testify that Muḥammad is His slave and messenger', except that all eight doors of Paradise are opened for him, and he can enter into it through whichever one he pleases.[255]

In this ḥadīth, there is an indication that *du*ʿ*ā* at this time has a greater chance of being responded to, as all the doors of Paradise are opened to the beleiver.

15. Before Drinking Zam Zam

Before drinking Zam Zam, one is encouraged to make *du*ʿ*ā*, as the Prophet (ﷺ) said:

> The water of Zam Zam is for whatever it has been drunk for.[256]

---

[254] Reported by al-Bukhārī (# 1154) and others.

[255] Reported by Muslim (# 234) and others.

[256] Narrated by Aḥmad (3/357) and Ibn Mājah (# 3062). Al-ʿIjlūnī considered it to be a good *isnād* and al-Albānī considred it *ṣaḥīḥ* (*Ṣaḥīḥ al-Jāmi*ʿ, # 5502).

The meaning of this ḥadīth is that whatever *du'ā* you make before drinking Zam Zam, it will be given to you.

16. *Du'ā* During Ramaḍān

The month of Ramaḍān is a blessed month, during which the Qur'ān was revealed, and the process of inspiration started upon the Prophet (ﷺ). Therefore, the *du'ā* of Ramaḍān is a blessed *du'ā*, and this can be inferred from the Prophet's (ﷺ) ḥadīth:

> When Ramaḍān comes, the Doors of Mercy (in one narration: of Paradise) are opened, and the Doors of Hell are closed, and the Shayāṭīn are chained up.[257]

So it can be inferred from this ḥadīth that *du'ā* during Ramaḍān has a greater chance of being accepted, as the Gates of Paradise and Mercy are opened.

17. *Du'ā* on 'The Night of Decree'

During this blessed night,[258] when the angels descend down to earth with the angel Jibrīl, and when the earth is overwhelmed with peace and serenity until the break of dawn, and when the doors of Paradise are opened, the worshipper is encouraged to turn to Allāh, and to ask of his needs for this world and the Hereafter.

As Allāh says:

إِنَّآ أَنزَلْنَٰهُ فِى لَيْلَةِ ٱلْقَدْرِ ﴿١﴾ وَمَآ أَدْرَىٰكَ مَا لَيْلَةُ ٱلْقَدْرِ ﴿٢﴾
لَيْلَةُ ٱلْقَدْرِ خَيْرٌ مِّنْ أَلْفِ شَهْرٍ ﴿٣﴾ تَنَزَّلُ ٱلْمَلَٰٓئِكَةُ وَٱلرُّوحُ
فِيهَا بِإِذْنِ رَبِّهِم مِّن كُلِّ أَمْرٍ ﴿٤﴾ سَلَٰمٌ هِىَ حَتَّىٰ مَطْلَعِ ٱلْفَجْرِ ﴿٥﴾

> We have revealed it (the Qur'ān) on the Night of Decree. And what will make you understand what the Night of Decree is?

---

[257] Reported by al-Bukhārī (# 1899), Muslim (# 1079) and others.

[258] The Night of Decree is one of the odd nights of the last ten nights of Ramaḍān.

> The Night of Decree is better than a thousand months. The angels come down, and the Holy Spirit, in it, with the Permission of their Lord, with all decrees. Peace! (It lasts) Until the break of dawn.[259]

ʿĀ'ishah narrated that she asked the Prophet (ﷺ): "O Messenger of Allāh! What *duʿā* should I make on *Laylat al-Qadr* (the Night of Decree)?" He (ﷺ) answered:

> "Say, 'O Allāh! You are Forgiving, and love to forgive, so forgive me!'"[260]

18. *Duʿā* Inside the Kaʿbah

The Kaʿbah is the holiest of all places, and the first mosque to be built for mankind. It is a sanctuary that has no comparison in the entire world. Therefore, it is no surprise that *duʿā* at this blessed place has greater chances of being answered.

Usāmah ibn Zayd reported: "When the Prophet (ﷺ), entered the House (Kaʿbah), he made *duʿā* in all of its corners".[261]

Of course, the obvious question that everyone will ask in our times is: "But it is not possible to go inside the Kaʿbah except with great difficulty!" Know then that the *ḥijr* (the semi-circular attachment that is opposite the Yemeni-corner and Black-stone wall) is actually a part of the Kaʿbah, and prayer inside the *ḥijr* is exactly the same as praying inside the physical structure of the Kaʿbah. This because of the fact that the *original* Kaʿbah built by Ibrāhīm was a rectangle, and its foundations included the area that is now the *ḥijr*. The only reason that the *ḥijr* is not included in the present structure is because the Quraysh, when they re-built the Kaʿbah, ran out of materials to complete its original structure. Therefore, they were forced to leave out the portion that is known today as the *ḥijr*. When

---

[259] Sūrah *al-Qadr*.

[260] Narrated by al-Tirmidhī, Ibn Mājah, and al-Ḥākim and authenticated in *Ṣaḥīḥ al-Jāmiʿ* # 4423.

[261] Reported by Muslim (2/968) and others.

the Prophet (ﷺ) re-conquered Makkah, he expressed his desire to ʿĀ'ishah that he wanted to rebuild the Kaʿbah upon the original foundations of Ibrāhīm, but he feared that the new Muslims would not be able to handle such a dramatic change, so he left it on its present foundations.

Therefore, one should be eager to pray in the *ḥijr*, and make *duʿā* in it as well, for it is equivalent to praying in the actual Kaʿbah.

19. *Duʿā* at Ṣafā and Marwa

It is narrated in the authentic Sunnah that the Prophet (ﷺ) would make long *duʿās* at Ṣafā and Marwa,[262] so the Muslim who is eager to follow the Sunnah of the Prophet (ﷺ) should do likewise.

20. *Duʿā* After Stoning the Jamarāt

Likewise, it is narrated that the Prophet (ﷺ) would stone the small *Jamarah* (one of the three pillars that is stoned in the last three days of Hajj), then face the qiblah, raise his hands, and make *duʿā* for a long time. He would then stone the middle *Jamarah* and do the same. When he stoned the large *Jamarah*, he would depart without making any *duʿā*.[263]

21. *Duʿā* on the Day of ʿArafah

Although *duʿā* during the entire Ḥajj is a great act of worship, *duʿā* on this particular day is of even greater importance. The Day of ʿArafah is the essence and pinnacle of Ḥajj. On this great and momentous day, when millions of worshippers gather together at one plain, from every single corner of the globe, with only one purpose in mind – to respond to the call of their Creator – during this auspicious day, Allāh does not refuse the requests of His worshippers.

---

[262] Reported by Muslim (# 1218) and others.

[263] Reported by al-Bukhārī (#1753) and others.

ʿAmr ibn al-ʿĀs narrated that the Prophet (ﷺ) said:

> "The best of all *duʿās* is the one given on the Day of ʿArafah, and the best statement that I or any of the prophets before me have said, is, 'There is no deity worthy of worship, He is One, and He has no Partners. To Him belongs the Dominion, to Him is given all Praise, and He is aware of all things".[264]

22. The First Ten Days of Dhul-Ḥijjah

The Prophet (ﷺ) stated:

> There are no days during which good deeds are more beloved to Allāh than during these ten days.[265]

This ḥadīth shows the general superiority of this time, and as *duʿā* is one of the most beloved acts of worship, we are encouraged to make *duʿā* during these ten days.

23. While Visiting the Sick

Umm Salamah narrated that the Prophet (ﷺ) said:

> "When you visit the sick, or the dead (body before its burial) then say good, because the angels say, *Āmīn* to whatever you say."[266]

24. When the Soul of a Person is Taken

During this frightening occasion, when a person is in the last stages of life, and is about to enter his life of eternity, bystanders should not make any *duʿā* except for good. This because the angels of death are waiting nearby, to take the soul of the person, and they say *Āmīn* to every *duʿā* made at this occasion.

Umm Salamah narrated that the Prophet (ﷺ) entered upon Abū Salamah (while he was on his death bed), and his eyes had fixed

---

[264] Narrated by al-Tirmidhī, from ʿAbdullāh ibn ʿAmr ibn al-ʿĀṣ, and authenticated by al-Albānī in *Ṣaḥīḥ al-Jāmiʿ* # 3274.

[265] Reported by al-Bukhārī (# 969) and others.

[266] Reported by Muslim (# 2126) and others.

into a stare (i.e. he had died), so the Prophet (ﷺ) closed his eyelids, and said:

> "When the soul leaves the body, the eyes follow it".

At this, the people of Abū Salamah's house began crying, and the Prophet (ﷺ) further said:

> "Do not ask for yourselves anything but good, for the angels will say *Āmīn* to all that you ask for. O Allāh, forgive Abū Salamah, and raise his ranks among those who are guided..."[267]

Therefore, whenever a person is in the presence of one who is about to die, he should pray to Allāh for all that is good, for the dying person, his family, and for himself.

This ḥadīth also explains why the eyes of those who are dead are always found to be in a stare, looking upwards, since the eyes follow the soul as it leaves upwards in the hands of the angels of death.

25. When Rain Falls

This is a time when the blessings of Allāh descend from the Heavens, and so it is also one of the times when the *duʿā* of a worshipper is accepted.

Sahl ibn Saʿd narrated that the Prophet (ﷺ) said:

> "Two are the *duʿās* that are never returned: the *duʿā* made when the prayer is being called, and at the time of rainfall".[268]

Plus there is the *ḥadīth* that has already been given, namely:

> "Seek the response to your *duʿās* when the armies meet, and the prayer is called, and when rain falls".[269]

---

[267] Narrated by Muslim, Abū Dāwūd and Aḥmad, as mentioned in *Ṣaḥīḥ al-Jāmiʿ* # 7266.

[268] Narrated by Abū Dāwūd (# 3540) and al-Ḥākim (2/114), who considered it to be *ṣaḥīḥ*, al-Dhahabī agreed with him, as did al-Albānī in *Ṣaḥīḥ al-Jāmiʿ* # 3078.

[269] Reported by al-Shāfiʿī in his *al-Umm* (1/223); authenticated in *al-Ṣaḥīḥah*, # 1469.

26. Before *Ẓuhr*

The Prophet (ﷺ), would pray four *raka'ahs* after the sun had reached its zenith (but before *Ẓuhr*), and he said,

> This is an hour during which the gates of the skies are opened, and I like that some of my good acts are raised up (at this time).[270]

In this ḥadīth is an indication that a *du'ā* at this time (after the sun reaches its zenith but before the time of *Ẓuhr*) has more chances of being responded to, as the gates of the Heavens are opened.

27. At the Crowing of a Rooster

Abū Hurayrah narrated that the Prophet (ﷺ) said:

> "When you hear a rooster crowing, then ask Allāh for His Bounties, for it has seen an angel, and when you hear a donkey braying, then seek refuge in Allāh from *Shayṭān*, for it has seen a *Shayṭān*."[271]

Qāḍī 'Iyāḍ said, in reference to this ḥadīth:

> "It is as if (the reason that one is asked to make *du'ā* when he hears the rooster crow) is that it is likely that the angel will say *Āmīn* to the person's *du'ā*, and ask for his forgiveness, and testify to his sincerity and humbleness. And when (he hears a donkey braying), he should seek refuge from Allāh for the evil that the *Shayṭān* can cause him, and the evil thoughts that he can whisper to him, so at this occasion the worshipper is told to turn to Allāh for protection..."

---

[270] Reported by Aḥmad (3/411), al-Tirmidhī (# 478) and others. Al-Tirmidhī considered it *ḥasan gharīb*, and Aḥmad Shākir considered it *ṣaḥīḥ* (2/343).

[271] Narrated by al-Bukhārī, Muslim and Aḥmad, as mentioned in *Ṣaḥīḥ al-Jāmi'* # 611.

CHAPTER VIII

Conditions During Which *Du ͑ā* is Answered

After a discussion of the times during which the *du ͑ā* is likely to be answered, it is relevant to discuss the conditions during which a worshipper's *du ͑ā* is likely to be responded to.

1. The Person who has been Wronged

If a person has been wronged by someone, Allāh accepts the *du ͑ā* of that person against the person that wronged him. This 'wrong' could be that he was cheated of his rights, oppressed, persecuted, slandered, or any other form of wrong that a person may be inflicted with.

The Prophet (ﷺ) mentioned in numerous *aḥādīth* that a Muslim should fear the *du ͑ā* of he who has been wronged, for he (ﷺ) said:

> "Fear the *du ͑ā* of he who has been wronged, for verily it ascends to the skies faster than sparks (of light)".[272]

And Anas ibn Mālik reported that the Prophet (ﷺ) said:

> "Fear the *du ͑ā* of he who has been wronged, even if he is a disbeliever, for there remains no veil between it".[273]

This ḥadīth means that there is no veil between it and Allāh, and Allāh responds to the *du ͑ā* of the person who has been wronged.

---

[272] Narrated by al-Ḥākim from Ibn ͑Umar, and authenticated in *Ṣaḥīḥ al-Jāmi ͑* # 118.

[273] Narrated by Aḥmad and Abū Ya ͑la, and authentiated in *Ṣaḥīḥ al-Jāmi ͑* # 119.

This ḥadīth also shows that there is no difference between doing wrong to a Muslim or to a disbeliever, and that both of their *duʿās* are answered by Allāh. If this is the case of the disbeliever, then how much more so the sinful Muslim! In fact, the Prophet (ﷺ) said:

> The *duʿā* of one who has been wronged is responded to, even if he is a *fāsiq* (evil person), for his evil will only be against himself.[274]

So even a sinful Muslim will be responded to, for his sin will be against him, and will not prevent his *duʿā* from being answered.

In another narration we are told,

> Three people's *duʿās* are never rejected: the one who is fasting, until he breaks his fast; the just ruler; and the one who has been wronged. Allāh raises it above the clouds, and the doors of the skies are opened for it, and the Lord says, 'By My Honour and Glory! I will help you, even if it be after some time!'[275]

This is a very severe warning to the one who wrongs others, and a comfort and solace to one who has been wronged. Allāh has sworn that He will, of a surety, come to the aid of the one who has been wronged.

It is appropriate here to quote the story of the noble Companion, Saʿd ibn Abī Waqqās, when ʿUmar appointed him governor over Kūfah. Some people of Kūfah complained to ʿUmar about Saʿd, so ʿUmar sent forth his servants to go around the *masjids* of Kūfah, asking the people's opinion about Saʿd. Wherever the messengers went, they could only find people praising Saʿd, except in one *masjid*, where a man by the name of Abū Saʿd stood up and said: "If you are really asking us by Allāh, then know that he was not just in his

---

[274] Reported by al-Ṭayālisī in his *Musnad* (# 1266). See *al-Ṣaḥīḥah*, # 767.

[275] Reported by al-Tirmidhī (# 3598), who declared it to be *ḥasan*. However, al-Albānī pointed out that it has a very slight weakness in it in *al-Ḍaʿīfah*, # 1358. Although it is weak with this wording, the phrase pertinent to the response of the *duʿā* is definetely authentic, as al-Albānī himself points out in *al-Ṣaḥīḥah*, # 870.

judgements, nor did he distribute the booty equally, nor was he easy with us".

At that, Sa'd stood up and said: "O Allāh! If he is lying, then take away his sight, and give him a long life, and make trials afflict him!"

The narrator of this event states: "I saw him after a long time, blind, his eyelids were drooping (out of old age), and he used to harass the little girls as they walked in the alleys. Whenever he was asked, 'How are you?' he would respond, 'I am an old man, great trials have befallen me! The *du'ā* of Sa'd has been inflicted upon me'".[276]

In another incident, a woman accused Sa'id ibn Zayd, one of the Prophet's (ﷺ) famous Companions of stealing some of her property. They appeared before the ruler, and Sa'id prayed, "O Allāh! If you know her to be lying, then make her blind, and make her grave in her own house". The narrator of this incident said, "I saw her (later on), blind. She used to walk touching the walls, and say, 'The *du'ā* of Sa'id has afflicted me!' Once, she passed by a well inside her house, and fell into it, so it became her grave".[277]

In these narrations we see the great miracle that Allāh blessed both Sa'd and Sa'id with, and we also see the dangers of abusing others. Is there not a lesson in this story for those who wrongly accuse other Muslims of matters that they are free of? And how many situations have occurred, where the one that has been wronged has raised his hands to Allāh, and seen with his own eyes the response of his *du'ā*? So beware, O Muslim, of oppressing other people in any form, and take comfort and solace, O you who have been wronged, that Allāh will indeed respond to your *du'ā*.

2. The One in Severe Circumstances

When a person finds himself in a grave crisis, and his heart is about to shatter with grief and fear, at this point, he turns to Allāh

[276] Reported by al-Bukhārī (# 755), Aḥmad (1/175) and others.

[277] Reported by Muslim (# 1610), and others.

with a heart like that of no other person. The quality of sincerity that he displays, and the desperate need that he feels for the Mercy of his Lord, is so strong and pure that it is a *duʿā* that is answered in all situations, regardless even of whether the person is a Muslim or not! Yes, even the *duʿā* of the *kāfir* is sometimes accepted, and that is part of the perfection of Allāh's Lordship, for He is the *Rabb* of the Muslim and the *kāfir*.

Allāh describes Himself as:

أَمَّن يُجِيبُ ٱلْمُضْطَرَّ إِذَا دَعَاهُ

> Is not He (the One) who responds to the distressed one when he calls out to Him?[278]

So if Allāh responds even to the disbeliever in this situation, then how about the sinful Muslim? And how about the sincere, pious believer, how can he give up hope of being answered?

Al-Qurṭubī wrote: "Allāh has guaranteed the response of the *duʿā* of the one in distress, as He Himself informed us of this (guarantee). And the reason for this is that the one in distress will turn to Him with a pure sincerity, cutting his hope off from all other sources. And sincerity to Him is the cause of (gaining) His protection, regardless of whether it emanates from a *kāfir* or Muslim, evil or pious!"[279]

3. After a Calamity

One of the occasions in which the *duʿā* of a person is answered is after a calamity has befallen him. However, it is necessary that the person display patience and satisfaction at Allāh's decree, and not wail or lament over his misfortune.

Umm Salamah narrated that the Prophet (ﷺ) said:

> There is no Muslim that is afflicted with a calamity, and he says what Allāh has commanded him to say: 'To Allāh we be-

---

[278] Sūrah *al-Naml*, 62.

[279] *Al-Jāmiʿ li Aḥkām al-Qur'ān*, 13/223.

> long and to Him we will return! O Allāh! Give me the rewards (of being patient over) this calamity, and grant me something better than it to replace it,' except that Allāh will give him something better to replace it.

Umm Salamah said, "So when (my husband) Abū Salamah died, I said this *du'ā*, but could not help thinking, 'Who is better than Abū Salamah (i.e. no one can replace Abū Salamah)?' Then the Prophet (ﷺ) himself sent me a messenger proposing to me, so Allāh blessed me with someone better than Abū Salamah".[280]

4. The Traveller

The person who has left his house, and is on a journey, is a stranger in the land that he travels to, alone and away from his family and friends. As such, Allāh, all Glory and Praise be to Him, sends His Mercy upon a traveller, especially if he is travelling for the sake of knowledge or with the intention of performing any other act of worship, such as pilgrimage or *jihād*.

A traveller has been guaranteed that his *du'ā* will be answered, for the Prophet (ﷺ) said:

> "Three are the *du'ās* that are responded to, there is no doubt concerning them: the *du'ā* of he who has been wronged, the traveller, and the *du'ā* of the father for his son".[281]

If this is the case of the average traveller who is travelling for worldly reasons, then it applies even more when the person is travelling for religious reasons, such as desiring to increase his knowledge, or visit his parents, or visit a Muslim brother.

---

[280] Narrated by Muslim (# 918), Abū Dāwūd (# 3119), al-Tirmidhī (# 3511) and others. The addition of Umm Salamah's story is found in some of the books of *sīrah*.

[281] Narrated by Abū Dāwūd (# 1535), al-Tirmidhī (# 1905), and Aḥmad, and authenticated in *Ṣaḥīḥ al-Jāmi'* # 3031.

5. The Father Against his Son or for his Son

The proof for this condition has been mentioned in the previous ḥadīth. In another wording of the ḥadīth, the Prophet (ﷺ) said:

> Three are the *duʿās* that are responded to ... the *duʿā* of the father against his son.[282]

The *duʿā* of a father for his son could be a *duʿā* of blessings and mercy for him if the father is content and happy with his son. On the other hand, the father can make a *duʿā* against his son, if the son does not treat his father properly. In this, there is a strong encouragement to Muslims to treat their parents with kindness, and to avoid causing distress to them in any way. This is also a warning to parents not to rush in making a *duʿā* against their children, for they might make a *duʿā* in a state of anger which they would later regret.

The *duʿā* of the mother is also included in this ḥadīth, for the right of the mother is even greater than that of the father. The *duʿā* of the parents for their daughters comes under this ḥadīth as well, since the rulings applicable to men also apply to women unless there exists evidence to the contrary.

The story of Jurayj and his mother was mentioned earlier, and this story also proves this point. When Jurayj's mother prayed against him because he did not obey her, Allāh responded to her *duʿās*.

6. The Son for the Father

While the father is alive, the son can benefit from him by pleasing him, thus ensuring that he makes *duʿā* for his son. After the father dies, then the son must repay some of the sacrifices that the father made for him, and part of this can be done by sincerely praying for him after his death.

---

[282] Narrated by al-Bukhārī in his *Adab al-Mufrad* (# 481) and authenticated in *Ṣaḥīḥ al-Adab* (# 372).

The Prophet (ﷺ) said:

> When a person dies, all of his actions are cut off except from three (matters): a *sadaqah jāriyah*,[283] or a pious son that prays for him, or some knowledge (that he gave) that others still benefit from.[284]

The Qur'ān itself commands this, for Allāh says:

> وَٱخْفِضْ لَهُمَا جَنَاحَ ٱلذُّلِّ مِنَ ٱلرَّحْمَةِ وَقُل رَّبِّ ٱرْحَمْهُمَا
> كَمَا رَبَّيَانِي صَغِيرًا ﴿٢٤﴾

> And lower unto them the wings of humility and mercy, and say, 'O My Lord! Have mercy on them, even as they took care of me while I was young'.[285]

So the pious son should make a point of regularly praying for his deceased parents, for this is the least that he can do to repay them for their kindness and care. Likewise, the daughter too should pray for her parents, as the ḥadīth applies to both son and daughter.

This does not mean that a person should not pray for his parents if they are alive, for of course this too is one of the rights that the parents have over the child.

7. The One who is Fasting

The Prophet (ﷺ) said:

> Three *du'ās* are never rejected: the *du'ā* of the father, and the *du'ā* of the one fasting, and the *du'ā* of the traveller.[286]

In another narration, it is reported that he (ﷺ) said:

> Three people's *du'ās* are never rejected: the one who is fasting,

---

[283] An act of charity that lasts for a period of time, such as building a *masjid*, or a Muslim school, etc.

[284] Reported by Muslim (# 1631), Abū Dāwūd (# 2880) and others.

[285] Sūrah *al-Isrā'*, 24.

[286] Reported by al-Bayhaqī in his *Sunan* (3/345) and others. Al-Albānī declared it to be authentic in *al-Ṣaḥīḥah*, # 1797.

until he breaks his fast; the just ruler; and the one who has been wronged. Allāh raises it above the clouds, and the doors of the skies are opened for it, and the Lord says, 'By My Honour and Glory! I will help you, even if it be after some time!'[287]

The preceding ḥadīth shows that the one who is fasting can make *duʿā* throughout the day, and his *duʿā* will be responded to. In a third ḥadīth, the time just before breaking the fast has been specified, so a person should strive even more at this particular time to be sincere in his *duʿā*. The Prophet (ﷺ) said:

> Indeed, the one who is fasting has – while he is about to break his fast – a *duʿā* that is not rejected".[288]

8. The Person Reciting the Qur'ān

It has been authentically narrated that peace and tranquility descend on the one who recites the Qur'ān, as do the angels. Therefore, after reciting any portion of the Qur'ān, we are encouraged to make a *duʿā*, as it is more likely to be responded to.[289]

Likewise, when we finish reciting the entire Qur'ān, we are also encouraged to make a *duʿā*, just as the famous Companion, Anas ibn Mālik, did when he called his family, and made a *duʿā* as soon as he had finished reciting the Qur'ān.[290]

---

[287] Reported by al-Tirmidhī (# 3598), who declared it to be *ḥasan*. However, al-Albānī pointed out that it has a very slight weakness in it in *al-Ḍaʿīfah*, # 1358.

[288] Reported by Ibn Mājah (# 1753) and others. Al-Būṣṣayrī said (2/350), "Its *isnād* is *ṣaḥīḥ,*" and al-Ḥāfiẓ Ibn Ḥajr declared it to be *ḥasan* (see al-Qaḥṭānī, p. 121). However, al-Albānī did not agree with them, and declared it to be *ḍaʿīf* in his *al-Irwā*, # 921. It seems that the ḥadīth has a very slight weakness in it, and Allāh knows best.

[289] Bakr Abū Zayd, *Taṣ-ḥīḥ al-Duʿā*, p. 33.

[290] For this report, and others, see the excellent tract by Shaykh Bakr Abū Zayd, *Marwiyyāt Duʿā al-Khatm al-Qur'ān*. It should be mentioned that those narrations in which the Prophet (ﷺ) is reported to have said that there is a *duʿā* that is accepted after finishing the Qur'ān are all fabricated, or very weak.

9. The Person Performing Ḥajj, ʿUmrah or *Jihād*

These three types of people have all left their homes solely for the sake of performing an act of worship to please Allāh, and, thus, they are like Allāh's guests. Therefore, as soon as they leave their homes, they are under the special protection and care of Allāh.

The Prophet (ﷺ) said:

> "The person who is fighting in the way of Allāh, and the person going for Ḥajj, and the person going for ʿUmrah are (like) Allāh's delegates. Their *duʿās* are responded to, and their requests are given."[291]

In another wording of this ḥadīth, the Prophet (ﷺ), said,

> The people performing Ḥajj and ʿUmrah are the delegates of Allāh. He called them and they responded, and they asked Him, so He gave them (their requests).[292]

Such is the Mercy and Generosity of Allāh, that He considers these three people to be like His delegates, and treats them with the utmost kindness, granting their every request.

10. The *Duʿā* for a Person in his Absence

Abū al-Dardā' reported that the Prophet (ﷺ) said:

> "There is no Muslim worshipper who prays for his brother (Muslim) in his absence except that an angel says, 'And to you be the same!'"[293]

And Ṣafwān ibn ʿAbdillāh narrated: "I went to Syria, and visited Abū al-Dardā' in his home, but he was not present when I arrived. Umm al-Dardā' asked me, 'Are you going to perform Ḥajj this year?' I replied that I was, so she said, 'In that case, do not forget to pray to Allāh for us for good, for the Prophet (ﷺ) used to say:

---

[291] Reported by Ibn Mājah, Ibn Ḥibbān, and al-Ṭabarānī, from Ibn ʿUmar, and authenticated in *Ṣaḥīḥ al-Jāmiʿ* # 4171.

[292] Reported by al-Bazzār (# 1153). See *al-Silsilah al-Ṣaḥīḥah*, # 1820.

[293] Reported by Muslim and Abū Dāwūd, from Abū al-Dardā', as mentioned in *Ṣaḥīḥ al-Jāmiʿ* # 5737.

"The *du'ā* of a Muslim for his brother in his absence is responded to. There is an angel in front of him that has been assigned to him; every time he makes a *du'ā* for his brother with good, the angel assigned to him says, '*Āmīn*! And to you the same'".[294]

In this situation, the *du'ā* must be purely for the sake of Allāh, since a Muslim will love his brother Muslim only for the sake of Allāh, and this is the only factor that will cause him to make a *du'ā* for his brother in his absence.

One of the scholars wrote, "In this ḥadīth there is a point of benefit to be obtained, and that is: if your *du'ā* is responded to because your brother is absent from you, then we hope that the angel's *du'ā* for you will also be responded to because you are absent from the angel!"[295]

It is reported that the pious predecessors would make a *du'ā* for their brothers when they themselves were in need of that *du'ā*, since they knew that this type of *du'ā* was responded to.

One can imagine what effects such true brotherhood stir up in a Muslim community – where every Muslim is praying for his brother Muslim for the good in this life and in the Hereafter.

11. The One who Remembers Allāh Constantly

The Prophet (ﷺ) narrated:

> Three (people's) *du'ās* are not rejected: the one who remembers Allāh frequently, and the one who has been wronged, and a just ruler.[296]

It is only befitting that the one who remembers Allāh constantly be remembered by Allāh at his time of need.

---

[294] Reported by Muslim, Ibn Mājah, and Aḥmad, from Abū ad-Dardā', as mentioned in *Ṣaḥīḥ al-Jāmi'* # 3380.

[295] See the quote in al-Hilālī, p. 68.

[296] Reported by al-Bayhaqī in his *Shu'ab al-Īmān* (2/399), and it is authentic. See *al-Ṣaḥīḥah*, # 1211.

12. The Just Ruler

This is based on the above ḥadīth. When a person whom Allāh has placed in a position of control and power over people is able to restrain his emotions and desires, and rules them with justice and honesty, then Allāh blesses him, and causes his *duʿā* to be answered.

CHAPTER IX

Factors that Aid a Person's *Du'ā* in being Answered

There are certain factors that assist a person's *du'ā* being accepted by Allāh. These factors are explicitly mentioned in the texts of the Qur'ān and Sunnah as being factors that guarantee, or greatly increase, the chances that one's *du'ās* are accepted. Therefore, every person that makes *du'ā* must see whether these factors are present in him or not, and if not, he should strive until he implements all of them.[297]

Although some of these factors have already been mentioned, they will be listed again here for the sake of benefit.

1. Sincerity

There is no doubt that the single greatest factor which aids a person's *du'ā* in being answered is his sincerity. The more sincere a person is while making *du'ā*, the greater are his chances of response.

Ponder over the story of Yūnus and the whale, the 'Companion of the fish', as he is referred to in the Qur'ān. He was thrown overboard, and then swallowed by a whale, only to be taken to the very depths of the ocean. Darkness covered with darkness – the darkness of the whale's belly, along with the darkness of the sea, along with the darkness of the night! But he did not despair, and instead called out, with a pure sincerity the like of which we cannot even imagine:

[297] This section is based on al-Ḥamad, pp. 85-90.

فَنَادَىٰ فِي ٱلظُّلُمَٰتِ أَن لَّآ إِلَٰهَ إِلَّآ أَنتَ سُبْحَٰنَكَ إِنِّي كُنتُ مِنَ ٱلظَّٰلِمِينَ ﴿٨٧﴾

Then he cried out from the darkness: Verily, there is no deity worthy of worship except You, You are glorified and above all deficiencies! Verily I was of the wrongdoers.[298]

So what was the response from Him who heard him from the depths of the ocean, inside the whale's stomach?

فَٱسْتَجَبْنَا لَهُۥ وَنَجَّيْنَٰهُ مِنَ ٱلْغَمِّ ۚ وَكَذَٰلِكَ نُـۨجِى ٱلْمُؤْمِنِينَ ﴿٨٨﴾

So We responded to his call, and saved him from the distress (that he was in). And likewise do We save the believers.[299]

So the One who responded to the Companion of the Fish is the same One that responds when we call out to Him, but where is our sincerity in comparison to that of Yūnus?

وَٱدْعُوهُ مُخْلِصِينَ لَهُ ٱلدِّينَ

And make *du'ā* to Him, sincerely, for to Him is the religion.[300]

Ibn 'Aqīl al-Ḥanbalī wrote: "It is said a *du'ā* is never responded to quickly except for a person who is sincere, or one who has been wronged".[301]

2. To Expect the Best from Allāh

This point too has been discussed previously.

One of the strongest factors that aids a person's *du'ā* in being accepted is that he expect, in fact, be certain, that Allāh will of a

---

[298] Sūrah *al-Anbiyā'*, 87.

[299] Sūrah *al-Anbiyā'*, 88.

[300] Sūrah *al-A'rāf*, 29.

[301] Al-Ḥamad, p. 85.

surety respond to his *duʿā*. When he expects the best from Allāh, then Allāh treats him the way that he expects, and this is from the Perfection of Allāh's Nature, and an indication of His Beautiful Names.

One of the ways that a person can increase this feeling in himself is to read the Qur'ānic *āyahs* (verses) that talk about Allāh's Power, so that he realises that Allāh is indeed capable of all things. As Allāh says:

إِنَّمَآ أَمْرُهُۥٓ إِذَآ أَرَادَ شَيْـًٔا أَن يَقُولَ لَهُۥ كُن فَيَكُونُ ﴿٨٢﴾

> Verily, His command, when He wishes to do something, is to only say, 'Be!' and it is.[302]

A believer should realise that everything that he desires is with Allāh.

وَإِن مِّن شَيْءٍ إِلَّا عِندَنَا خَزَآئِنُهُۥ

> And there is not a single thing except that We have its treasures.[303]

Just ponder over the meanings of this one ḥadīth in order to get a glimpse at the vast treasures of the One whom you ask, for the Prophet (ﷺ) said that Allāh said:

> O My Servants! If the first of you, and the last of you; if the *jinn* of you, and the men of you, were to stand on one plain, and ask Me, and I gave every single person what he wanted, then all of that would not decrease anything from My kingdom, except like a needle (decreases the amount of water) when it is placed in the ocean (and then taken out).[304]

So this ḥadīth is an indication of the completeness of His Power and Kingdom. If Allāh were to give every single creation, from amongst men and *jinn*, all that they desired, that would not de-

---

[302] Sūrah *Yā Sīn*, 82.

[303] Sūrah *al-Ḥijr*, 21.

[304] Reported by Muslim (# 2577) and others.

crease anything out of His vast treasures and kingdom, just as when a person inserts a needle in an ocean and takes it out, the needle does not take away anything from the ocean's waters.

The Companions understood this concept of expecting the best from Allāh. And hence why ʿUmar ibn al-Khaṭṭāb said: "I am not worried about whether my *duʿā* will be responded to, but rather I am worried about whether I will be able to make *duʿā* or not. So if I have been guided (by Allāh) to make *duʿā*, then (I know) that the response will come with it".[305]

Another scholar stated: "I do not have any example to give for the believer (and his hope for response) except that of a person, stranded in the middle of the ocean, clinging on to a plank of wood, crying out, 'O my Lord! O my Lord!' hoping that Allāh might save him."[306]

Such indeed is the hope of the believer – hope beyond hope, and expectation beyond expectation.

3. Doing Good Deeds

The Prophet (ﷺ) said:

> Make the orphan come close to you, and be nice to him, and wipe his head, and feed him from your food. That will cause your heart to be soft, and your needs to be fulfilled.[307]

Once Anas ibn Mālik was asked by someone to make *duʿā* for him. He replied, "Verily, *duʿā* is raised up (to Allāh) by good deeds",[308] indicating that the questioner should strive to do good deeds if he wants his *duʿās* to be answered. And Wahb ibn Munabbih said: "The example of the one who makes *duʿā* without doing any deeds is like the one who tries to shoot arrows without a bow".[309]

---

[305] Al-ʿAwāyishah, p. 117.

[306] Reported by Imām Aḥmad in his *al-Zuhd*; see *al-Dā'*, p. 46.

[307] Narrated by al-Ṭabarānī in his *al-Kabīr* and others. See *al-Ṣaḥīḥah*, # 854.

[308] Al-ʿAwāyishah, p. 55.

[309] Ibn al-Mubārak, *al-Zuhd*, # 322.

So the person who wishes to have his *du'ā* responded to should increase the quantity and quality of the good deeds that he does.

4. Fulfilling the Rights of Parents

One of the best deeds that a person can do, in fact, the most important and greatest act of worship after worshipping Allāh, is that he be dutiful to his parents. The rights of parents are indeed very great, and it is because of this that the person who fulfils these rights earns a very high status with Allāh. Of the blessings that such a person has is that his *du'ās* are answered.

This is indicated in Uways al-Qarnī's ḥadīth, who among the *tābi'ī*[310] has the highest status of all. 'Umar ibn al-Khaṭṭāb narrated, "I heard the Prophet (ﷺ) say:

> There will come to you (a man by the name of) Uways ibn 'Āmir, with some people from Yemen. He is from (the tribe of) Murād, then from Qarn. He was afflicted with leprosy (all over his body) except for one part, the size of a *dirham*. He has a mother to whom he is very dutiful. If he were to swear by Allāh, Allāh would fulfil his oath. If you are able to ask him to seek your forgiveness, then do so".[311]

When 'Umar heard this, he waited until Uways came to Madīnah, and then asked him to make a *du'ā* for him.

This ḥadīth shows that being dutiful to one's parents is a cause of one's *du'ā* being accepted, as the reason that Uways's oath was responded to was because of the devotion that he used to display to his mother.

Also, the story of the three people that were trapped in the cave further proves this point, since one of them mentioned his good character to his parents as a means of *tawassul* (this story is mentioned in a subsequent chapter regarding *tawassul*).

---

[310] A person who met one or more of the Companions, but did not see the Prophet (ﷺ).

[311] Reported by Muslim (4/1968) and others.

5. To Make *Duʿā* at All Times

The Prophet (ﷺ) stated:

> "Whoever wishes that Allāh responds to his *duʿā* at times of hardship, then let him increase his *duʿā* at times of ease!" [312]

And Ibn ʿAbbās narrated that he was once riding behind the Prophet (ﷺ) on a mount when he (ﷺ) said:

> "O youth! Do you not wish that I should teach you some advice that Allāh will benefit you with?

I responded, "Yes!" He then said:

> Protect (the commandments) of Allāh, and Allāh will protect you, protect (the commandments) of Allāh, and you will find Him ever in front of you. Know Him when you are in a state of contentment, and He will know you when you are in a state of need". [313]

The meaning of this ḥadīth is that if a person worships Allāh and remembers Him at times of ease, then Allāh will remember and help him at times of hardship.

Constant remembrance of Allāh is a sign that a person loves Allāh. Imagine a son who only comes to his parents when he needs their help, and does not remember them when he is not in need of them. Is it not more likely that they will help him if he continually remembers them, and shows his care towards them?

This is why one of the signs of a disbeliever is that he only remembers Allāh when he is in a state of need, as will be mentioned in a later section.

There is a beautiful narration from one of the scholars of the past in which he illustrated this point. Al-Dhahāk ibn Qays said, "Remember Allāh at times of ease, and He will remember you at times

---

[312] Reported by al-Tirmidhī (# 3382), al-Ḥākim (1/544) and others. See *al-Ṣaḥīḥah*, # 593.

[313] Reported by Aḥmad (1/307), al-Tirmidhī (# 2516) and others. See *Ṣaḥīḥ al-Jāmiʿ* (# 2958).

of hardship. For indeed, the prophet Yunus would remember Allāh constantly, and so when he was swallowed by the whale (he was rescued). And this is what Allāh says:

فَلَوْلَآ أَنَّهُۥ
كَانَ مِنَ ٱلْمُسَبِّحِينَ ﴿١٤٣﴾ لَلَبِثَ فِى بَطْنِهِۦٓ إِلَىٰ يَوْمِ يُبْعَثُونَ ﴿١٤٤﴾

> 'And were it not for the fact that he was amongst those who glorified Allāh (constantly); he would have remained in its stomach until the Day of Resurrection.' [314]

And the Pharaoh was a tyrant who never remembered Allāh. So when he was about to drown, and he proclaimed his belief, Allāh said,

ءَآلْـَٔـٰنَ وَقَدْ عَصَيْتَ قَبْلُ وَكُنتَ مِنَ ٱلْمُفْسِدِينَ ﴿٩١﴾

> 'Now?! And you were disobedient before, and were amongst the transgressors?'"[315, 316]

So Allāh saved Yunus from the depths of the ocean because of his constant worship, and He caused Pharaoh to drown while he was walking on dry land due to his rejection of Allāh's remembrance.

6. To do Extra Voluntary Acts After the Obligatory Ones

This is one of the greatest ways that a person can increase the chances of his *duʿā* being answered. This is based on the ḥadīth *qudsī* that states:

---

[314] Sūrah al-Ṣāffāt; 143-144.

[315] Sūrah Yūnus; 91.

[316] Reported by Ibn Rajab in his *Nūr al-Iqtibās*, p. 43,

> Whoever shows enmity to one of My *walī*,[317] then I have declared war against him. And My servant does not cease to draw closer to Me by doing voluntary acts, until I love him. And when I love him, I become his hearing by which he hears, and his eyes by which he sees, and his hands by which he grasps, and his feet by which he walks. And if he asks Me, I will give it to him, and if he seeks refuge in Me, I will give him refuge.[318]

So when a person increases his voluntary good deeds, such as prayer, and fasting, and giving charity, then Allāh loves him, and when Allāh loves him, all his *duʿās* are answered.

7. Repenting From Previous Sins

Sins are one of the factors that prevent a person's *duʿā* from being accepted. Therefore, one of the ways that a person can increase the chances of his *duʿā* being answered is by repenting to Allāh. This must be a sincere repentance, for all of the previous sins that he has committed. This is done by having sincerity towards Allāh, feeling guilty for the sins that he has performed, asking for Allāh's forgiveness, and making a sincere determination not to return to that sin. Additionally, if the sin involved transgressing the rights of others, it is required to return those rights or an equivalent amount of good to the person from whom it was taken.

Nūḥ told his people:

فَقُلْتُ ٱسْتَغْفِرُوا۟ رَبَّكُمْ إِنَّهُۥ كَانَ غَفَّارًا ﴿١٠﴾
يُرْسِلِ ٱلسَّمَآءَ عَلَيْكُم مِّدْرَارًا ﴿١١﴾ وَيُمْدِدْكُم بِأَمْوَٰلٍ وَبَنِينَ وَيَجْعَل
لَّكُمْ جَنَّـٰتٍ وَيَجْعَل لَّكُمْ أَنْهَـٰرًا ﴿١٢﴾

---

[317] The *walī* is one who has earned the protection and pleasure of Allāh, by being sincere in his actions, and acting according to the Sunnah.

[318] Reported by al-Bukhārī, # 6502, and others.

> I told them, "Seek Allāh's forgiveness, for verily He is the One that forgives frequently. He will then send the skies upon you (with rain) in abundance. And He will increase your wealth and children, and bestow upon you gardens, and bestow upon you rivers".[319]

We also have, in the story of the one who prayed to Allāh while he was on a long journey, but whose prayer was rejected because he had wronged others and fed himself with impure money. The only way he could correct that state was by repenting.

8. Having a Humble Appearance

One of the factors that aids a person's *du'ā* in being answered is to have a dishevelled, humbled appearance. This is referred to in the ḥadīth of the traveller on a long journey, who raises his hands and cries out, 'O my Lord! O my Lord!' The Prophet (ﷺ), described him as having a dirty, dishevelled look, as this is one of the factors that aids a person's *du'ā* in being accepted. This because it shows a person's poverty and need of Allāh, and proves that he is not concerned about his appearance or looks, but rather about the response to his *du'ā*.

Ibn 'Abbās, in describing the state in which the Prophet y went to pray the rain prayer when the inhabitants of Madīnah were suffering from a drought, said: "The Prophet exited [the city], wearing modest clothes, in a state of humbleness and displaying neediness [to Allāh]..."[320]

In another ḥadīth which also proves this point, the Prophet (ﷺ) said;

> It is possible that a person who is dusty and dishevelled, wearing only two coarse garments, will be responded to by Allāh if he swears by Allāh (for a *du'ā*).[321]

---

[319] Sūrah *Nūḥ,* 10-12.

[320] Reported by Abu Dawud (# 1165) and authenticated by al-Albānī in *Irwā' al-Ghalīl* (3/133).

[321] Reported by Muslim (# 2622).

However, this does not mean that a person should purposely tear his clothes up, and throw dust on his body, before making a *duʿā*! What is meant is that when such a condition exists – the result of factors beyond the control of the person himself – then such a *duʿā* is more likely to be responded to.

9. Making *Duʿā* at Holy Places

Allāh has blessed certain places over others, so one of the ways that a person can increase his chances of being answered is by making *duʿā* in these places.[322]

For example, mosques are preferred by Allāh over houses and market-places. Likewise, the places of Ḥajj during Ḥajj time (Mina, Muzdalifah and ʿArafāt) are places that the Prophet (ﷺ) would make *duʿā* in, as has been stated above. Other places include: the Mounts of Safa and Marwa, inside the Kaʿbah, and of course the *Ḥarams* of Makkah and Madīnah.

It is important, though, not to exaggerate in this regard, by considering places that are *n*ot blessed as blessed, such as mosques that are built on graves of famous saints, or have such graves inside them or connected to them. Such places are not holy in the slightest. In fact, prayer in such mosques is not allowed due to the explicit narrations from the Prophet (ﷺ) in which he prohibited the Muslims from praying over mosques built over or around graves.[323]

10. Conforming with the Etiquette of *Duʿā*

It is essential that the one making *duʿā* conforms to all the preconditions and etiquettes that have been mentioned before, in particular praying only to Allāh, and concentrating on one's *duʿā*, and praying during the blessed times and occasions during which one's *duʿā* is more likely to be responded to.

---

[322] Al-Arūsī, p. 218.

[323] See *Fundamentals of Tawḥīd*, pp. 138-175 for a more detailed discussion of this point.

In conclusion, we quote Ibn al-Qayyim:

"If the *du'ā* is combined with the following factors:

- the presence of the heart, and its full concentration on the *du'ā*
- making *du'ā* at one of the times of response
- a meek heart, one that is broken and humiliated in the presence of Allāh, full of humbleness and softness
- facing the qiblah
- in a state of *wuḍū*
- raising one's hands to Allāh
- starting the *du'ā* with praise to Allāh
- following that up with salutations upon the Prophet (ﷺ)
- preceding the *du'ā* with repentance and seeking forgiveness for past sins
- preceding the *du'ā* by giving some charity
- and finally entering in upon Allāh, and being persistent in asking Him, and calling upon Him in a state of fear and hope, and performing *tawassul* with His Names and Attributes

then this *du'ā* is hardly ever left, but rather responded to, especially if the *du'ā* is using the supplications that the Prophet (ﷺ) informed are likely to be responded to."[324]

---

[324] Paraphrased from *al-Dā' wa al-Dawā'*, p. 48.

CHAPTER X

Factors that Prevent *Duʿās* from being Answered

One of the greatest tests and trials that a Muslim might be afflicted with is that his *duʿā* is not answered! Hence why the Prophet (ﷺ) would pray to Allāh that his *duʿā* not be amongst those *duʿās* that are not responded to. In particular he (ﷺ) would pray:

> O Allāh! I seek your refuge from knowledge that is without benefit, and from a heart that does not become fearful, and from a soul that is never satisfied, and from a *duʿā* that is not responded to![325]

So the Prophet (ﷺ) would actually make a *duʿā* that his *duʿā* be answered!

There are a number of factors that have been mentioned in the *aḥādīth* that cause one's *duʿā* not to be accepted. Although some of these factors have been given above, for the sake of completeness they will be listed here again.

1. *Ḥarām* Sustenance

Abū Hurayrah narrated that the Prophet (ﷺ) said:

> "O People! Allāh is *al-Ṭayyib* (Pure), and He only accepts that which is pure! Allāh has commanded the believers what He has commanded the Messengers, for He said,
>
> "O Messengers! Eat from the pure foods, and do right",
>
> and He said,

[325] Reported by Muslim and others.

> "O you who believe! Eat from the pure and good foods We have given you".
>
> Then the Prophet (ﷺ) mentioned a traveller on a long journey, who is dishevelled and dusty, and who stretches forth his hands to the sky, saying, "O my Lord! O my Lord!" – while his food is unlawful, his drink is unlawful, his clothing is unlawful, and he is nourished unlawfully; how can he be answered?[326]

In this ḥadīth, we are informed about one of the greatest causes of one's *duʿā* not being responded to. Consider the example that the Prophet (ﷺ) gave of this man who combined in him many of the factors that aid the *duʿā* in being accepted. Firstly, he was travelling, and not just a small journey, but rather a long one. He was away from his family for a long time, and the land that he was in is far-away. Secondly, his appearance was one that extracts sympathy for his situation, for he was dishevelled and dusty, tired and dirty. Thirdly, he raised his hands to the sky – to the *al-Ḥayi*, The Shy – hoping that they would not be returned empty. Fourthly, he made *tawassul* with one of Allāh's most powerful and comprehensive Names, that of *'al-Rabb*,' which is one of the best Names to use in a *duʿā*. Fifthly, he repeated his *duʿā* and the Name of Allāh, so that it had more chance of being accepted.

Yet, despite all of these factors and regardless of his following the necessary etiquette, his *duʿā* was not responded to. Not only that, but the Prophet (ﷺ) made a point of stressing how ridiculous it was that he expected his *duʿā* to be answered, for he stated',...how can he be answered,' implying that the sin of eating *ḥarām* sustenance is so great that there is no point in him hoping to have his *duʿā* accepted.

So it is essential that one who wishes that his *duʿā* be accepted ensure that he eats from pure money, money that has been earned

---

[326] Reported by Aḥmad, Muslim, and al-Tirmidhī from Abū Hurayrah, as mentioned in *Ṣaḥīḥ al-Jāmiʿ* # 2744.

with permissible means, and that he eats pure food, food that he is allowed to eat.[327]

Sa'd ibn Abī Waqqās, one of the Prophet's (ﷺ) famous Companions was once asked, "Why is it that your *du'ās* are responded to, amongst all of the other Companions?" He replied, "I do not raise to my mouth a morsel except that I know where it came from and where it came out of".[328]

2. Sins

There is no doubt that a person's sins come between him and the response of his *du'ā*. Therefore, when a person makes *du'ā* for long periods of time, without receiving a response, this should cause him to turn towards himself, and examine his actions. Perhaps there is something that he is doing that is the cause of his *du'ā* being unanswered?

This is referred to in the following ḥadīth,

> The skies of the heavens are opened in the middle of the night, and a crier calls out: Is there any person making *du'ā*, that he be responded to? Is there any that asks, that he be given? Is there any that is in straightened circumstances, that it be lifted from him? And there is no Muslim that makes a *du'ā* (at this time) except that Allāh will respond to him, except for a fornicatress that is striving (to sell) her private parts, or a tax-collector".[329]

So in this ḥadīth, we are informed that every single Muslim that makes a *du'ā* at this time will be responded to, except a prostitute that is selling her body, and a tax-collector that is taking other people's money unjustly. So these two sins are the cause of their *du'ās* being rejected.

---

[327] For further details on this point, see the author's book, *15 Ways to Increase your Earnings from the Qur'ān and Sunnah*, al-Hidaayah Publications, 2002.

[328] *Sharḥ al-Arba'īn*, p. 275.

[329] Reported by al-Ṭabarānī in his *al-Awsaṭ*. See *al-Ṣaḥīḥah*, # 1073.

Once, Sufyān al-Thawrī was asked: "Why do you not make *duʿā* (for such and such a matter)?" He responded, "Leaving sins is, in and of itself, *duʿā*",[330] implying that, just as sins come between a person and his *duʿā*, likewise leaving sins makes the path of response easier.

A poet versified this concept when he wrote,

We call upon our Lord at every disaster,
And yet when rescue arrives, Him do we forget!
How can you expect that your duʿā be responded to,
When you have, with sins, its path blocked?

3. Leaving Advice to Others

Part of one's *īmān* is that one loves for one's brother what one loves for oneself. This necessitates one's wanting good for one's brother, and averting evil from him. So, when one sees one's brother doing something that is not allowed, it becomes obligatory on one to try to prevent him, even if one has to do so physically (if one is able to do so without harm or any adverse consequences). Similarly, one has to advise and exhort him to do good deeds if he is being lax in performing them.

This obligation is one of the factors that has made our nation the greatest nation out of all Allāh's nations.

كُنتُمْ خَيْرَ أُمَّةٍ أُخْرِجَتْ لِلنَّاسِ تَأْمُرُونَ بِالْمَعْرُوفِ
وَتَنْهَوْنَ عَنِ الْمُنكَرِ وَتُؤْمِنُونَ بِاللَّهِ

You are the best of peoples ever raised for mankind; you enjoin what is good and forbid what is evil, and believe in Allāh.[331]

So leaving this obligation brings about Allāh's anger and punishment, and part of this punishment is that our *duʿās* are not answered.

---

[330] *Jāmiʿ al-ʿUlūm wa l-Ḥikam,* 1/276.

[331] Sūrah *Āl-ʿImrān*, 110.

The Prophet (ﷺ) said:

> I swear by Him in whose Hands is my soul, you will of a surety command what is good, and forbid what is evil, or else it is very possible that Allāh will send upon you His punishment, so you will make *duʿā* to Him, and you will not be responded to.[332]

4. Being Hasty

This point has already been mentioned, and is one of the factors that the Prophet (ﷺ) informed us that causes a *duʿā* to be rejected.

> "The *duʿā* of any worshipper will continue to be responded to, as long as he does not ask for a sin or breaking the ties of kinship, and as long as he is not hasty."

It was asked, "O Messenger of Allāh? And what does it mean to be hasty?" He (ﷺ) responded:

> "A worshipper says, 'I have prayed and prayed, and I don't see that it will be accepted', so he gives up hope of being answered, and leaves *duʿā*".[333]

> A worshipper should never give up hope of getting a response to his *duʿā*. Even if he has prayed for years and years, he should continue to pray, for how does he know that the response will not come tomorrow? Some of the wisdom behind delaying the response to a *duʿā* are mentioned in the next chapter.

5. Becoming Tired

In other words, a person makes *duʿā* for so long that he becomes tired and gives up, due to lack of enthusiasm and energy.

In one wording of the above ḥadīth, the Prophet (ﷺ) said at the end,

---

[332] Reported by al-Tirmidhī (# 2169) who said that it was *ḥasan ṣaḥīḥ*, as did al-Albānī in *Ṣaḥīḥ al-Jāmiʿ*, # 7070.

[333] Narrated by Muslim from Abū Hurayrah, as mentioned in *Ṣaḥīḥ al-Jāmiʿ* # 7705.

"A worshipper says, 'I have prayed, but no response came!' At that, he becomes tired and leaves *duʿā*".[334]

And that is why the angels have been praised in the Qur'ān that they never tire of Allāh's worship.

وَمَنْ عِندَهُۥ لَا يَسْتَكْبِرُونَ عَنْ عِبَادَتِهِۦ وَلَا يَسْتَحْسِرُونَ ﴿١٩﴾

And those that are with Him (i.e. the angels in the Heavens) are not arrogant to worship Him, nor do they get tired.[335]

6. Asking for Something Prohibited

The above ḥadīth also mentions that asking for something *ḥarām*, or asking for breaking the ties of kinship, is a factor that causes the *duʿā* to be rejected.

7. A Man Married to an Evil Woman, One who Gave a Loan but Did not Take Precautions, and a Man who Gave his Money to a Fool

These three categories of people are mentioned in the following ḥadīth, narrated by Abū Mūsa al-Ashʿarī:

> Three people make *duʿās*, but they will not be answered! (The first is) a man who had under him (in marriage) a woman who had an evil character, yet he did not divorce her. (The second is) a man who gave some money as a debt to another man, yet he did not use any witnesses. (The third is) a man who gave his money to a fool, even though Allāh says,
>
> وَلَا تُؤْتُوا۟ ٱلسُّفَهَآءَ أَمْوَٰلَكُمُ
>
> And do not give fools your money.[336, 337]

---

[334] Reported by Muslim (# 2735) and others.

[335] Sūrah *al-Anbiyā'*, 19.

[336] Sūrah *al-Nisā'*, 5.

[337] Reported by al-Ḥākim (2/302) who declared it authentic, and al-Dhahabī agreed with him, as did al-Albānī (see *al-Ṣaḥīḥah*, # 1805).

So in this narration, we are informed of three categories of people whose *duʿā* is not responded to.

The first is a man who is married to a woman who has very lax morals. Such a woman might flirt with other men, and not guard her husband's honour and property in his absence. If this is the case, and the man cannot correct her, then she should be divorced, for it is possible that she might bring great shame to him and his household. If he does not divorce her, then he exposes himself to Allāh's anger, and his *duʿās* are not responded to.

The second is a person who is not wise in giving loans. He gives loans to people that are not trustworthy, and on top of that, he does not take the necessary precautions, for it is advised that a person giving a loan ensures there are two witnesses to the transaction. This ensures that no dispute arises if the two parties disagree about the amount of the loan. So, if a person does not take these necessary precautions, then he only has himself to blame, and his *duʿā* will not be responded to.

The third is a person who is not responsible with his money, and gives it to people who are not intelligent or wise in business dealings. He might enter into a contract with a business partner, or engage in buying and selling, with one who is foolish in these affairs. So once again, he only has himself to blame if his money is lost, and his *duʿā* are not answered.

8. Abandoning the Etiquette of *Duʿā*

If a person opposes the proper etiquette of *duʿā*, then this is a very obvious cause of his *duʿā* not being responded to. So it is important that a person check his *duʿā* with all of its attendant preconditions and etiquettes, and be thorough in conforming to the manners of a proper *duʿā*.

In conclusion, we quote Ibn al-Qayyim: "And such is *duʿā*, for it is one of the strongest factors that repels evil, and brings about desired good. However, it is possible that its effects are not seen, either because of a weakness in the *du'ā* – for example, the *du'ā* is not beloved to Allāh, since it contains in it transgression, or because of a weakness in the heart of the one making *du'ā*. So the heart does not turn to Allāh, and unify its energy in asking for it while it makes the *du'ā*, so it is like a very weak bow, from which the arrow leaves with weakness. Another cause for which the *du'ā* is not answered is the presence of a preventing factor, such as eating *ḥarām* sustenance, or being unjust, or there being a layer of filth due to sins over the heart, or that the heart has been overtaken by play and heedlessness".[338]

Furthermorethe famous ascetic and worshipper, Ibrāhīm ibn Adham was once asked, "Why is it that we make *du'ā*, yet they are not responded to?" He replied:

> "Because you know Allāh, yet do not obey Him.
> And you know the Prophet (ﷺ), but do not follow his Sunnah.
> And you know the Qur'ān, but you do not act upon it.
> And you eat from the blessings of Allāh, but you do not express gratitude for it.
> And you know Paradise, yet do not strive for it.
> And you know the Fire of Hell, yet do not run away from it.
> And you know Shayṭān, but you do not fight him, and instead obey him.
> And you know death, but you do not prepare yourselves for it.
> And you bury the dead, but do not learn a lesson from it.
> And you have left your own faults, and instead busy yourself with the faults of others."[339]

338 *Al-Dā' wa al-Dawā'*, p. 39.

339 Al-Radi, p. 31.

CHAPTER XI

The Wisdom Behind A Delayed Response

It is indeed a great trial for a Muslim to make *duʿā*, sincerely and properly, continually, for a long period of time, and yet see no sign of response. Here, a person's *īmān* in Allāh is truly tested. And here is the opportunity that *Shayṭān* uses to try to sow his whispers, and plant his doubts in a believer's heart. In this way a person might start thinking evil thoughts about his Creator, or start doubting the wisdom of the Divine Decree.

So whoever falls into this, should immediately seek Allāh's refuge from *Shayṭān*, and turn to Allāh sincerely, making yet another *duʿā*: that he be saved from *Shayṭān's* evil plots, and that he be granted patience to withstand the test that he is undergoing. He should also ponder over his own limited knowledge and intelligence, and realise the infinite Knowledge of Allāh, and the extreme wisdom behind any Divine act.

At the same time, he should realise the great blessings that Allāh has given to mankind when He guaranteed a response to all *duʿās*, as long as the *duʿā* conforms to all the necessary etiquettes, and there are no prohibiting factors found in the one making it. So every *duʿā al-ʿibādah* is responded to by giving the doer rewards in this life and the Hereafter, and every *duʿā al-mas'alah* is responded to by giving what was asked, or something equivalent to it, or by averting some evil that was to befall the one making *duʿā*, or by giving him reward equivalent to his *duʿā* on the Day of Judgement. So even when one's *duʿā* is apparently not responded to, he should realise that the actual response might not be what he presumes, and it is, in fact, possible that his *duʿā* has already been answered, without his even knowing it!

A Muslim should understand that there are many wisdoms behind the delayed response of a *duʿā*, whether he realises it or not. All of Allāh's decrees are wise, and, although it is not possible that we fully and truly comprehend all the Divine Wisdom behind an act, it is possible that we can glean some of the benefits of a Decree. The following points have been mentioned by some scholars:[340]

1. Allāh is the *Mālik*

Allāh is the true King, the Owner of All Kingdoms. No one can interfere in His decisions, and no one can question His resolutions. As Allāh says in the Qur'ān,

لَا يُسْـَٔلُ عَمَّا يَفْعَلُ وَهُمْ يُسْـَٔلُونَ ﴿٢٣﴾

> He is not questioned regarding what He does, but rather they will be questioned (regarding what they do).[341]

He also says:

وَٱللَّهُ يَحْكُمُ لَا مُعَقِّبَ لِحُكْمِهِۦ ۚ وَهُوَ سَرِيعُ ٱلْحِسَابِ ﴿٤١﴾

> And Allāh judges, and there is none that can change His judgement. And He is the Ever-Swift in Reckoning.[342]

So the Muslim does not question the Will of Allāh, rather he accepts it, and is pleased with it.

One of the scholars wrote: "So there is none of us who can escape from the Will of Allāh and His Decree. And no one can avert His judgement or His trials (upon us). Verily, we all belong to Allāh, we are His slaves and (part of His) possessions. He does with us as He pleases, and what He wills".[343]

---

[340] Paraphrased from al-Ḥamad, pp. 93-107 and al-Khudarī, pp. 87-91.

[341] Sūrah *al-Anbiyā'*, 23.

[342] Sūrah *al-Raʿd*, 41.

[343] Al-Ḥamad, p. 94.

2. Man does not have a Right Over his Creator

The one making *duʿā* should realise his lowly status, and know that he does not have a right over his Creator that his *duʿā* be responded to. He should be wise enough to contemplate his own many faults and shortcomings with regards to the rights that Allāh has over him. This will make him appreciate that he does not have any rights over Allāh!

Ibn al-Qayyim wrote:

> So one of the greatest matters of benefit to the heart is that it looks into the rights that Allāh has over His slaves, because this will cause him to look at his own self in a despicable and lowly manner. It will make him avoid self-conceit and vanity concerning his actions, and instead open for him the door to humility and meekness. He will be submissive before his Lord, and give up hope of his own self, for he will realise that success will only come about through the Mercy of Allāh and His Blessings. For His right (upon the soul) is that He be obeyed, and not disobeyed, and remembered, and not forgotten, and thanked, and not rejected. So whoever looks into this right that his Lord has upon him, then he will know – a most certain knowledge – that he is not fulfilling the rights of his Lord in a way that he should, and that nothing can save him except divine aid and forgiveness. So if he were to rely upon his own actions, he would be destroyed! So this is what those who have knowledge of Allāh look upon, and this is what has caused them to give up hope of attaining any good from themselves, and made them put all of their hope in the Mercy and Forgiveness of Allāh.
>
> But if you were to look at the status of the majority of people, you will find them to be the exact opposite of this! They examine the 'rights' that they have upon Allāh, and they ignore the rights that Allāh has upon them! And because of this, they have cut themselves off from Allāh, and their hearts have been sealed up from recognising Him, or loving Him, or being eager to meet Him. And this is the height of ignorance that a man can have with regards to his Lord, and even with regards to himself.[330]

[344] Paraphrased from *Ighāthat al-Lahfān*, p. 97-98.

3. A Delay in Response is a Trial

When the response of a *duʿā* is delayed, this is a type of test and trial that is inflicted upon the servant. This necessitates his being patient during this trial. So a person should realise that, just like his entire life is a trial and test for him, so too is this delayed response. This is just one of the many trials that he has to face if he eventually wishes to enter Paradise and please his Creator.

As Allāh says:

وَنَبْلُوكُم بِٱلشَّرِّ وَٱلْخَيْرِ فِتْنَةً ۖ وَإِلَيْنَا تُرْجَعُونَ ﴿٣٥﴾

> And We test you, with good and evil, as a *fitnah*. And to Us you will return.[345]

So both good and evil is a test, a *fitnah*, for us, to see whether we are patient when afflicted with evil, and whether we use the good that we have been given properly.

4. Allāh is the Most-Wise

Of Allāh's many beautiful Names is *al-Ḥakīm*, or The Most-Wise. So to Allāh belongs the greatest wisdom; all of His Decrees are Wise. When He gives, He gives with wisdom, and when He prevents, He prevents with wisdom. As Allāh says:

حِكْمَةٌۢ بَٰلِغَةٌ ۖ

> Perfect (or Complete and All-Encompassing) Wisdom.[346]

So it is possible that what a person desires is not wise for him to have. And because of this, he is not granted it, or it is delayed until such a time that it is suitable for him. It is possible that the *duʿā* might be responded to at a later time, due to factors that Allāh alone is aware of. For example, a couple might pray for a child, and their *duʿā* is not answered for a number of years, since Allāh knows that it would be better for them to be blessed with a child at a later date.

---

[345] Sūrah *al-Anbiyā'*, 35.

[346] Sūrah *al-Qamar*, 5.

So the believer accepts the Divine Wisdom of Allāh, and does not cause a delay in response to swerve him from the true *īmān* in Allāh.

5. The Matter Might Bring Evil

Following up from the last point, it is possible that Allāh knows that a certain matter, although apparently might appear to bring good, in reality will lead to evil consequences. So, a person might desire to have money, and in his heart he feels that he will spend this money for the sake of Allāh, and yet Allāh knows that if this person were to be given money, he would spend it in *ḥarām* ways, and that it would ruin his *īmān*. So he would become like the one that is mentioned in the Qur'ān:

وَمِنْهُم مَّنْ عَٰهَدَ ٱللَّهَ لَئِنْ
ءَاتَىٰنَا مِن فَضْلِهِۦ لَنَصَّدَّقَنَّ وَلَنَكُونَنَّ مِنَ ٱلصَّٰلِحِينَ ﴿٧٥﴾
فَلَمَّآ ءَاتَىٰهُم مِّن فَضْلِهِۦ بَخِلُوا۟ بِهِۦ وَتَوَلَّوا۟ وَّهُم مُّعْرِضُونَ
﴿٧٦﴾ فَأَعْقَبَهُمْ نِفَاقًا فِى قُلُوبِهِمْ إِلَىٰ يَوْمِ يَلْقَوْنَهُۥ بِمَآ أَخْلَفُوا۟
ٱللَّهَ مَا وَعَدُوهُ وَبِمَا كَانُوا۟ يَكْذِبُونَ ﴿٧٧﴾

> And of them are some who made a promise with Allāh (saying): if He bestowed on us out of His Blessings, then we will of a surety give charity, and we will surely become amongst the righteous! Then, when He gave them of His Blessings, they became miserly (in spending for the sake of Allāh), and turned away, averse (out of arrogance). So because of this He punished them by putting hypocrisy in their hearts, until the Day when they shall meet Him, because they broke which they promised Allāh, and because they used to lie (to Allāh)![347]

So beware, O Muslim, of getting angry, or complaining, against Allāh's Decree, for it is possible that the matter that you so desire might be the very cause of your destruction!

---

[347] Sūrah *al-Tawbah*, 75-77.

Shaykh al-Islām Ibn al-Qayyim, the master of spiritual diseases and their cures, writes:

> The Divine Decree related to the believer is always a bounty, even if it is in the form of withholding (something that is desired), and it is a blessing, even if it appears to be a trial, and an affliction that has befallen him is in reality a cure, even though it appears to be a disease! Unfortunately, due to the ignorance of the worshipper, and his transgressions, he does not consider anything to be a gift or a blessing or a cure unless he can enjoy it immediately, and it is in accordance with his nature. If he were only given a little bit of understanding, then he would have counted being withheld from as a blessing, and the sickness as a mercy, and he would relish the trouble that befalls him more than he relishes his ease, and he would enjoy poverty more than he enjoys richness, and he would be more thankful when he is blessed with little than he is when he is blessed with a lot.[348]

Note that a believer does not *ask* for problems and trials, but when they occur, the true believer relishes them more than he would an apparent blessing, because he realises and expects the great reward that he will obtain through his patience and perseverance.

6. Allāh's Choice is Better than the Choice of the Servant

This is a great secret that very few people appreciate or implement in their lives. For verily, Allāh is more Merciful to His servants than a mother is to her child, and He will only Decree for them what is best for their needs in this world and the Hereafter. So even when a trial or tribulation afflicts a Muslim, this is better for him than it not having happened.

So, O servant of Allāh, next time your *du*ʿ*ā* is not answered, ask yourself: "Is it not possible that Allāh knows that this matter which I am asking for is not for my benefit? And is He not the Most Mer-

---

[348] *Madārij al-Sālikīn*, 2/215-216.

ciful of all that have mercy? So, in this prevention of my *du'ā* being answered, there might be great good for me!"

Just like a parent must not fulfil all the desires of his child since some of them are harmful for him, so too – and to Allāh belongs the greatest example – must a person realise that not all of his *du'ās* are really for his benefit. And once a person truly and fully realises this, that Allāh cares for him more than he cares for himself, then he has gone a long way towards perfecting his *īmān*.

The great sage and ascetic Sufyān al-Thawrī said: "Verily, when He withholds, He actually gives, because He did not withhold on account of miserliness or stinginess, but rather He looked at the benefit of the servant. So the fact that He withheld is actually His choice for the servant and His excellent decision".[349]

7. Man does not Know the Result of His *Du'ā*

This is another factor that a person should take into consideration, and that is that he does not know the consequences of any *du'ā* that he makes. It is only Allāh, the *'Alīm*, the Knower of All, Who knows the result of a person's *du'ā*.

Ponder over the story of the youth that was killed by Khadir, Mūsa's teacher. Without a doubt, the youth's parents must have suffered greatly at his death. Yet, Allāh knew that, had the boy lived, he would have caused great distress and hardship to his parents. Therefore, it was Allāh's Mercy that the youth was not allowed to grow up to harm his parents, for had he done so, and turned to disbelief, the grief caused to such pious parents would have been worse than the grief of an innocent death.

وَأَمَّا ٱلْغُلَٰمُ فَكَانَ أَبَوَاهُ مُؤْمِنَيْنِ فَخَشِينَآ أَن يُرْهِقَهُمَا
طُغْيَٰنًا وَكُفْرًا ﴿٨٠﴾

[349] *Madārij al-Sālikīn*, 2/215.

And as for the boy, his parents were believers, and We feared lest he should oppress them by rebellion and disbelief.[350]

Therefore, it can be seen that a person's knowledge of good and evil is relative, whereas Allāh's knowledge is infinite. So a person should resign himself to the fact that His Creator knows the actual consequences of his *duʿā*, and as such his Lord's decision is better than his own.

8. Trials Bring One Closer to Allāh

The Prophet (ﷺ) said:

> The greatness of reward is based on the severity of the trial. And if Allāh loves a person, He tests him, so whoever is pleased (with Allāh), then he will have the Pleasure (of Allāh), but whoever is angry, then he will receive the Anger (of Allāh).[351]

So the fact that a person's *duʿā* is not responded to is a trial from Allāh, and this should make a person optimistic that he is from amongst those whom Allāh loves. Such a test should make him increase in his patience and draw him closer to Allāh.

9. Something Hated Sometimes Brings Good

When a person's *īmān* is strong, then he will realise that everything that Allāh has decreed for him is good, even if he does not see the wisdom behind a certain Decree. So, when an affliction befalls him, he will know and realise that hidden in it is great good and benefit for him. As Allāh states:

فَعَسَىٰٓ أَن تَكْرَهُوا۟ شَيْـًٔا وَيَجْعَلَ ٱللَّهُ فِيهِ خَيْرًا كَثِيرًا ﴿١٩﴾

> For it is possible that you hate something, yet Allāh places in it a lot of good (for you).[352]

---

[350] Sūrah *al-Kahf*, 80.

[351] Reported by al-Tirmidhī (# 2396), Ibn Mājah (# 4031) and others. Authenticated in *Ṣaḥīḥ al-Tirmidhī* 2/286.

[352] Sūrah *al-Nisā'*, 19.

And Allāh also stated about *jihād*:

كُتِبَ عَلَيْكُمُ ٱلْقِتَالُ وَهُوَ كُرْهٌ لَّكُمْ ۖ وَعَسَىٰٓ أَن تَكْرَهُوا۟
شَيْـًٔا وَهُوَ خَيْرٌ لَّكُمْ ۖ وَعَسَىٰٓ أَن تُحِبُّوا۟ شَيْـًٔا وَهُوَ شَرٌّ لَّكُمْ ۗ
وَٱللَّهُ يَعْلَمُ وَأَنتُمْ لَا تَعْلَمُونَ ﴿٢١٦﴾

> "*Jihād* is ordained for you (Muslims) though you dislike it. And it may be that you dislike a thing even though it is for your good, or that you like a thing even though it is for your evil. And Allāh knows, whereas you do not know.[353]

So when a person realises that something that is disliked might cause or lead to something that is desired, this will ease for him the fact that his *duʿā* has not been responded to, and sow in his heart the patience that is necessary to overcome this matter.

Ponder over the wise statement of Sufyān ibn ʿUyaynah, who stated: "What the slave detests is better for him than what he loves! This is because what he detests will cause him to increase in his *duʿā*, whereas what he loves will distract him (from worshipping Allāh)".[354]

10. It Causes the Believer to Reflect on Himself

When a person's *duʿā* is apparently not answered, it causes him to contemplate his life, the good and the bad. It causes him to examine his *duʿā*, and why he is making it. It causes him to examine his life, and what he wants with it. It causes him to examine his money, how he earns it and how he spends it. It causes him to examine his good deeds, and how few they actually are. It causes him to examine his evil deeds, and how numerous they are. It causes him to turn to Allāh in repentance, and change his lifestyle. And these effects only occur to the true believer.

---

[353] Sūrah *al-Baqarah*, 216.

[354] Al-Ḥamad, p. 101.

So this delay in response is actually a cleansing experience and a purification for the Muslim, for it forces him to re-examine his relationship with Allāh, and try to strengthen it. And had his *duʿā* been responded to immediately, then this examination would not have occurred, nor would any extra good come out of it. But in this delay, a person, as it were, finds himself, and this, in and of itself, is a great blessing from Allāh.

11. The *Duʿā* Might Actually Have been Responded To

We have already mentioned the ḥadīth in which the Prophet (ﷺ) guaranteed that a person's *duʿā* will be accepted. However, the 'acceptance' of a *duʿā* might be in a manner that is not apparent. It is possible that Allāh will give him the reward of his *duʿā* on the Day of Judgement, and this reward will be more beloved to him on that Day than the response of his *duʿā* in this life. It is also possible that Allāh blesses him with something else that he did not ask for, as a result of his *duʿā*. Lastly, it is possible that Allāh averts an evil that was predestined for him because of his *duʿā*.

So when a person realises this, then how can he despair at his *duʿā* not being answered? Does he not realise that the response of the *duʿā* is guaranteed by Allāh? Perhaps the *duʿā* has been responded to in ways that he does not see, but of a surety, if he is performing *duʿā* properly, it must be answered.

12. The *Duʿā* Might be Weak

Ibn al-Qayyim's quotation concerning the relationship of *duʿā* with the Divine Decree has already been given above. Ibn al-Qayyim mentioned that there are three possibilities with regards to the *duʿā* and Divine Decree. Firstly, it is possible that the *duʿā* is stronger than the Decree, and thus repels it permanently. Secondly, it is possible that the *duʿā* is weaker than the Decree, so the Decree occurs, but the *duʿā* causes it to soften a little bit. Thirdly, they be equal in strength, so each one prevents the other from acting.[355]

---

[355] *Al-Dāʾ wa al-Dawāʾ*, p. 42.

Therefore, a person should examine whether the *duʿā* is fulfilling the conditions for the acceptance of a *duʿā*. He should see if there are any impediments that prevent his *duʿā* from being answered.

13. The Manifestation of Allāh's Names and Attributes

The fact that a person's *duʿā* is responded to or not is an indication and manifestation of many of Allāh's Names and Attributes.

Of these Names is: *al-Mu'ṭī* (the One that Gives), *al-Māniʿ* (the One that Withholds), *al-Ḥakam* (the One that Judges and Decrees), *al-ʿAdl* (the All-Just), *al-Karīm*, (the Ever-Generous), *al-Ḥakīm* (the All-Wise), and many others. Whether a person's *duʿā* is answered or not, all of these Names, and more, are manifested in Allāh's Decrees. So when He gives, He gives out of Generosity, and Wisdom, and Justice, and when He withholds, He withholds out of Power, Wisdom, and Justice. So a person should keep the Names and Attributes of Allāh in mind when his *duʿā* is not responded to, for in this is a great manifestation of these Names and Attributes.

14. The Perfection of Worship

Finally, one of the greatest benefits and wisdoms of a delayed response is that it perfects a person's worship and *īmān* of Allāh. And this is the very purpose of creation! So when a person's *duʿā* is not responded to, let him ponder over the ways that this increases his *īmān*, and sharpens his servitude to Allāh, and perfects his humbleness to the Creator. Some of the ways that this is done are as follows:

i. Waiting for a Response:

When a person eagerly and anxiously awaits a response to his *duʿā*, this necessitates a strong hope in Allāh, and an optimism of Allāh's Mercy and Blessings. This feeling is, in and of itself, an act of worship, and the longer that the response is delayed, the stronger these feelings become if the person wishes to continue in his *duʿā*. In this way his *īmān* is strengthened without him even realising it!

ii. Showing One's Need to Allāh

The essence of worship is to humble one's self before Allāh, and realise one's extreme need of Allāh's Help and Mercy. And when the response to a *duʿā* is delayed, this increases this awareness, and a person realises that there is no one besides Allāh that can help him, or respond to his *duʿā*, so his *īmān* in Allāh increases in this manner. Simultaneous with this realisation comes the awe and meekness that is required in Allāh's presence,along with humility and humbleness, for a person realises his own weak and fragile nature.

Had every *duʿā* of a person been answered immediately, this would lead to arrogance, and cultivate a feeling of self-sufficiency and conceit! It would cause the person to forget the relationship that he should have with Allāh, and, in fact, might even lead to him to think that he has a *right* upon Allāh to answer his prayers. If a person were to become so arrogant, then there would be no hope for him in the Hereafter, for no person will enter Paradise with an ounce of arrogance in his heart.

Shaykh al-Islām Ibn Taymiyyah said: "So the servant is always in need of his Lord, from every perspective. This because He is the object of his worship, and the source of all of his help. So no one can bring him any good except Him, and nothing can better the situation of the servant except His worship. And on top of all this, the servant is sinning, and there is no way that he can avoid this. So he is always in need, sinning, and he is in need of the One who always Forgives, the One who is Ever-Merciful. The One who always Forgives (*al-Ghafūr*) will forgive his sins, and the Ever-Merciful (*al-Raḥīm*) will show him mercy and bless him and be kind to him. So the servant is eternally between the blessings of his Lord and the sins of his soul".[356]

---

[356] Al-Ḥamad, p. 104.

iii. Pleasure at Allāh's Decree

One of the most important pillars of *īmān* is to be content with Allāh's Decree. This is because the slave realises and appreciates that whatever Allāh has chosen for him is for his own good, whether he can see this good or not. So there is a blind faith in whatever Allāh decrees, and a total satisfaction with whatever occurs.

Therefore, the delay in responding to a *du'ā* is one of the opportunities in which a believer must display his contentment at the decree of Allāh, and not show anger or annoyance. The one who is pleased with Allāh as his Lord, and with the Decrees of Allāh in his life, will attain the pleasure of Allāh in this world and in the Hereafter, but the one who is displeased and angry, will only attain Allāh's displeasure and anger.

iv. Humility in Front of Allāh

When the response of a *du'ā* is delayed, the believer becomes even more humiliated and humble in front of the All-Mighty. And this humility is one of the primary pillars of worship, for *'ibādah*, is defined as 'the height of humility along with the height of love.' The three pillars upon which a Muslim worships Allāh are: love, fear and hope; and humility is one of the ways in which this fear and love is displayed.

So this delay in response is in fact a means to draw out the servant's meekness and humility from his heart. Had the *du'ā* been responded to, the servant would not feel such sincere humility, nor would he feel a need of being humble in the presence of the Divine One.

v. Enjoying a Private Conversation with Allāh

Amongst the many benefits of *du'ā* is that *du'ā* opens up a private channel between the servant and his Lord, as has been discussed previously. So the longer the response of the *du'ā* is delayed, the stronger and more powerful this relationship and channel becomes. Finally, a stage is reached, by a very select and blessed few, in which the pleasures of this communication become more pleasing to the soul than the actual response of the *duʿā* would be! So, a person actually *wishes* for a delay in response to his *duʿā*, since he knows that this relationship that he has with his Lord will not continue when his *duʿā* is responded to. And the longer the delay, the longer his conversation and relationship will continue.

vi. Combating the Plots of Shayṭān

Without a doubt, *Shayṭān* stoops to all levels, and tries all plots so that a person will turn away from worship of Allāh. And is there any opportunity greater for him to seize than when a servant's *duʿā* is not answered?! For here is the servant, weak and humble in front of Allāh, calling and crying out to him, 'O my Lord! O my Lord!' Yet, there is no response! So *Shayṭān* seizes this opportunity, and plants his whispers and seeds of doubt in the son of Adam, until he thinks every evil thought about his Lord!

But the true believer, the one who is ever-aware and cautious of *Shayṭān's* plots, sees the dangers of this situation, and, instead of letting it be a cause of him going away from worship of Allāh, seizes it as an opportunity to attack *Shayṭān* and increase in his worship of Allāh! So he turns to Allāh, again and again, and seeks refuge from *Shayṭān*, for he realises that his only hope for safety is through Allāh, and his only refuge and haven is in Allāh's Protection! So in this intense battle between *Shayṭān* and the son of Adam, the weapon that is used is *duʿā* to Allāh, and the armour that is worn is seeking refuge in Allāh.

15. Conclusion

These are only some of the benefits and wisdoms that scholars have stated as regards which a *duʿā* might be not be answered, or its response delayed. Without a doubt, there are far more benefits than can be imagined, but in these few pages, there should be a reminder for the believer, and a solace for the Muslim.

Furthermore, although the general rule is that the more pious a person is, the greater are his chances of being answered, this is not always the case. It is possible that a disbeliever, or an evil sinner, is responded to, and it is possible that the *duʿā* of the most pious is not answered. So just because a person's *duʿā* is not answered is not an indication that the person is not pious.

If even the Prophet's (ﷺ) *duʿā* was sometimes not responded to, then where do we stand in comparison to him? The Prophet (ﷺ) said,

> I asked my Lord for three things, but He gave me two of them, and prevented me from one. I asked my Lord that my nation not be destroyed by a drought, so He gave it to me. And I asked Him that my nation not perish by drowning, so He gave it to me. And I asked Him that fighting not occur between them, but He did not give it to me.[357]

And this is a clear indication that not every single *duʿā* of a person is responded to.

Additionally, these 'wisdoms' that are mentioned above should not be taken as an excuse to give up *duʿā*, for the Prophet (ﷺ) explicitly prohibited this. The purpose behind these explanations is such that a person might be comforted when the response is delayed, and not give up the continuance of *duʿā*.

In conclusion, it is appropriate to quote a lengthy passage form one of Ibn al-Jawzī's works,[358] a passage full of wisdom and beneficial advice.

Ibn al-Jawzī wrote:

> I was once in a situation of distress, so I regularly made *duʿā* to Allāh to relieve me from my distress, and to bless me with relief and freedom. Yet, the response seemed to be postponed, so my soul started getting agitated and restless.
>
> I told it 'Woe to thee! Consider your situation: are you one who

---

[357] Reported by Muslim (# 2890) and others.

[358] *Ṣayd al-Khāṭir*, v. 2, p. 291

is a maid-servant or are you a queen?[359] Are you one who is controlled (by Allāh), or are you the controller? Do you not know that this world is the place of trials and tests? And if you ask for something and it is not responded to, and you are impatient at this, then where is the test? After all, are not trials and tests merely the opposite of our own goals and desires? If only you were to understand this responsibility, then that which is difficult will appear easy for you, and the unbearable will become light.'

After it pondered over this, it quietened down a bit.

I then told it, 'I also have a second answer, and that is that you are asking (Allāh) your wishes and desires, but neglecting to ask yourself what it is obligated to do. This is the essence of ignorance, for it is appropriate for you to do the opposite, since you are a servant, and the intelligent servant strives to fulfil the rights of his master, knowing that it is not obligatory for the master to grant any desire.'

After I told it this, it achieved more peace.

I then told it, 'I have yet a third response, and that is that you have delayed the response, as you have blocked its path with your sins. So if only you were to open the path, the response would be hastened. Do you not know that the cause of peace is *taqwa*? Have you not heard the statement of Allāh:

وَمَن يَتَّقِ ٱللَّهَ يَجْعَل لَّهُۥ مَخْرَجًا ۝٢ وَيَرْزُقْهُ مِنْ حَيْثُ لَا يَحْتَسِبُ

And whoever fears Allāh, He will provide for him an escape. And he provides for him from sources that he never could imagine? [Sūrah *al-Ṭalāq*, 2-3]

Have you not understood that the opposite also applies, (that if you are immersed in your sins, your matter will be made difficult). Woe to the intoxication of thoughtlessness that is stronger than all other intoxicants, and prevents the water that is desired

[359] The soul is feminine in the Arabic language, hence the feminine gender.

from reaching the garden of one's goals![360]

So my soul realised the truth, and became content.

I then said, 'I have yet a fourth response, and that is that you are asking for something for which you do not know the consequences of. In fact, it might be harmful for you. Your example is that of a child, stricken with fever, and asking for sweets. The one in charge of you is more aware of your betterment than you are. Has not Allāh said,

وَعَسَىٰٓ أَن تَكْرَهُوا۟ شَيْـًٔا وَهُوَ خَيْرٌ لَّكُمْ

And it is possible that you hate something and it is for your good?

[Sūrah *al-Baqarah*, 216]

After the truth became clear to my soul, it settled in its contentment.

I then said to it, "I have a final – fifth – response, and that is that this wish of yours will decrease your reward (with Allāh), and lower your status. Therefore, the prevention of the response is actually the increasement of your good. If you were only to ask what benefits your Hereafter, it would be better for you.

Understand, therefore, all that I have told you.'

It then replied, 'I have been grazing in the gardens of your response, and the understanding (that you have given me) has caused me to be ecstatic with joy!'

So see, dear reader, how this great scholar, Ibn al-Jawzī, was able to transform the pain and anguish that his soul was feeling, into joy and ecstasy, only because of his knowledge and *īmān*!

---

[360] This beautifuly eloquent phrase requires some explanation! Basically, Ibn al-Jawzī is comparing one's *duʿā* to the fruits of a garden, and the factors that facilitate the response of the *duʿā* to the water that is needed for those fruits to grow. So the fruits (the *duʿā*) will only ripen if water is given to the garden. He then compares one's own heedlessness (in sins) to being intoxicated, and this intoxication prevents the person from realising that he is, with his own hands, preventing the water from reaching the garden, thus stating that sins lead to one's *duʿā* not being answered.

CHAPTER XII

Permissible Acts of *Du*ʿ*ā*

There are certain acts that people might presume are prohibited, but are in fact allowed. Some of these are listed below.

1. To Pray for a Person without Praying for One's Self

This is permissible since the Prophet (ﷺ) prayed for a number of Companions without making a *du*ʿ*ā* for himself. Examples of this have already been given above. In one such case, Abū Mūsa al-Ashʿarī reported that the Prophet (ﷺ) said:

> "O Allāh! Forgive ʿUbayd Abī ʿĀmir. O Allāh! Forgive ʿAbdullāh ibn Qays his sins and enter him on the Day of Judgement to a good place".[361]

2. To Wish For Death in Severe Circumstances

The proof for this is found in the ḥadīth quoted above, in which Anas ibn Mālik reported that the Prophet (ﷺ) said:

> None of you should wish for death due to any calamity that has befallen him. If he has no choice but to wish for death, then let him say, 'O Allāh! Grant me life as long as life is better for me, and take me away (in death) whenever death is better for me!'[362]

This ḥadīth shows that it is permissible, under extreme situations, to wish for death.

---

[361] Narrated by al-Bukhārī (4323).

[362] Reported by al-Bukhārī, Muslim and Aḥmad, as mentioned in *Ṣaḥīḥ al-Jāmi*ʿ # 7611.

Imām al-Bukhārī, due to the many difficulties that he encountered from people who were jealous of him, wished for death towards the end of his life, and made this *du'ā*, after which Allāh granted him his desire.

3. To Pray For and Against Non-Muslims

The prayer for non-Muslims can only be when they are alive, for after they are dead, Allāh has prohibited us from praying for them. The Qur'ān says:

مَا كَانَ لِلنَّبِيِّ وَالَّذِينَ ءَامَنُوٓا۟ أَن
يَسْتَغْفِرُوا۟ لِلْمُشْرِكِينَ وَلَوْ كَانُوٓا۟ أُو۟لِى قُرْبَىٰ مِنۢ بَعْدِ
مَا تَبَيَّنَ لَهُمْ أَنَّهُمْ أَصْحَٰبُ ٱلْجَحِيمِ ﴿١١٣﴾

> "It is not proper for the Prophet and those who believe to ask Allāh's forgiveness for the pagans after it has become clear to them that they are the dwellers of the Hell-fire".[363]

During their lifetimes, however, it is permissible to pray that Allāh guide them to Islām.

Abū Hurayrah reported that Ṭufayl ibn 'Amr came to the Prophet (ﷺ) and said: "O Messenger of Allāh (ﷺ)! (The tribe of) Daws has disobeyed and refused (to enter Islām), so pray against them!" So the people thought that the Prophet (ﷺ) would pray against them, but instead he (ﷺ) said:

> "O Allāh! Guide Daws, and bring them (to Islām)".[364]

As for praying against non-Muslims, this too has been narrated in many of the Prophet's (ﷺ) *aḥādīth*. Such *du'ās* may be done when they have arrogantly rejected the truth after it has been made clear to them, and when they continue to cause harm to Muslims. For

---

[363] Sūrah *al-Tawbah*, 113.

[364] Reported by al-Bukhārī (6397).

example, Mūsa prayed to Allāh concerning Pharaoh:

رَبَّنَا ٱطْمِسْ عَلَىٰٓ أَمْوَٰلِهِمْ
وَٱشْدُدْ عَلَىٰ قُلُوبِهِمْ فَلَا يُؤْمِنُوا۟ حَتَّىٰ يَرَوُا۟ ٱلْعَذَابَ ٱلْأَلِيمَ ﴿٨٨﴾

"Our Lord! Destroy their wealth, and harden their hearts, so that they will not believe until they see the painful torment".[365]

The Prophet (ﷺ) prayed against certain members of the Quraysh, as also against the Confederate Tribes who had gathered and encamped outside of Madīnah to attack the Muslims.

However, in general, it should be left to scholars and students of knowledge to decide when a non-Muslim should be cursed or prayed against.

4. To Request a Pious Person to Perform a *Duʿā*

It is permissible to ask a person that one feels is more pious than oneself to make a *duʿā* for one.

This topic is discussed in greater detail in the next chapter.

[365] Sūrah *al-Yūnus*, 88.

CHAPTER XIII

TAWASSUL

The concept of *tawassul* has been referred to many times in this treatise. It is one of the most important etiquettes of *du'ā*, and one of the greatest factors that increase the chances of a *du'ā* being accepted.

Since many people have an incorrect understanding of this concept, and because of it fall into *shirk* or innovation, it is important that this topic be given greater attention.[366]

Linguistically, *tawassul* means to come closer to an objective and to gain proximity to a desired goal. In Islamic terms, it signifies the act of trying to come closer to Allāh through manners that have been prescribed by the Qur'ān and Sunnah. In other words, it is a means of seeking nearness to Allāh. This concept is referred to in the following verse:

يَٰٓأَيُّهَا ٱلَّذِينَ ءَامَنُوا۟ ٱتَّقُوا۟ ٱللَّهَ وَٱبْتَغُوٓا۟ إِلَيْهِ ٱلْوَسِيلَةَ
وَجَٰهِدُوا۟ فِى سَبِيلِهِۦ لَعَلَّكُمْ تُفْلِحُونَ ﴿٣٥﴾

> O you who believe! Do your duty to Allāh and seek the means to approach Him (*wasīlah*), and strive hard in His cause so that you may be successful.[367]

When used in the context of *du'ā*, *tawassul* takes on a more specific meaning. It then refers to seeking a means of having one's

---

[366] Due to the nature of this book, the topic of *tawassul* can only be dealt with briefly. The reader is strongly encouraged to read al-'Allāmah Muḥammad Nāṣir al-Dīn al-Albānī's book *Tawassul: Its Types and Rulings* (al-Hidaayah Publishing & Distribution, United Kingdom, 1995).

[367] Sūrah *al-Mā'idah*, 35.

duʿā accepted, or increasing the chances of one's *duʿā* being accepted.

There are a number of ways that are prescribed in the *Sharīʿah* for *tawassul*. These are as follows:

1. *Tawassul* through Allāh's Names and Attributes

This is one of the most powerful means of *tawassul*, and has been mentioned many times in this small treatise.

The Prophet (ﷺ) heard a man say in his *tashahhud*: "O Allāh I ask You by virtue of the fact that all praise belongs to You, none has the right to be worshipped but You, alone, having no partner. The Great Bestower of all blessings, O Originator of the heavens and the earth, O Possessor of Majesty and Honour, O Ever-Living, O Sustainer and Protector of all that exists. Indeed I ask You for Paradise and I seek Your refuge from the Fire". So the Prophet said to his Companions:

> Do you know what he has supplicated with?

They said: 'Allāh and His Messenger know best'. He said:

> By Him in Whose Hand is my soul! He has supplicated to Allāh by His Great Name (and in a narration: by His Greatest Name), the one that, if He is called upon by it, He responds, and if He is asked by it, He gives".[368]

In another ḥadīth, the Prophet (ﷺ), said,

> Whoever is greatly troubled and says: "O Allāh! I am Your Slave, son of Your male slave and female slave. My forelock is in Your Hand. Your Judgement is continually operative upon me. Your sentence concerning me is just. I ask You by every Name which is Yours with which You named Yourself, (regardless of whether) You have taught it to anyone from Your creation, or sent it down in Your Book, or have kept it to Yourself in the knowledge of the Hidden with You, that You make the Qur'ān the spring of my heart, the light of my chest, the

---

[368] Reported by Abū Dāwūd, al-Nasā'ī and Aḥmad and others with *ṣaḥīḥ isnād*.

> removal of my sadness and of my anxiety!" then Allāh will remove his anxiety and sorrow, and replace it with joy.[369]

An example of *tawassul* through Allāh's Attributes is in the ḥadīth in which the Prophet (ﷺ) prayed with the following *du'ā*:

> O Allāh! (I ask you) by Your knowledge of the unseen, and Your power to create, that You cause me to live as long as living is better for me, and that You cause me to die when You know that death is better for me.[370]

So in this *du'ā*, *tawassul* was sought through the Attributes of Knowledge, and Power.

2. *Tawassul* by Mentioning Allāh's Favours

Another manner in which a person may do *tawassul* is by mentioning the favours of Allāh upon him. So, for example, a person might say: "O Allāh! You have guided me to Islām, and placed in me a love for knowledge and its people! O Allāh! Cause me to increase in this knowledge, and cause me to be amongst the righteous scholars!"

This principle is shown in the *du'ā* of Zakariyya, when he asked Allāh to bless him with a child.

قَالَ رَبِّ إِنِّي وَهَنَ ٱلْعَظْمُ مِنِّي وَٱشْتَعَلَ ٱلرَّأْسُ شَيْبًا
وَلَمْ أَكُنۢ بِدُعَآئِكَ رَبِّ شَقِيًّا ﴿٤﴾

> He said: O My Lord! Indeed, my bones have grown feeble, and grey hair has spread over my head. And I have never been unblest in (or deprived of) my *du'ā* to You, O my Lord![371]

Shaykh al-Islām Ibn Taymiyyah said: "The meaning is: you have made me accustomed to receiving your response, and You have not deprived me by rejecting me and cutting off (your help) from me.

---

[369] Reported by Aḥmad (# 3712) and the wording is his, and al-Ḥākim (1/509) and others. Authenticated in *al-Ṣaḥīḥah* (# 199).

[370] Reported by al-Bukhārī (# 5671) and Muslim (# 2680).

[371] Sūrah *Maryam*, 4.

So it is a *tawassul* to Allāh by the blessings that He has previously given, of answering his *duʿās*, and His good. And this is very apparent here".[372]

3. *Tawassul* by Mentioning Ones State

Another means of *tawassul* is by mentioning to Allāh the dire circumstances that one is in, and the desperate need that one has for His Mercy and Blessings.

In the *duʿā* of Zakariyya quoted above, we find him saying:

قَالَ رَبِّ إِنِّي وَهَنَ ٱلْعَظْمُ مِنِّي وَٱشْتَعَلَ ٱلرَّأْسُ شَيْبًا
وَلَمْ أَكُنۢ بِدُعَآئِكَ رَبِّ شَقِيًّا ﴿٤﴾

> He said: O My Lord! Indeed, my bones have grown feeble, and grey hair has spread over my head. And I have never been unblest in (or deprived of) my *duʿā* to You, O my Lord![373]

So he begins by mentioning the state that he is in of old age, and that he needs to be blessed with a son, for he might be on the verge of death.

The Prophet Nūḥ, when he was rejected by his people, cried out:

فَدَعَا رَبَّهُۥٓ أَنِّي مَغْلُوبٌ فَٱنتَصِرْ ﴿١٠﴾

> Then he made a *duʿā* to his Lord: I have been overpowered, so help (me)![374]

So he mentioned the appalling circumstance that he was in – that he had been overpowered by his enemies – and used that as a *tawassul* so that his *duʿā* would be responded to. Likewise, when Mūsa was in the valley of Midyan, alone and with no supporter or helper, he cried out to Allāh,

---

[372] *Majmūʿ al-Fatāwa*, v. 15, p. 14.

[373] Sūrah *Maryam*, 4.

[374] Sūrah *al-Qamar*, 10.

رَبِّ إِنِّي لِمَآ أَنزَلْتَ إِلَيَّ مِنْ خَيْرٍ فَقِيرٌ

> O My Lord! Verily I am *faqīr* (needy) for whatever good that you can send down upon me.[375]

And this type of *tawassul* is even used amongst people! For does not a beggar, when he stands up to ask for money, announce, "I am a person with a large family, and I have many debts to pay back, and cannot find work...?" All of this is used in order for him to obtain more sympathy from the people that hear him, and indeed to Allāh belongs the greatest example.

4. *Tawassul* Through Good Deeds

Tawassul can also be made through mentioning one's good deeds. So, one can say: "O Allāh! Because of my love for Your religion, and love for You and Your Prophet, forgive me!" Or, "O Allāh! Because of the charity that I gave to so-and-so, out of pleasing You, then grant me my *duʿā*".

The Qur'ān is replete with this type of *tawassul*. In one verse, the believers are described as:

ٱلَّذِينَ يَقُولُونَ رَبَّنَآ إِنَّنَآ ءَامَنَّا فَٱغْفِرْ لَنَا ذُنُوبَنَا
وَقِنَا عَذَابَ ٱلنَّارِ ﴿١٦﴾

> Those that say: 'O Allāh! We have believed, so forgive us our sins, and save us from the Fire of Hell!'[376]

In this *duʿā*, *tawassul* is sought because of one's *īmān* in Allāh and His religion, and there is no doubt that the greatest good deed that a person can use is his *īmān* in Allāh.

This principle has also been confirmed in the story of the companions of the cave, as is reported by ʿAbdullāh ibn ʿUmar, who said: "I heard Allāh's Messenger say:

---

[375] Sūrah *al-Qaṣaṣ,* 24.

[376] Sūrah *Āl-ʿImrān*, 16.

Three men, amongst those who came before you, set out until night came, and they reached a cave, so they entered it. But a boulder rolled down from the mountain and blocked the entrance of the cave. So they said: nothing can rescue you from this rock except that you supplicate to Allāh by mentioning righteous deeds you have done. (And in the narration of Muslim: so one of them said to the others: think of righteous deeds which you have done purely for Allāh by making mention of them, that He might release you).

So one of them said: "O Allāh! I had two elderly parents, and I had not used to give precedence over them to my family and slaves in giving them milk to drink. But one day I was delayed in seeking after something (in the narration of Muslim: for fodder) and I did not return with the flock until they (my parents) had slept. So I milked the animals for my family and slaves before them, and I waited with the bowl in my hand for them to awake, even though my family and children were crying out of hunger. I disliked waking them up, and I also disliked leaving them hungry (by giving the milk to my family and leaving my parents with nothing to drink). I waited for them to wake up until, finally, with the break of dawn, they awoke and drank their milk. O Allāh if I did that seeking Your Face, then relieve us from this situation caused by the rock'. So it moved slightly, and they could see the sky, but they were unable to escape.

The next said: "O Allāh! My uncle had a daughter and she was the most beloved of the people to me, and I tried to persuade her to have sexual relations with me, but she refused me until she suffered from a year of famine. Then she came to me and I gave her a hundred and twenty deenars on the condition that she would comply with my desire for her, so she agreed. But when I was about to fulfil my desire she said: 'It is unlawful for you to break the seal except by lawful means'. So I felt ashamed to commit the crime against her, so I left her alone, and she was the most dear of all people to me, and I (also) left the gold which I had given her. O Allāh if I did that seeking Your Face then release us from the situation we are in'. So the rock opened further but they were still unable to escape.

> And the third said: 'O Allāh! I employed some labourers and paid them their wages except a single man who did not take his wages and went away. I invested his wages and it grew into a great deal of property. Then after some time he came to me and said: 'O servant of Allāh, give me my wages'. So I said to him: 'All the camels, cows, sheep, and slaves that you see are your wages'. So he said: 'O servant of Allāh, do not mock me'. So I said: 'I am not mocking you'. So he took all of that and led them away and did not leave any of it. O Allāh if I did that seeking Your Face, then release us from our situation'. So the rock moved and they walked out of the cave.[377]

This ḥadīth is clear proof that one of the means of *tawassul* is mentioning one's good deeds while making *du'ā*. And this fact is, in and of itself, a great incentive for one to do deeds purely for the sake of Allāh, so that one may use them as a means of *tawassul* when one is in dire need of a *du'ā* being answered.

5. *Tawassul* Through Mentioning the Effect of the *Du'ā*

Tawassul can also be made by attaching the response of the *du'ā* to a good deed or benefit. So, for example, a person can say: "O Allāh! I ask you to increase me in knowledge, so that I may teach my family and relatives your religion." Or, he might pray: "O Allāh! Increase my wealth so that I can spend it in your way!"

This principle is shown by the ḥadīth in which the Prophet (ﷺ), said,

> When a person comes to visit the sick, then let him say: O Allāh! Cure your servant so-and-so, for he will then inflict a wound on an enemy, or walk for your sake to the prayer.[378]

It is also shown in the *du'ā* of Ibrāhīm when he left Ḥājar and Ismā'īl in the barren valley of Bakkah, later to be called Makkah:

---

[377] Reported by al-Bukhārī (3/260/), Muslim (# 6607), al-Nasā'i and others, with various wordings and additions.

[378] Reported by Abū Dāwūd (# 3107). See *Ṣaḥīḥ al-Jāmi'*, # 466.

رَّبَّنَآ إِنِّيٓ أَسۡكَنتُ مِن ذُرِّيَّتِي بِوَادٍ غَيۡرِ ذِي زَرۡعٍ عِندَ بَيۡتِكَ
ٱلۡمُحَرَّمِ رَبَّنَا لِيُقِيمُواْ ٱلصَّلَوٰةَ فَٱجۡعَلۡ أَفۡـِٔدَةٗ مِّنَ ٱلنَّاسِ
تَهۡوِيٓ إِلَيۡهِمۡ وَٱرۡزُقۡهُم مِّنَ ٱلثَّمَرَٰتِ لَعَلَّهُمۡ يَشۡكُرُونَ ٣٧

O My Lord! I have left my family to live in a valley that has no fruits, close to your Sacred House, so that they may establish the prayer. Our Lord! Therefore cause a group of people to love them, and provide them with fruits so that they may give thanks.[379]

So Ibrāhīm asked that Allāh bless them with fruits, and cause a community of people to live with them, so that they could establish prayer and give thanks to Allāh.

This is also demonstrated in Mūsa's *duʿā* :

وَٱجۡعَل لِّي وَزِيرٗا مِّنۡ أَهۡلِي ٢٩ هَٰرُونَ أَخِي ٣٠ ٱشۡدُدۡ بِهِۦٓ أَزۡرِي ٣١
وَأَشۡرِكۡهُ فِيٓ أَمۡرِي ٣٢ كَيۡ نُسَبِّحَكَ كَثِيرٗا ٣٣ وَنَذۡكُرَكَ كَثِيرًا ٣٤
إِنَّكَ كُنتَ بِنَا بَصِيرٗا ٣٥

O My Lord! Give me a helper from my family. My brother Hārūn. Increase my strength through him. And let him share my task. That we may glorify you a lot. And remember you much. Verily, you are ever a Well-Seer over us.[380]

Mūsa asked Allāh to bless him with Hārūn as a helper so that both of them could thank Him and praise Him.

6. *Tawassul* by Asking a Living Person to Make *Duʿā*

It is allowed to make *tawassul* by asking a living person to make *duʿā* on your behalf, if you feel that such a person is a true and righteous person. So, it is permissible to go to a scholar, and say, for example: "O so-and-so! I ask that you make a *duʿā* to Allāh that he cure my son from such-and-such an illness".

---

[379] Sūrah *Ibrāhīm*, 37.

[380] Sūrah *Ṭā Hā*, 29-35.

Safwān ibn ʿAbdillāh narrated: "I went to Syria, and visited Abū al-Dardā' in his home, but he was not present when I arrived. Umm al-Dardā' asked me, 'Are you going to perform Ḥajj this year?' I replied that I was, so she said: 'In that case, do not forget to pray to Allāh for us for good, for the Prophet (ﷺ) used to say:

> "The *duʿā* of a Muslim for his brother in his absence is responded to. In his presence there is an angel that has been assigned to him; every time he makes a *duʿā* for his brother with good, the angel assigned to him says, '*Āmīn*. And to you the same'".[381]

In this narration, Umm al-Dardā asked Safwān to remember her and her husband while making *duʿā*.

Jābir ibn ʿAbdillāh reported that a woman came to the Prophet (ﷺ) and said: "Pray for me and my husband". So the Prophet (ﷺ) responded:

> "May Allāh have mercy on you and your husband".[382]

Once, during the caliphate of ʿUmar ibn al-Khaṭṭāb, there was a severe drought that afflicted Madīnah. The Muslims, under the leadership of ʿUmar, went outside the city to perform *ṣalāt al-istisqā*, the prayer for rain. After finishing the prayer, ʿUmar said: "O Allāh! We used to perform *tawassul* through the Prophet (ﷺ), (while he was alive), and now we will perform *tawassul* through the Prophet's (ﷺ) uncle, ʿAbbās ibn ʿAbd al-Muṭṭalib". So saying, he commanded ʿAbbās to make a *duʿā* to Allāh for rain, and indeed, Allāh responded to his *duʿā*, and it rained in Madīnah.[383]

Although it is permissible to ask others to make *duʿā* for one's self, it is better not to do so for personal *duʿās* (this is in contrast to

---

[381] Reported by Muslim, Ibn Mājah, and Aḥmad, from Abū al-Dardā, as mentioned in *Ṣaḥīḥ al-Jāmiʿ* # 3380.

[382] Reported by Abū Dāwūd (1530). The Arabic wording is '*Ṣalla Allāhu ʿalayḳi...*', which shows the permissibility of using this phrase for other than the Prophet (ﷺ). This because, when used for the Prophet (ﷺ), this is a *duʿā* to Allāh to honour and bless him, but when used for someone else, it is a general prayer to have mercy on him.

[383] Reported by al-Bukhārī (4/209) and others.

duʿās that are related to the benefit of the entire *ummah*, such as the preceding example, in which ʿUmar asked ʿAbbās to make a *duʿā* for the Muslims of Madīnah).

This for the following reasons:

1. The general rule is that the person should pray for himself. Just like he does his other acts of worship, and takes care of his own affairs of this world, so too should he make his own *duʿā*.

2. Asking others is a type of request that is done to other than Allāh, and shows a need or poverty that a person feels towards mankind. In this there might be a type of humiliation for a person, and a degradation of his status as he beseeches others.

3. There is no one that will feel more sincerity than the one making *duʿā* for himself and his loved ones. It cannot be expected that a friend or distant acquaintance will feel the same sincerity and emotions that the person himself is feeling. And yet it is these very emotions that are the cause of any *duʿā* being accepted. So how is it that a person will go to a total stranger, and ask him to pray to Allāh about a problem that he himself is facing?

4. This act leads many people to leave *duʿā* themselves, as they then rely on others to make *duʿā* for them. This fact was mentioned earlier.

5. It might lead to arrogance on the part of the person being asked. For it is possible that he will feel that he is holy and pious, and hence why people come to him to ask him to make *duʿā* for them.

6. It has not been reported that any of the major Companions ever asked the Prophet (ﷺ) to make *duʿā* for them regarding a personal, worldly benefit that they desired. They would ask him to make *duʿā* regarding a matter that was of benefit to all of the Muslims (such as ʿUmar's request to the Prophet (ﷺ), to make *duʿā*

to bless the Muslims with food when the army ran short of it during the Battle of Tabūk), or of a religious benefit (such as Abū Hurayrah asking the Prophet (ﷺ) to make *duʿā* to guide his mother to Islām), but there is no reported incident in which they came to the Prophet (ﷺ) to ask for a personal, worldly benefit.[384]

It has been reported that once a person came to Mālik ibn Dīnar, one of the famous scholars of his time. He asked Mālik: "Make *duʿā* for me, as I am in severe circumstances". Mālik responded, "In that case, make *duʿā* for yourself, as He is the One Who responds to the distressed who is in severe circumstances". In another incident, Ṭāwūs, one of the scholars of the *tābiʿīn*, visited a sick person, who asked him: "O Ṭāwūs, please make a *duʿā* for me". Ṭāwūs replied: "Pray for yourself, for He is the One that responds to the one in distress".[385]

These narrations show that it is a mistake to ask someone to make *duʿā* on your behalf, and then rely on that person's *duʿā*, without making *duʿā* yourself.

So these are the six ways that are found in the Qur'ān and Sunnah by which *tawassul* can be done.[386]

---

384 Arūsi, p. 203.

385 Al-Ḥamad, p. 76.

386 It should be mentioned that some scholars only mention three ways of performing *tawassul* (Shaykh al-Albānī), others mention four (Shaykh Bakr), and yet others mention seven (Shaykh Ibn al-ʿUthaymīn). In reality, there is no contradiciton in these various categorisations, and if one ponders over them, one will see that many of these categories are merely sub-categories of other types. For example, *tawassul* by mentioning Allāh's favours can be considered a type of *tawassul* through Allāh's Names and Attributes (since the favour is an *effect* of Allāh's Names), and *tawassul* by mentioning the good effect of one's *duʿā* can be considered *tawassul* through a good deed (since it is the *intention* to do a good deed in the future, which, in and of itself, is a good deed). However, these six categories that are mentioned here seem, and Allāh knows best, to be the simplest way of expressing the various types of *tawassul*.

7. Other Types of *Tawassul*

The types of *tawassul* mentioned above are the only types sanctioned by the Qur'ān and Sunnah. All other types of *tawassul* are not sanctioned by Islām. This because all acts of worship, including *tawassul,* must be based on authentic texts of the Qur'ān and Sunnah, and not upon opinion or desire.

So if a person does *tawassul* by a means other than what has been mentioned, then without a doubt he will either fall into *shirk* (associating partners with Allāh) or *bid*ʿ*ah* (innovation). For example, if a person makes *tawassul to* another object or false deity, this is one of the greatest types of *shirk*! To make *tawassul* through idols and other false deities is exactly what the pagan Arabs did before the Prophet's (ﷺ) advent.

Similarly, if a person makes *tawassul* to Allāh, but by means of something that has not been sanctioned in religion, this will be an innovation. The most common type of *tawassul* that is done in our times, and yet is not sanctioned by the Qur'ān and Sunnah, is *tawassul* through the status of the Prophet (ﷺ).

Without a doubt, the Prophet (ﷺ) is the one single person that all Muslims love the most. He is the best of creation, and the most noble of mankind. He is our leader in this world and on the Day of Judgement, and he is the most righteous of all Adam's children. All of this, however, should not cause us to raise him above the level that Allāh Himself chose for His Prophet, and that the Prophet (ﷺ) himself was content with. One only needs to look at the Christians and the consequences that have occurred when they raised ʿĪsa ibn Maryam above the status that he deserved, to see the dangers of this line of thinking.

With this in mind, we say that *tawassul* through the Prophet (ﷺ) can be divided into three categories. The first type is *tawassul* through one's love for the Prophet (ﷺ). This type comes under *tawassul* through one's good deeds, and is allowed. The second type comes under *tawassul* through the Prophet's (ﷺ) *du*ʿ*ā* while he was alive. This comes under *tawassul* by asking a pious person to make *du*ʿ*ā*, and without a doubt the Prophet (ﷺ) is the most noble and pious of Adam's children. However, after the Prophet's (ﷺ) death, it is not possible to use this type of *tawassul* any more, as the Prophet (ﷺ) cannot hear a person's *du'ā* while he is in his grave. (This is in contrast to a person sending *salām* upon the Prophet (ﷺ) for Allāh has assigned angels to convey these *salāms* to him as has been narrated in authentic traditions. As for anything other than *salāms* then there is no authentic narration that such information is conveyed to him.) The third type of *tawassul* with regards to the Prophet (ﷺ) is *tawassul* through his status. So, a person would say: 'O Allāh, I ask you by the status of the Prophet (ﷺ), with You, that you grant me such-and-such'.

Tawassul through the status of the Prophet (ﷺ) is a matter that has not been mentioned in the Qur'ān, or in the authentic Sunnah. Therefore, this act is a dangerous innovation into the religion of Islām. In addition, there are no authentic narrations from the first three generations of Islām – the three generations that the Prophet (ﷺ) praised in many authentic narrations – that show that any one of the great scholars and worshippers of these generations practised this type of *tawassul*. So this, in and of itself, is clear proof that *tawassul* through the status of the Prophet (ﷺ) is an innovation, and it is irrelevant who amongst the later scholars sanctioned it. For no group of people loved the Prophet (ﷺ) more than the Companions, and yet none of them, even when they were in dire need, performed this type of *tawassul*. And the Muslim has, in the Prophet (ﷺ), and his Companions, a model to follow and imitate.[387]

---

[387] For further details on this topic, and refutation of the more common evidences that are used in order to justify this type of *tawassul* (in particular, the 'ḥadīth of the blind man'), see the book on the subject by Shaykh al-Albānī, previously mentioned.

CHAPTER XIV

Du'ā and its Relationship with Destiny

The topic of *du'ā* and its relationship to destiny (*qadr*) is a very important one, and one around which much confusion exists. Many people ask: "If everything has already been destined to occur, then of what use is *du'ā*, as, if Allāh has written what I want, I will get it without making *du'ā*, and if it is not written for me, then I will never get it no matter how much *du'ā* I make?"

The response to this question lies in understanding that the outcome of anything is dependent on the performance of the efforts that are necessary to procure it. In other words, it has already been decreed, for example, that a seed will give fruit if planted, but this will not occur unless the farmer takes the appropriate efforts in irrigating the crop, maintaining it, protecting the seedling as it grows, and ensuring as much as he can that the factors are amenable for the plant to give fruit.

So even though a person believes in the Divine Decree, he must at the same time strive all he can to ensure that the desired goal occurs. So *du'ā* is the *means* that one uses to achieve the desired goal that one has, and this means in no way contradicts the destiny that has been written for that person.

This stance is clarified by the Prophet's (ﷺ) ḥadīth reported by Thawban, that he (ﷺ) said:

> "Nothing increases one's life-span except good deeds, and nothing repels Divine Decree except *du'ā*. And verily, a person may be deprived of sustenance due to a sin that he does!"[388]

---

[388] Narrated by Ibn Mājah # 90, and Shaykh al-Albānī said in *Ṣaḥīḥ Ibn Mājah* (73): "It is authentic without the addition, 'And verily...'; see *al-Ṣaḥīḥah*, # 154."

In other words, the performance of good deeds is a cause of increasing one's life span, so if a person puts in the necessary effort, the results will be achieved, and this is also destined. So both the *means* to achieve a goal, and the *fulfilment* of the goal itself, are already decreed.

If someone were to ask: "How can *du'ā* repel Divine Decree?" we would respond, "The fact that you may be ill has already been decreed by Allāh for you, as has the fact that you will ask Allāh to cure you of this illness (i.e. both the illness and your asking to cure the illness has been decreed). In a similar manner, a person may be deprived of his sustenance that was decreed for him, since Allāh's eternal knowledge encompassed the fact that this person would perform a sinful deed that would cause the deprivation of his sustenance. All of this, then, is from the decree of Allāh, all Glory and Praise be to Him".

There are a number of *aḥādīth* that clarify this point. For example, Mu'ādh ibn Jabal reported that the Prophet (ﷺ) said:

> "Caution will be of no benefit against Divine Decree, but *du'ā* benefits all things, whether they come down or not. I therefore advise you to make *du'ā*, O servants of Allāh!"[389]

So no matter how cautious a person is, he cannot escape what is written for him, simply because Allāh controls everything, and nothing escapes His Knowledge or Power. However, by turning to Allāh through *du'ā*, it is possible to avert something that might have been decreed. Salmān al-Fārsī narrated that the Prophet (ﷺ) said:

> "Nothing repels Divine Decree except *du'ā*, and nothing increases one's life-span except good deeds".[390]

This ḥadīth informs us in no uncertain terms that the only way that we can repel some Divine Decree is through the means of *du'ā*.

[389] This ḥadīth is weak. It was narrated by Aḥmad, Abū Ya'la, and al-Ṭabarānī in *al-Kabīr,* as has been mentioned in *Ḍa'īf al-Jāmi'* # 4785.

[390] Authentic, reported by al-Tirmidhī and al-Ḥākim from Salmān, and is in *Ṣaḥīḥ al-Jāmi'* # 7687.

So it is possible that some unpleasant matter has been preordained for us, but *only if we do not make duʿā to avert it from us*. So if *duʿā* is made, then this matter will not occur or be fulfilled, whereas if *duʿā* is left, the misfortune will occur.

Another narration in al-Tirmidhī also supports this. The Prophet (ﷺ) said:

> "There is no Muslim on the face of the earth that asks Allāh for anything except that Allāh gives it to him, or averts from him a similar evil, as long as he does not ask for something evil or for breaking the ties of kinship".[391]

From this narration, the benefits of *duʿā* are made clear, and its value is understood. For not only is a person rewarded for making a *duʿā*, but it is also a cause of repelling an evil that was destined for him, and in obtaining the good that he was expecting.

Ibn Ḥajr, commenting on the benefits of *duʿā*, said: "And the benefit of performing *duʿā* is the attainment of reward by obeying the command (of Allāh to make *duʿā*), and also by the attainment of what is asked for, for there is a possibility that the request is dependent on the *duʿā*, since Allāh is the Creator of both the effort and result of the effort!"[392]

Therefore, the proper response to the question posed at the beginning of the chapter is, in the words of Ibn al-Qayyim, as follows:

> "The logical consequences of such a reasoning leads to a rejection of all efforts. It can, therefore, be said to a person who holds this view, 'If the satisfaction of your hunger and thirst has already been destined for you, then it will be fulfilled, whether you eat or not. On the other hand, if it has not been destined for you, it will never occur, whether you eat or not. And, if a son has been destined for you, then you will be granted one, whether you have intercourse with your wife or not. On the other hand, if a son has not been destined for you, then

[391] Authentic, narrated by al-Tirmidhī from ʿUbādah ibn Ṣāmit, as is mentioned in *Ṣaḥīḥ al-Jāmiʿ* # 5637.

[392] *Fatḥ al-Bārī*, 11/95.

> you will never be granted one. In this case, there is no point in you getting married...!'
>
> "Now, will any sane person agree with all of these conclusions?"[393]

To summarise, then, Divine Decree (*qadr*) cannot be used as an excuse not to make *du'ā*. For, just as one strives to ensure that one attains worldly needs, of food, drink and family, so too must one strive in one's religious deeds to attain the desired goal. *Du'ā* is intrinsically related to *qadr*; in fact, it is a *part* of one's *qadr*. Allāh has already decreed that a certain matter will be granted to a servant, or an evil averted from him, *if he makes du'ā*, so if he were to leave *du'ā*, then the desired goal would not be reached.

Hence why it was the Sunnah of the Prophet (ﷺ) to make the following *du'ā* during the *witr* prayer:

> "...Bless me in what You have given me. And avert and turn away from me the evil that has been decreed for me, for verily You Decree (all things), and none can decree against You..."[394]

So the Muslim turns to Allāh and prays to Him so that any and all evil can be averted from him.

Additionally, it should be remembered that the concept of Divine Decree is one that a human can never fully understand, due to his limited intellect and finite capabilities. The true Muslim does not delve too deeply into the philosophical ramifications of Divine Decree. Rather, he accepts all that has occurred to him in the past as having been destined for him, and he strives to obtain what he desires in the future (as long as it is permissible for him). Since he does not know what has been written for him in the future, he expects the best from Allāh, and does everything in his power to ensure that what he wants is granted him. Just like going to work

---

[393] *Al-Jawāb al-Kāfī*, Ibn al-Qayyim, p. 13.

[394] Reported by al-Tirmidhī (# 464), al-Nasā'ī (# 1725) and others, with an authentic chain.

every day will ensure, if Allāh wills, that he gets his pay-cheque at the end of the month, so too does making *duʿā* ensure, if Allāh wills, that he achieves his desired goal.

CHAPTER XV

Miscellaneous Topics

1. *Du'ā* and its Inherent Proof of Allāh's Transcendency

The fact that Allāh is above us is a matter that does not require much proof, for every single creature, whether Muslim or not, already has ingrained in him this simple fact. In addition, the texts of the Qur'ān and Sunnah that explicitly mention this matter are so numerous that they number in their thousands. For example, Allāh states, describing the believers:

يَخَافُونَ رَبَّهُم مِّن فَوْقِهِمْ

They fear their Lord, who is above them.[395]

He also states:

وَهُوَ ٱلْقَاهِرُ فَوْقَ عِبَادِهِۦ

And He is the *Qāhir* (the Irresistible), above His worshippers.[396]

Likewise, this concept is affirmed in many *aḥādīth* of the Prophet (ﷺ). For example, when the Prophet (ﷺ) went on his miraculous journey of *al-Isrā wa l-Mi'rāj*, he *ascended* up from Jerusalem to the seven heavens, and then to the Divine Presence, where Allāh spoke to him directly from behind a veil of light.

On another occasion, the Prophet (ﷺ) once tested a slave-girl to see whether she was a Muslim or not, and asked her:

> "Where is Allāh?"

---

[395] Sūrah *al-Naḥl*, 50.

[396] Sūrah *al-An'ām*, 18.

She responded: "In the skies". In some narrations of this ḥadīth, she pointed upwards with her forefinger.

He then asked her,

> "Who am I?"

She responded: "The prophet of Allāh".

So the Prophet (ﷺ) said:

> "Free her, for verily she is a believer".[397]

The point of this ḥadīth is that the Prophet (ﷺ) bore witness that she was a believer, based on her simple testimony that Allāh was transcendent above creation and that he was Allāh's Messenger.[398]

Although the proofs for the transcendency of Allāh over His creation are so clear, various groups that ascribed themselves to Islām deviated in this understanding, and, based on Greek logic and Aristotelian principles, declared that Allāh cannot be described by any means or direction. They stated that Allāh, '...is neither above the world, nor below it, nor to the left of it, nor to the right of it, nor in front of it, nor behind it...' believing that, by doing so, they were affirming Allāh's perfect Uniqueness from creation. In reality, such a line of thinking actually negates the very existence of Allāh, as it alludes to the belief that Allāh is *nowhere*! Groups such as the *Muʿtazilah*[399] and the *Ashʿarīyah*[400] made this claim.

---

[397] This ḥadīth is reported, with various chains and various wordings, in almost all of the major works of Ḥadīth, thus the attempt by certain sects to try to cast doubt on its authenticity are ludicrous. This particular wording is reported in Muslim (1/1094).

[398] For further proofs of this matter, and the danger of believing that Allāh is everywhere, refer to Bilāl Philips' *Fundamentals of Tawḥīd*, pp. 107-125.

[399] A philosophical group that tried to rationalise Islām with Greek philosophy, in particular the views of Aristotle and Socrates. This group, as a whole, does not exist in our times, although many incorrect views that exist in other groups can be traced back to the *Muʿtazilah*.

[400] A group that formed as a counter-response to the *Muʿtazilah*, and tried to refute the *Muʿtazilah* based on the principles of Greek philosophy. Al- =

In contrast to this extreme position, certain groups went in the exact opposite direction, and claimed that Allāh is *everywhere*. The most striking example of this are the extreme *Sūfīs*, such as Ibn ʿArabī and al-Ḥallāj, who both claimed that Allāh in-dwells in creation, such that creation as a whole is the *essence* of Allāh, and Allāh is the essence of creation.

Although a detailed discussion of this concept and its historical development, and the implications of these deviations, is beyond the scope of this work, the point that is relevant is that *duʿā* is one of the simplest and most powerful proofs that Allāh is, in fact, *above* creation.

This because a person raises his hands *up* to Allāh, and his heart automatically and subconsciously 'reaches up' to Allāh, expecting a response. This natural and innate feeling is a part of a person's *fiṭrah*, or the natural disposition that Allāh puts in every man. Therefore we find that even the non-Muslim, when he prays, finds his heart directed upwards, and his hands reaching out for the skies, beseeching Allāh.

The proof of Allāh's transcendency in *duʿā* has been narrated by numerous authorities of the early generations.

The great Imām Abū Ḥanīfah (d. 150 A.H.) was asked about a person who claims that he does not know whether the Throne that Allāh has risen over is in the skies, or on earth. Abū Ḥanīfah replied: "He is a disbeliever, for he has denied that Allāh is above the skies... and because *duʿā* is said to Him directed *upwards*, not downwards".[401]

Imām Abū Muḥammad ʿAbdullāh ibn Kullāb (d. 241 A.H.) wrote, while refuting those who claim that Allāh is everywhere, "So we have not seen anyone, whether Arab or non-Arab, or Muslim or

= though the early *Ashʿarīs* were very close to the Sunnah, over time, it too evolved into a pure philosophical School of Thought, especially as regards the areas of the Names and Attributes of Allāh. This School of Thought is very widespread to this day.

[401] Reported by Imām al-Dhahabī in his *al-ʿUluww*, p. 136.

non-Muslim, when he is asked, 'Where is your Lord?' except that he will say, 'Above the skies,' or he will point upwards with his finger... and we have not seen any person, when he makes a *duʿā*, except that he raises his hands up to the skies".[402]

ʿUthmān ibn Saʿid al-Dārimi (d. 282 A.H.) wrote: "And so there is unanimous consensus amongst the Muslims and non-Muslims that Allāh is above the heavens... even the little children that have not yet come of age know this! For you find, if one of them is distressed with a matter, that he raises his hands upwards, to the skies, making a *duʿā* to Allāh, and he does not point in any other direction".[403]

Imām Abū Bakr ibn Khuzaymah (d. 311 A.H.), the famous scholar of ḥadīth and compiler of *Ṣaḥīḥ Ibn Khuzaymah*, entitled one of the chapters in his work *Kitāb al-Tawḥīd* as follows: "The Chapter concerning the evidences that Allāh is above the skies, as He has informed us in His Clear Revelation, and upon the tongue of the Prophet (ﷺ), and as is understood by the innate nature of all Muslims, whether they be scholars or laymen, free men or slaves, male or female, old or young, for everyone who makes a *duʿā* to Allāh raises his face towards the skies, and stretches his hands up to Allāh, pointing upwards, not downwards".[404]

Even Abū al-Ḥasan al-Ashʿari (d. 324 A.H.) himself, whom the *Ashʿarīs* claim that they follow, wrote: "And we have seen all of the Muslims raising their hands up to Allāh, towards the skies, because Allāh is above His Throne, which is above the seven heavens. So if Allāh were not above the Throne, they would not have raised their hands up to Him."[405]

---

[402] Reported in *Siyar Aʿlām al-Nubalā*, 11/175.

[403] Reported in his *al-Radd ʿalā al-Marrīsī*, p. 25.

[404] *Kitāb al-Tawḥīd*, p. 110.

[405] In Abū al-Ḥasan's book *al-Ibānah*, p. 107. Although Abū al-Ḥasan al-Ashʿari is the founder of the *Ashʿarī* School of Thought, in reality the modern-day *Ashʿarīs* have deviated greatly from his original philosophies, most of which he himself rejected before he died.

Other scholars who explicitly mentioned the *du'ā* as evidence of the transcendency of Allāh are: Ibn Qutaybah (d. 276 A.H.), Ibn Abī Shaybah (d. 297 A.H.), al-Khaṭṭābī (d. 388 A.H.), al-Bāqillānī (d. 403 A.H.), Abū Ya'la (d. 458 A.H.), Ibn 'Abd al-Barr (d. 463 A.H.), and many others.[406]

Perhaps one of the most famous of these references is the incident that occurred with Muḥammad al-Hamadhānī (d. 531 A.H.), one of the famous scholars of *Ahl al-Sunnah*. While he was attending a lesson by Imām al-Ḥaramayn Abū al-Ma'alī al-Juwaynī (d. 478 A.H.), one of the scholars who re-defined the *Ash'arī* creed and evolved it into what it is today, al-Juwaynī started to explain his ideology that Allāh cannot be described by any direction, and even interpreted away the explicit verses to the effect that Allāh is above us. Hearing this, al-Hamadhānī responded: "Relieve us of all of these advanced refutations! Just explain to me how we should rid ourselves of this innate feeling that all of us have. For never does a person make a *du'ā* and cry out , 'O my Lord!' except that he finds his heart and soul, even before his tongue utters the cry, direct straight up; neither does it go left nor right, but rather it goes upwards. So tell me, what should we do about this feeling, so that we can rid ourselves of the 'up' and 'down'.[407]" Hearing this, al-Juwanyī was dumbstruck, and was unable to respond, and uproar broke out in the entire gathering, and the lecture was stopped. Al-Juwaynī started hitting himself on the forehead, a sign of confusion and helplessness, and cried out, '*Ḥayyarani al-Hamadhānī*,' or, 'Al-Hamadhānī has indeed confused me'.[408]

---

[406] For a more detailed discussion of this concept, the reader is referred to al-Arūsī, pp. 280-291.

[407] The 'up' and 'down' refers to the *Ash'arī* phrase, '...and He is neither above us nor below us'.

[408] Reported in many famous works, including *al-Siyar* of al-Dhahabī, 18/477, with a chain that is continuous with *ḥuffāẓ*, or Hadīth masters, so there is absolutely no doubt with regards to its authenticity.

So the point is that no matter what advanced logic or complicated philosophy that these groups try to use in order to prove that Allāh is nowhere, mankind simply cannot rid himself of the *fiṭrah,* the innate nature, that Allāh has endowed him with, and part of this *fiṭrah* is that Allāh is above us; He is not everywhere, nor is He nowhere.[409]

---

[409] Here it is necessary to comment on two 'evidences' that are used by those who claim that Allāh cannot be described with a direction in order to justify their position. The first 'evidence' is their saying: "The sky is the qiblah for *duʿā*, just like Makkah is the qiblah for *ṣalāt*." The second 'evidence' is their saying, "Just like the prostration of a person to the ground does not mean that Allāh is under the ground, likewise raising the hands up does not mean that Allāh is transcendent above us".

So as for the first 'evidence' that is raised, the following points can be used to show the futilty of it:

i- The statement that the sky is the qiblah for *duʿā* is not found in the Qur'ān, Sunnah or from any of the major scholars of the pious predecessors, so how can such a statement be made without any real evidence?

ii- The actual qiblah of *duʿā* is Makkah, as has been stated in the etiquette of *duʿā*. So the one who makes a *duʿā* turns his body towards the Kaʿbah, just like the one in ṣalāt does. Therefore, there are not two qiblahs while making *duʿā* – one towards Makkah and the other towards the sky – there is only one proper qiblah.

iii-The qiblah is a matter that is related to the legal law of the Sharīʿah, and changes from one religion to another. This is why the Jews during the time of Mūsa had a certain qiblah that Allāh legislated for them, and the Muslims have another qiblah. Likewise, most religions have various 'holy' directions that they face during their acts of worship. The transcendency of Allāh, however, is a universally agreed upon fact, and members of all religions, while making a *duʿā* to the Supreme Creator, raise their hands towards the sky, and their hearts 'reach out' above them to call their Creator. This matter proves that the transcendency of Allāh is a matter that is ingrained in every created being, unlike the qiblah.

As for the second 'evidence', then it can be refuted by the following:

i- It is agreed upon by all of mankind that prostrating on the ground does not imply that the object or deity that is being worshipped is *underneath* the person, but rather that it is in front of him and above him. Does the =

2. Wiping One's Face After Finishing the *Duʿā*.

There are a number of narrations in which it is stated that the Prophet (ﷺ) would wipe his face with his hands after finishing a *duʿā*. However, scholars of Ḥadīth have differed about the authenticity of these narrations, some of which are as follows:

ʿUmar ibn al-Khaṭṭāb reported that whenever the Prophet (ﷺ) raised his hands in *duʿā*, he would not lower them until he had wiped his face.[410] Al-Tirmidhī, when he reported this ḥadīth, said, "This ḥadīth is *ṣaḥīḥ gharīb*."[411]

Ibn ʿAbbās reported that the Prophet (ﷺ) said:

> Ask Allāh from the palms of your hands, and do not ask Him from the back of your hands, and when you finish, then wipe your hands over your faces.[412]

Abū Dāwūd said: "This ḥadīth has been reported from other than this chain, on the authority of Muḥammad ibn Kaʿb, and all of them are very weak. This particular chain is the best, and it too is weak".

= Hindu, when he prostrates in front of a statue, claim that the statue is *below* him? Or does the worshipper of the Sun, when he prostrates and the sun is at its zenith, believe that the sun is *below* him? Rather, prostration is an act of worship that is done to show humilty to a deity that is *above* and *in front of* the one prostrating.

ii- Even if it is said, for argument's sake, that the face of the person is facing the ground while he is prostrating, the fact of the matter is that a person's *heart*, while he is making *duʿā* in that situation, reaches *up* and directs itself to the transcendency of Allāh above him.

[410] Reported by al-Tirmidhī (# 3386).

[411] Ibid. In some manuscripts of al-Tirmidhī, only the phrase, '*gharīb*' occurs, and this seems more correct.

[412] Reported by Abū Dāwūd (# 1485) and Ibn Mājah (# 3866).

There are also a number of other *aḥādīth* and statements of the *salaf* with regards to wiping one's hands over the face after *du'ā*.[413] However, all of the *aḥādīth* are without a doubt weak. The difference of opinion occurs in whether these *aḥādīth*, put together, raise them to the status of *ḥasan* (acceptable) or not.

Therefore, based on their opinion about the status of these *aḥādīth*, various scholars have held different opinions about the permissibility of wiping one's face.

Some scholars stated that it is recommended to wipe one's face after one makes *du'ā*. These include al-Ghazālī, al-Ḥalīymī, al-Nawawī (in one of his opinions) al-Ḥāfiẓ Ibn Ḥajr, al-Ṣan'ānī and others. Ibn Ḥajr writes in his *Bulūgh al-Marām*, after mentioning some of these *aḥādīth*, "All of these *aḥādīth* taken together demonstrate that this ḥadīth is *ḥasan* (acceptable)."[414] Al-Ṣan'anī commented, "In this ḥadīth, there is evidence that it is allowed to wipe one's hands after finishing one's *du'ā*. And it is said that the reason for this is that, since Allāh will not allow the hands to return empty, then it is as if His Mercy has reached them. So it is appropriate to let these blessings be transmitted, as it were, to the face, which is the most noble of all organs, and the most deserving of respect."[415] Al-Bayhaqī states in his *Sunan* that this act has been narrated from a number of *salaf*, but only outside of the ṣalāt (i.e. there is no narration that they would wipe their hands over their face while they were praying).[416] Some scholars have found narrations from the following scholars of the *salaf* who allowed or practised wiping of the face: al-Ḥasan al-Baṣrī, Abū Ka'b al-Baṣrī, Ma'mar ibn Rāshid,

---

[413] In fact, Shaykh Bakr Abū Zayd has written a booklet in which he compiled all of the *aḥādīth* and narrations pertaining to this topic, called *Juz fī Maṣ-ḥ al-Wajh bi al-yadayn ba'da al-Du'ā*. He found seven *aḥādīth* of the Prophet, and over a dozen narrations from the *salaf*, some of whom approved, and others who disapproved. In addition, he discussed the position of the four *madh-habs* concerning this act.

[414] *Subul al-Salām*, 4/427.

[415] *Subul al-Salām*, 4/428.

[416] *Al-Sunan*, 2/212.

ʿAbd al-Razzāq al-Ṣanʿānī (the author of the *Muṣannaf*), Isḥāq ibn Rahūyah, and Imām Aḥmad (in one opinion from him).[417]

Other scholars held the opinion that it is permissible to wipe one's hands over one's face, but only while one is not in prayer. As for a person making a *duʿā* during *ṣalāt* (for example, the *qunūt duʿā*), then he should not wipe it over his face. Shaykh Bakr Abū Zayd writes: "And if he wishes, he can wipe his face with his hands after finishing his *duʿā*, as long as he is *outside* of his ṣalāt, and not *while* he is praying".[418]

Yet others held the opinion that it is not recommended to wipe one's hand over one's face at all. These scholars considered the *aḥādīth* pertaining to the topic to be weak, or even very weak. Some of them even considered this act to be an innovation.

Some scholars who explicitly disliked any wiping are: Imām Mālik, ʿAbdullāh ibn al-Mubārak, Aḥmad ibn Ḥanbal (in one narration from him), and others. In fact, one later scholar even went so far as to say: "No one does this act except an ignorant person".[419]

---

[417] See Bakr Abū Zayd's *Juz fī Mas-ḥ al-wajh*, pp. 47-52.

[418] Abū Zayd, p. 27. Note: Although this quote is explicit in his book *Taṣḥīḥ al-Duʿā*, he says in his book, *Juz fī Mas-ḥ al-Wajh bi al-yadayn*, (p. 75), '...so based on all that has preceded, if a person does it occasionally while he is not praying, and does not make it a habitual practice, then there is some basis for it". So in this book he states that if a person does it, it should not be done habitually, and Allāh knows best. Also, Shaykh Bakr Abū Zayd himself holds the opinion that all of the ḥadīth narrated concerning this matter are weak, and, thus, there is no evidence for it from the texts.

[419] This is narrated from the al-ʿIzz ibn ʿAbd al-Salām. However, Imām al-Zarkashī stated, after quoting him: "This statement is held upon the fact that he (meaning al-ʿIzz) did not come across the *aḥādīth* narrated to this effect. And these *aḥādīth*, even though their *isnāds* are slightly weak, strengthen each other". See Abū Zayd, p. 55. Also, this act has been authentically narrated from a number of the scholars of the *salaf*, and great scholars, such as al-Ḥāfiẓ Ibn Ḥajr, have declared these *aḥādīth* to be authentic. Therefore, it is not proper to unconditionally label all those that wipe their hands over the face as ignorant, for this is a matter in which there is a legitimate difference of opinion.

Shaykh al-Islām Ibn Taymiyyah wrote: "As for wiping the face after finishing a *du'ā*, then there is no ḥadīth (narrated from the Prophet,(ﷺ) except for one, or two, and they do not qualify as proof (i.e. they are all weak)".[420]

Shaykh al-Albānī stated: "In this narration (of wiping over the face), the defect is in the name who is not mentioned. However, his name is mentioned in another narration in Ibn Mājah as Ṣalāḥ ibn Ḥasan and he is a very weak narrator, so this narration must be rejected. I have yet to find any supporting evidence (for this act). It seems that (this weakness) is the reason why al-'Izz ibn 'Abd al-Salām said: 'No one wipes his face (after a *du'ā*) except an ignorant person'. Even if this narration were only slightly weak, it would still not be permissible to act upon it, since it ordains an Islamic ruling, and that is the desirability of wiping one's face, so how can it be acted upon when it is extremely weak?"[421]

In conclusion, there is a legitimate difference of opinion over the permissibility of wiping one's hands over one's face after making *du'ā*. There are a number of *aḥādīth* narrated from the Prophet (ﷺ) concerning this matter (to be precise, seven); however, all of them are weak. So whoever believes that these *aḥādīth*, when taken together, strengthen one another and make the ḥadīth *ḥasan* – as is the opinion al-Ḥāfiẓ Ibn Ḥajr - has some basis for this act. However, it does appear that the weaknesses of these *aḥādīth* are quite severe, and that they do not support one another; therefore, it does not reach the level of *ḥasan*.

In any case, both the wiping of one's face, and the disapproval of this act, has been narrated from the scholars and Imāms of the *salaf*, so it is not appropriate to ignore this fact. So whatever opinion one takes, one has a basis for it, even though it appears that the stronger opinion is that one should *not* wipe one's hands over one's face after *du'ā*, and Allāh knows best.

---

[420] *Majmū' al-Fatāwa*, 22/519.

[421] *Silsilah al-Ṣaḥīḥah* (2/146).

3. For Every Prophet there is a Special *Du'ā*

One of the favours that Allāh has bestowed upon His prophets is that He has given each one of them one *du'ā* that will be answered.

Abū Hurayrah reported that the Prophet (ﷺ) said:

> "For every prophet, there is a *du'ā* which he makes that is answered. However, I wish to postpone my *du'ā* (to the Day of Judgement) as an intercession for my *ummah*."[422]

In another ḥadīth he (ﷺ) said:

> "For every prophet there is a *du'ā* that is responded to, and I have kept my *du'ā* as an intercession for my *ummah* on the Day of Judgement. And it will be for those, Allāh willing, who died without having associated partners with Allāh".[423]

This is an indication of the Prophet's (ﷺ) mercy and kindness to his *ummah*, since he will use his *du'ā* for his *ummah*, when they need it the most.

It should also be remembered that the *du'ā* referred to in the above ḥadīth are special *du'ās* of the prophets, and not every *du'ā* that they make is answered by Allāh. The proof for this is found in the ḥadīth in which the Prophet (ﷺ) said:

> "I asked my Lord three things. He gave me two of them, and refused one..."[424]

In this ḥadīth, it is shown that not every *du'ā* of a prophet is answered.

---

[422] Narrated by Aḥmad and al-Bukhārī, as mentioned in *Ṣaḥīḥ al-Jāmi'* # 5178.

[423] Narrated by Aḥmad, Muslim and al-Tirmidhī from Abū Hurayrah, as mentoned in *Ṣaḥīḥ al-Jāmi'* # 5176.

[4124] Narrated by Aḥmad, Muslim and others, from Sa'd, as mentioned in *Ṣaḥīḥ al-Jāmi'* # 3593.

4. The Most Important Matters to Ask For

The servant asks Allāh for his each and every matter, for the treasures of all matters belong to Allāh:

وَإِن مِّن شَيْءٍ إِلَّا عِندَنَا خَزَآئِنُهُۥ

And there is nothing except that We possess its treasures (or stores).[425]

However, without a doubt, certain matters have more right to be asked than others, for not all affairs are equivalent in importance. Of the matters that one should ask continuously and without fail are the following:[426]

i. Guidance

Every day, over twenty times a Muslim cries out to Allāh:

إِيَّاكَ نَعْبُدُ وَإِيَّاكَ نَسْتَعِينُ ﴿٥﴾

You Alone do we worship, and You alone do we ask for Help[427]

So it is of primary importance that we ask Allāh for help in worshipping Him, and that we be guided to the Straight Path, the Path of those whom He is pleased with, and not the Path of those who have gone astray. For Allāh alone is the only one that can guide:

مَن يَهْدِ ٱللَّهُ فَهُوَ ٱلْمُهْتَدِ ۖ وَمَن يُضْلِلْ فَلَن
تَجِدَ لَهُۥ وَلِيًّا مُّرْشِدًا ﴿١٧﴾

So whoever Allāh guides is the (only) one that is truly guided, and whoever He leads astray will never find a protector, or a guide.[428]

---

[425] Sūrah *al-Ḥijr*, 21.

[426] See al-Qaḥṭānī, pp. 137-145.

[427] Sūrah *al-Fātiḥah*, 5.

[428] Sūrah *al-Kahf*, 17.

Hence why the Prophet (ﷺ) would regularly pray in his *Witr* prayer:

> O Allāh! Guide me along with those whom You have guided.[429]

He (ﷺ) would also pray:

> O Allāh! I ask you for guidance, and that you cover up (my shortcomings and mistakes).[430]

ii. Forgiveness

No matter how pious a person becomes, or how rightly guided he is, he is bound to fall into error occasionally, for he is only human. The righteous person realises this, and is ever-quick to turn to Allāh in repentance, doing so frequently and sincerely. And in doing so, he keeps in front of him Allāh's statement as follows:

وَإِنِّي لَغَفَّارٌ لِّمَن تَابَ وَءَامَنَ وَعَمِلَ صَٰلِحًا ثُمَّ ٱهْتَدَىٰ ﴿٨٢﴾

> And I am indeed Ever-Forgiving to the one that repents, and believes, and does good deeds, and then is rightly guided.[431]

And the Prophet (ﷺ), the most perfect of the Children of Adam, informed us of his own situation, and commanded us to follow it, when he said:

> O Mankind! Repent to Allāh and seek forgiveness, for verily I ask for Allāh's forgiveness a hundred times a day![432]

iii. Paradise

The ultimate goal of every believer should be to earn the pleasure of Allāh, and, through it, Paradise. So if this really is the goal of the believer, he should ask for it in every single *duʿā* that he makes,

---

[429] Reported by al-Tirmidhī; see *Ṣaḥīḥ al-Tirmidhī*, 1/144.

[430] Reported by Muslim, 4/209.

[431] Sūrah *Ṭā Hā*, 82.

[432] Reported by Muslim, 4/2076.

day and night, morning and evening. And if a person finds that he does not ask frequently for Paradise, then he must ask himself how important it is to him, and re-evaluate the priorities that he has made for himself.

Ponder over the wisdom of the Companion of the Prophet (ﷺ), Rabīʿah ibn Kaʿb al-Aslamī, who served the Prophet (ﷺ), and attended to his needs. Once, the Prophet (ﷺ), impressed with his dedication, said:

> "Ask (whatever you want)".

So see what his response was, and his great maturity and wisdom, when, without a second's hesitation or doubt, he responded, "I wish that I be with you in Paradise". The Prophet (ﷺ) said:

> "Anything else besides this?"

So he said, "No, that is what I want". Then the Prophet (ﷺ) responded:

> "Then help me with your (request) by numerous prostrations".[433]

So he did not even ask for anything else, since to him this was his ultimate goal and desire, thus he had no need of anything else.

Asking Allāh for Paradise necessitates seeking His protection from the Fire of Hell. Therefore the Prophet (ﷺ) would often combine these two requests.

---

[433] Reported by Muslim, 1/353. This ḥadīth should not be interpreted to mean that the Prophet (ﷺ) had complete control over everything, and thus the decision of who will enter Paradise will be his. It was merely a request from the Prophet (ﷺ) to Rabīʿah to inform him of what he wanted, and, once Rabīʿah did so, that the Prophet (ﷺ) would try his best to give it to him. In this case, this would have been accomplished by *duʿā* to Allāh – and whose *duʿā* has a greater chance of being accepted than the Prophet's (ﷺ)? Hence why the Prophet (ﷺ) asked him to *help* him in getting this *duʿā* accepted, by increasing the number of voluntary prayers he performed, thus making himself more worthy of accompanying the Prophet (ﷺ) in Paradise.

Once he (ﷺ) asked a Bedouin which *du'ās* he recited in his prayer? The Bedouin responded: "I say my *tashahhud*, and then I ask Allāh for Paradise, and seek His refuge from the Fire of Hell. For verily, by Allāh, I am not able to comprehend (and memorise) your humming or the humming of Mu'ādh!" So the Prophet (ﷺ) responded, bemusedly:

> And around these two requests we hum![434]

So this poor Bedouin, who used to pray behind the Prophet (ﷺ) and Mu'ādh ibn Jabal, admitted that he did not know the 'complicated' *du'ās* that the Prophet (ﷺ) used to recite, and, therefore, was forced to ask something very simple. The Prophet (ﷺ) responded that all of these 'complicated' *du'ās* that he (ﷺ) used to make were, in reality, summarised in his simple request for Paradise, and seeking refuge from the Fire of Hell.

iv. Protection from Afflictions

One of the comprehensive matters that the Prophet (ﷺ) exhorted us to ask for is protection from afflictions, or *'āfiyah*. This is a comprehensive word that denotes good health and protection from major affliction and tribulation in this world and the Hereafter.

Once, the Prophet's (ﷺ) uncle, 'Abbās, asked him to teach him a comprehensive *du'ā* that he should ask of Allāh. So the Prophet (ﷺ) responded:

> Ask Allāh for *'āfiyah*.

He pondered over this for a few days, but felt that there was something more that he should ask as well. So he returned to the Prophet (ﷺ) with the same request, after which the Prophet (ﷺ) said:

> O 'Abbās! O Uncle of the Prophet of Allāh! Ask Allāh for *'āfiyah* in this life and the Next.[435]

---

[434] Reported by Abū Dāwūd, # 792, and authenticated in *Ṣaḥīḥ Abī Dāwūd*, 1/150.

[435] Reported by al-Tirmidhi; see *Ṣaḥīḥ al-Tirmidhī* 3/170.

And Abū Bakr narrated that he heard the Prophet (ﷺ) saying while he was on the pulpit giving the Friday *khuṭbah*:

> Ask Allāh for forgiveness and *ʿāfiyah*, for no one has been given, after certainty (i.e. *īmān*), anything better than *ʿāfiyah*.[436]

v. Perseverence in One's Faith

A person always strives to protect the valuables that he has, and takes every precaution that they are not taken away from him. And without a doubt, the greatest blessing that a Muslim has been given is the blessing of *īmān*, and hence why he continually asks Allāh to protect his *īmān*.

Umm Salamah once asked the Prophet (ﷺ): "O Messenger of Allāh! Why is it that most of your *duʿā* is (the phrase), 'O He who turns the hearts! Make my heart firm upon your religion'?" So the Prophet (ﷺ) responded:

> O Umm Salmah! There is not a single person of the Children of Adam except that his heart is between two of the Fingers from the Fingers of Allāh. So whoever Allāh wishes, He establishes and makes firm (the heart on His obedience), and whoever He wishes, He leads astray.[437]

There are many other important matters that one must always ask Allāh of, such as the continual attainment of Allāh's Mercy and Blessings, and patience at His Decree and contentment with whatever one has been blessed with, and other matters. The main point to realise is that a believer must prioritise his goals, and place the needs and requirements of his religion over those of this world. Although both worlds are sought from Allāh, one of them is temporary, and is a means and test to achieve happiness in the other one, so the wise person realises this, and asks Allāh accordingly.

---

[436] Reported by al-Tirmidhī; see *Ṣaḥīḥ al-Tirmidhī* 3/180.

[437] Reported by al-Tirmidhī; see *Ṣaḥīḥ al-Tirmidhī* 3/171.

5. The Disbeliever does not Remember Allāh Except in a State of Need

One of the signs of a person who does not truly love Allāh, or rejects the truth, is that he only calls upon Allāh when he is in a state of extreme desperation. This because he feels that when he is in a state of richness and contentment he has no need of his Creator, yet he does not realise that if Allāh willed, all of his richness and contentment could leave him immediately. Only a true believer realises that he is always in need of Allāh's blessings.

Allāh says describing the disbelievers:

وَإِذَا مَسَّ ٱلْإِنسَٰنَ ٱلضُّرُّ دَعَانَا لِجَنۢبِهِۦٓ أَوْ قَاعِدًا أَوْ قَآئِمًا
فَلَمَّا كَشَفْنَا عَنْهُ ضُرَّهُۥ مَرَّ كَأَن لَّمْ يَدْعُنَآ إِلَىٰ ضُرٍّ مَّسَّهُۥ ۚ
كَذَٰلِكَ زُيِّنَ لِلْمُسْرِفِينَ مَا كَانُوا۟ يَعْمَلُونَ ﴿١٢﴾

And when some harm befalls man, he calls upon Us, lying down, sitting and standing! Yet, when We remove his harm from him, he passes on his way as if he had never invoked Us for any harm! Thus it is made alluring to the transgressors that which they do.[438]

قُلْ مَن يُنَجِّيكُم مِّن ظُلُمَٰتِ ٱلْبَرِّ وَٱلْبَحْرِ تَدْعُونَهُۥ تَضَرُّعًا وَخُفْيَةً
لَّئِنْ أَنجَىٰنَا مِنْ هَٰذِهِۦ لَنَكُونَنَّ مِنَ ٱلشَّٰكِرِينَ ﴿٦٣﴾

Say: Who rescues you from the darkness of the land and the sea, when you call upon Him in humility and secret, 'If He (Allāh) only saves us from this (danger) we will truly be grateful'.[439]

[438] Sūrah *Yūnus*, 12.

[439] Sūrah *al-An'ām,* 63.

> وَإِذَا مَسَّ ٱلْإِنسَٰنَ ضُرٌّ دَعَا رَبَّهُۥ مُنِيبًا إِلَيْهِ ثُمَّ إِذَا خَوَّلَهُۥ
> نِعْمَةً مِّنْهُ نَسِىَ مَا كَانَ يَدْعُوٓا۟ إِلَيْهِ مِن قَبْلُ وَجَعَلَ لِلَّهِ أَندَادًا
> لِّيُضِلَّ عَن سَبِيلِهِۦ ۚ
>
> And when some evil touches man, he cries to his Lord, turning to Him in repentence, but when He bestows a favour from Himself upon him, he forgets what he was asking for before, and (instead) he sets up partners with Allāh, in order to mislead others from His path.[440]
>
> وَإِذَا مَسَّكُمُ ٱلضُّرُّ فِى ٱلْبَحْرِ ضَلَّ مَن تَدْعُونَ إِلَّآ إِيَّاهُ ۖ فَلَمَّا نَجَّىٰكُمْ
> إِلَى ٱلْبَرِّ أَعْرَضْتُمْ ۚ وَكَانَ ٱلْإِنسَٰنُ كَفُورًا ﴿٦٧﴾
>
> And when harm touches you upon the sea, those that you call upon besides Him vanish except Him (Allāh Alone). But when He brings you safely to the land, you turn away from Him, and man is ever-ungrateful.[441]
>
> وَإِذَا مَسَّهُ ٱلشَّرُّ فَذُو دُعَآءٍ عَرِيضٍ ﴿٥١﴾
>
> And when some evil afflicts him, then he (starts a) lengthy supplication![442]

These verses indicate the importance of sincerity, and that Allāh responds to the *duʿā* of disbelievers at these times, either because they are truly sincere or as a test and trial for them. They also indicate the danger of calling out to Allāh only at a time of need, as is the unfortunate case with many of today's Muslims.

Allāh says:

---

[440] Sūrah *al-Zumar*, 8.

[441] Sūrah *al-Isrā'*, 67.

[442] Sūrah *Fuṣṣilat*, 51.

وَإِذَا غَشِيَهُم مَّوْجٌ كَالظُّلَلِ دَعَوُا اللَّهَ مُخْلِصِينَ لَهُ الدِّينَ
فَلَمَّا نَجَّاهُمْ إِلَى الْبَرِّ فَمِنْهُم مُّقْتَصِدٌ

> And when a wave covers them like darkness, they (the disbelievers) invoke Allāh, making their invocations sincere towards Him. But when He brings them safe to land, they are among those who stop in the middle (between disbelief and belief).[443]

However, if a disbeliever makes a *duʿā* to Allāh without sincerity, or makes a *duʿā* to other than Allāh, then concerning such *duʿās* it is said:

وَمَا دُعَاءُ الْكَافِرِينَ إِلَّا فِي ضَلَالٍ ﴿٥٠﴾

> And the *duʿās* of the disbelievers is nothing but in error.[444]

All of these verses show that only a disbeliever calls Allāh when he feels in need of him; a true believer remembers and calls upon Allāh at all times.

Shaykh al-Islām Ibn Taymiyyah said,

> As for the believer, it is essential after his prayer is answered that he worships Allāh, and is sincere to Him, and turns to Him as he has been commanded. This can be achieved either by doing only the obligatory acts – and in this case he is among the pious – or by doing the obligatory and encouraged acts – and in this case he will be among those who are close to Allāh. And whoever leaves part of what he has been commanded with after his prayer has been answered, then he is among the sinners. And this in fact might enter into minor *shirk*, which most of the creation is tested with. Or, it might enter into *shirk* in Allāh's Oneness (*Rubūbiyyah*), or *shirk* in Allāh's right to be worshipped alone (*Ulūhiyyah*).[445]

---

[443] Sūrah *Luqmān*, 32.

[444] Sūrah *Ghāfir*, 50.

[445] *Qāʿidah fi Anwāʿ al-Istiftāḥ,* p. 17.

6. Sincere *Du'ā* for the Dead

Abū Hurayrah narrates that he heard the Prophet (ﷺ) say:

> "When you pray over the dead, then be sincere in your *du'ā*".[446]

Imām al-Shawkānī, commenting on this ḥadīth, said: "The phrase 'be sincere in your *du'ā*' shows that it is not necessary to limit the *du'ā* to the specific *du'ās* mentioned, and it is essential for the person praying for the dead person to ask sincerely for him, whether the dead person was known to be a pious person or an evil person. In fact, the person who was a sinner is in even more need of the prayer of his Muslim brothers, and is in dire need of their intercession. And due to this, he has now been brought forth in front of them, and has come to them..."[447]

7. The *Du'ā* of Yūnus

The *du'ā* that Yūnus (Jonah) made while he was in the whale's stomach is a special, blessed *du'ā*, and Allāh accepts the *du'ā* of any person if he makes the *du'ā* of Yūnus.

The Prophet (ﷺ) said:

> The *du'ā* of Dhū Nūn (i.e. the 'One of the Fish,' meaning Yūnus) while he was in the whale's stomach,
>
> 'There is no deity or object worthy of worship save you, You are glorified above all deficiencies! Verily, I was among the wrongdoers!'[448]
>
> – no Muslim can ever make this *du'ā* except that Allāh will answer him![449]

---

[446] Authentic, narrated by Abū Dāwūd, Ibn Mājah, Ibn Ḥibbān and others, from Abū Hurayrah, and authenticated by al-Albānī in *Ṣaḥīḥ al-Jāmi'* # 669.

[447] *Nayl al-Awṭār*, 4/78.

[448] *Lā ilāhā illā anta subḥānaka innī kuntu min al-ẓālimīn.*

[449] Narrated by Aḥmad, al-Tirmidhī and al-Nasā'ī, from Sa'd, and authenticated in *Ṣaḥīḥ al-Jāmi'* # 3383.

Therefore, this *du'ā* was not only a blessing for Yūnus, peace be upon him, but also for every single Muslim.

8. The *Du'ā* of Animals

Even animals make *du'ā* to Allāh for their needs and wants.

Mu'āwiyah ibn Khadīj said that he once passed by Abū Dharr al-Ghifārī while he was standing close to one of his horses, so he asked him why he was so worried about this horse. Abū Dharr responded, "I think that the *du'ā* of this horse has been responded to". So he asked, "And what is the *du'ā* of an animal amongst animals?" Abū Dharr said, "I swear by Him in Whose Hands is my life! There is not a single horse except that it makes a *du'ā* every morning: 'O Allāh! You have put me under the care of a servant amongst Your servants, and you have put my sustenance in his hands, therefore make me more beloved to him than his family, wealth and children".[450]

Abū Dharr based this statement on a ḥadīth of the Prophet (ﷺ) in which he said:

> "There is no Arabian horse except that it is allowed every dawn to make two *du'ās*. It says, 'O Allāh! You have put me under the care of the one whom you have put me under from amongst the Children of Adam, therefore make me amongst the most beloved of his family and money to him (or, the most beloved of his family and money to him)'".[451]

This ḥadīth also explains the phenomenon of why Arabian horses are the most prized horses in the world.

---

[450] An authentic narration by Aḥmad (5/162). Even though this is a Companion's statement, it takes on the status of a ḥadīth of the Prophet (ﷺ) since this type of knowledge cannot be obtained through personal reasoning. In addition, the following ḥadīth is additional evidence for it.

[451] Reported by Aḥmad, al-Nasā'ī and al-Ḥākim, and authenticated in *Ṣaḥīḥ al-Jāmi'* # 2414.

9. The *Duʿā* of the Prophet (ﷺ) Against a Person

The Qur'ān says:

وَمَآ أَرْسَلْنَٰكَ إِلَّا رَحْمَةً لِّلْعَٰلَمِينَ ﴿١٠٧﴾

> And We have only sent you O Muḥammad (ﷺ) as a mercy for all of the world.[452]

As part of this general mercy, the Prophet (ﷺ) did not curse or abuse any Muslim, and even on such rare occasions where such abuse occurred, the Prophet (ﷺ) prayed to Allāh to exchange these condemnations into blessings.

ʿĀ'ishah narrates: "Once, there entered upon the Prophet (ﷺ) two people, and they talked with him words which I could not hear, but they made the Prophet (ﷺ) very angry, and he cursed them. After they left, I said: "O Messenger of Allāh (ﷺ)! These two people will never be able to obtain any good." He (ﷺ) asked,

> "And how so?"

I said, "Since you cursed them". He (ﷺ) responded:

> "And do you not know the agreement that I have made with my Lord? I said, 'O Allāh! I am only a mortal, so any Muslim whom I curse or abuse, let it be a means of purification and a blessing for him!'"[453]

---

[452] Sūrah *al-Anbiyā'*, 107.

[453] Reported by Muslim (2600) and others.

CHAPTER XVI

INNOVATIONS OF *DU'Ā*

Amongst the worst evils that has afflicted the Muslim *ummah* is the evil of innovations; those acts concerning which the Prophet (ﷺ) said, "Whoever innovates something into this religion of ours will have it rejected".[454] Some of these innovations are based on weak aḥādīth - aḥādīth which cannot authentically be traced back to the Prophet (ﷺ), and should therefore not be acted upon. Others are based upon whims and desires. Some of these innovations even involve *shirk*!

Some of the more common innovations are mentioned below.

1. Habitually Reading Specified *Du'ās* Which Are Not Found in the Sunnah

There are some Muslim sects (in particular, those of the Sūfis) that make it a condition on their members to recite regular *dhikrs* and *du'ās*. Each sect or order amongst the Sūfis – without exception – obligates its members to recite such incantations at regular intervals. These incantations are called *wirds* (plural: *awrād*), or *ḥizbs* (plural: *ahzāb*). Most sects even have a hierarchy of such *wirds*, such that an apprentice to a particular Sūfi order is given a general, daily, *wird*, and each subsequent level given a higher, more intensive (and, many times, more full of *shirk*) *wirds*. So the *wird* also represents a person's status in the Sūfi hierarchy.

Such regular incantations have many problems.

Firstly, the act of habitually performing a specific routine, at regu-

---

[454] Reported by al-Bukhārī and Muslim

lar times and intervals, believing that such an act is pleasing to Allāh, is without a doubt an innovation into the religion of Islām. No one after the Prophet (ﷺ) has the right to legislate any specific acts of worship. In all such *wirds*, one finds various phrases, some Qur'ānic, some from the Sunnah, and some from the particular Shaykh of that order, which the follower must repeat a specific number of times, at various times of the day. Even if a *du'ā* is found in the Qur'ān or Sunnah, to repeat it a specific number of times, or at specific times of the day, believing that this is an act of worship, makes such an act an innovation into the religion (unless, of course, the Prophet (ﷺ) himself commanded us to repeat them or say them at specific timings).

Secondly, a person who recites such *wirds* rarely uses the *du'ās* found in the authentic Sunnah of the Prophet (ﷺ), and instead relies on the wordings and incantations of his Shaykh. The person who practices such *wirds* believes in his heart – though he dares not verbalize it – that these ramblings of his Shaykh are more blessed and have a greater chance of being responded to than the beautiful and concise speech of the Prophet (ﷺ). It is because of this that when you ask such a person to return to the prophetic *du'ā*, he feels a sense of disdain, believing that he has been given a more special *du'ā*, whereas the *du'ā* that the Prophet Muhammad (ﷺ) taught the Muslims is a *du'ā* for the 'commoners', meaning the Muslims at large. Shaykh al-Islām Ibn Taymiyyah writes, "And of the people who are the most deserving to be criticized are those who take a *ḥizb* which has not been narrated from the Prophet (ﷺ) - even if it be a *ḥizb* written by some *Shaykhs* - and leaves the prophetic *ḥizbs* that the leader of the children of Adam and the Imām of the prophets (ﷺ) used to say." [455]

---

[455] *Majmū' al-Fatāwa*, 22/232. Notice how Shaykh al-Islām encourages the Muslims to go back to the prophetic *du'ās*, and contrast this with the Sūfi Shaykhs and *Peers*, for each one only calls to his specific *wird*, believing it to be better than the *wirds* of all other Sūfi sects.

Thirdly, such *wirds* or *ḥizbs* usually containing meaningless phrases, or the beginnings of the Surahs (such as *Alif Låm Mīm*, *Hā Mīm*) repeated a specific number of times. Such chants have no basis in the Sunnah of our beloved Prophet (ﷺ), or in the actions of his Companions and those after them.

Fourthly, more often than not there is blatant *shirk* in such *wirds* (especially in the extreme Sūfi sects), and even if there is no *shirk*, there are almost always innovations and phrases that lead to *shirk* (such as performing *tawassul* with the status of the Prophet (ﷺ)).

Fifthly, the whole purpose of *du'ā* – that of feeling poverty to Allāh, and showing sincerity and need to his Creator – is destroyed when one parrots the same phrases hundreds of times in the course of a few days or weeks. Such people are more concerning about the *punctuality* and *quantity* of these *wirds*, rather than the *spirituality* and *quality* that a true *du'ā* is supposed to instill. Therefore, even if such *wirds* do not contain traces of *shirk* or innovation (and this is hardly ever the case), it conflicts with the true meaning and purpose of *du'ā* by concentrating on a specified wording of the tongue rather than inculcating humbleness and sincerity of *du'ā* in the heart.

In conclusion, ponder over the following passage from one of the scholars whose life was devoted to calling to the pure worship of Allāh, based on the Sunnah of the Messenger of Allāh (ﷺ), Shaykh al-Islām Ibn Taymiyyah:

> "There is no doubt that the remembrance of Allāh, and *du'ā* to Him, are of the greatest acts of worship. And all acts of worship are based on what is found (in the texts), and following (the Prophet (ﷺ)). So the *dhikr* and the *du'ā* that the Prophet (ﷺ) used to do are the best choices that any person who wishes to do *dhikr* and make *du'ā* can choose. Whoever sticks with them will find peace and contentment...Anything besides these may possibly be prohibited, or disliked, or even contain elements of *shirk* which most people will not be able to detect.
>
> No one has the right to legislate upon the people a specific routine of *dhikr* and *du'ā* which are not found in the Sunnah, making such incantations a regular and punctual act of wor-

ship that a person must adhere to, just as they adhere to the five daily prayers. Rather, such an act (of inventing these *wirds* and reciting them) is an innovation into this religion, and something which Allāh has not allowed. This is in contrast to some *du'ā* (not found in the Sunnah) that a person might make occasionally, without making it a recommended practice upon other people, for this is not prohibited...

As for taking a *wird* which has no evidence in the Islamic Law, and habitually reciting a *dhikr* which is not found in the Islamic texts, then this is a matter which must be prohibited against. Along with this, it should be borne in mind that the *dhikrs* and *du'ās* which are found in the Islamic texts fulfill the loftiest and most noble goals (that any person needs). So whoever replaces these (*du'ās* of the Sunnah) with other ones is either an ignoramus, or one who goes beyond the boundaries (of the Sacred Law)."[456]

2. Kissing One's Thumbs and Rubbing One's Eyes with them

It is all too common to see Muslims kiss their thumbs and then rub them upon their eyes when the Prophet's (ﷺ) name is mentioned. The basis of this act is the following fabricated narration:

'Abbās ibn Aḥmad ibn Abī Bakr, the Ṣūfī, reported with a chain of narrators full of unknown names, that Khidr, the Companion of Moses, said: "Whoever says when the *Mu'adhin* says, 'I testify that Muḥammad (ﷺ) is the Messenger of Allāh,' 'Welcome, my loved one, and the coolness of my eyes, Muḥammad (ﷺ),' then kisses his thumbs and rubs them on his eyes, will never have any eye diseases".

This is the source of the acts of the ignorant: a chain of unknown narrators, narrating on the authority of a person who lived thousands of years before them!

---

[456]Based on a passage in: *Majmu' al-Fatāwa*, 22/510-511.

3. *Duʿā* in a Group

This is amongst those innovations that have become so common that many Muslims actually believe it is a Sunnah. Yet, this act has no basis in the Qur'ān or Sunnah, not even a weak ḥadīth! In many *masjids*, a joint *duʿā* is made after every single ṣalāt; the imām says a *duʿā* out loud, and the entire congregation says, *'Āmīn'* behind him. There is no doubt that such an act is an innovation into this religion, as the Prophet (ﷺ) never did such a congregational *duʿā* after the ṣalāt, nor did the Companions after him, nor did the Successors after them.

In fact, quite the opposite is true! When a drought afflicted the Muslims during ʿUmar's Caliphate, ʿUmar himself was the one who made the *duʿā*, and he also ordered ʿAbbās to make an individual *duʿā*. He did not order all the Companions to make a joint *duʿā* with him, nor did any of the other Companions suggest this to him. This shows that such a concept was unknown to the Companions.

It has been narrated that one of the governors wrote to ʿUmar ibn al-Khaṭṭāb, 'There are a group of people here who come together, and make *duʿā* (in congregation) for the Muslims and the Caliph'. So ʿUmar ordered some of his servants to go with sticks and beat them, and in fact he helped them in this![457] This, despite the fact that they were actually making *duʿā for* him, as he was the Caliph at that time. This narration is clear proof that congregational *duʿā* is an innovation that was strongly disapproved of by the Companions.

It should be mentioned that congregational *duʿās* are permissible during certain occasions that the Sunnah has confirmed (such as during the *khuṭbah* on Friday, or during the Witr prayer when it is performed in congregation), but to make it a habit on other than such occasions makes it an innovation. Additionally, it directly contradicts many of the etiquettes of *duʿā*, and opens up the door for

---

[457] Reported by Ibn Abī Shaybah, # 6242. See Abū Zayd, p. 72.

riyā (showing off one's deeds). Such congregational *du'ās* make it easier for a person's thoughts to wander, as concentration can only be perfected when one makes the *du'ā* oneself.

4. To Clasp One's Hands to One's Chest During *Du'ā*

This is contrary to the proper manner of *du'ā*, as the Sunnah is to ask with the palms outwards. In fact, this act resembles the manner of prayer of the Christians.

5. *Tawassul* with the Status of the Prophet (ﷺ)

The way that a person does this is that he prays: O Allāh, I ask you by virtue of the status of Your Prophet (ﷺ) that you grant me such and such. This concept has already been discussed previously.

Shaykh al-Islām Ibn Taymiyyah wrote: "(*Tawassul* with the status of the Prophet (ﷺ) is incorrect) despite the fact that the status of the Prophet (ﷺ) is greater than the status of all prophets and messengers. However, the status of a created being with the Creator can never be compared with the status of a created being with another created being. None can intercede in front of Allāh except with His Permission. Yet mortals can intercede on behalf of one another without any permission, so the intercessor becomes like a partner in attaining the goal".[458] This too has already been discussed in detail.

6. To Specify the Unspecified

What is meant by this is that a person specifies a certain time, or a certain place, or a certain *du'ā*, that is not specified by the Sharī'ah, and believes that such an act will increase the chances of his *du'ā* being accepted. So, to make a habit of making *du'ā* on, say the

---

[458] Al-Ḥalabī, p. 95.

twelfth of Rabīʿ al-Awal, or at a certain location, is an innovation. Likewise, to specify a particular *duʿā* before or after doing an act is also considered an innovation (unless such a specification is found in the Sunnah). It is not allowed to add constraints or details that are not found in the Qur'ān or Sunnah, believing that such acts will be more rewarded by Allāh!

Another example that is common is that during the *ṭawāf* (circumambulation around the Kaʿbah) many people read specific *duʿās* for each round, believing that this is part of the Sunnah. Yet, there is nothing specific of this nature found in the Qur'ān or Sunnah, so if a person does this, believing that these specific *duʿās* are encouraged or more rewarding than others, then he has fallen into a *bidʿah*, or religious innovation.

Other examples of this include making a New Year's wish, or doing the same while blowing out candles, or at the beginning of spring and autumn, or any other occasions that have not been specified by the Sharīʿah.

The opposite of this principle is also true, so, if a specific *duʿā* has been narrated in the Sunnah for a specific occasion or after a certain act, then it should not be used habitually except for the circumstances that it has been narrated for. So, for example, the *duʿā* that is narrated from the Prophet (ﷺ) for entering the *masjid* should not be used every time a person enters any house or other structure, since the Sunnah has specified where this *duʿā* should be used.

7. The Statement "May Allāh Establish it and Preserve it"

This statement is made by many people after the statement of the *mu'adhin*: "The prayer has been established (*Qad qāmat al-ṣalāt*)".

However, the basis of this is a weak narration, reported by Abū Dāwūd and others.

CHAPTER XVII

Some Weak Ḥadīth Regarding *Du*ʿ*ā*

There are a number of weak or fabricated *aḥādīth* that are, unfortunately, circulated amongst the masses as authentic traditions of the Prophet (ﷺ). A Muslim should be cautious when he quotes any ḥadīth or accepts them without verification. He must realise that a ḥadīth is a statement attributed to the Prophet (ﷺ), thus it is essential that this attribution be correct.

Some of the more common of these are as follows.

1. The First Ḥadīth

"*Du*ʿ*ā* is the weapon of the believer, and the pillar of Islām, and the light of the heavens and earth".

This ḥadīth was narrated by al-Ḥākim (1/492), but as Ibn ʿAdī and al-Ḥaythamī pointed out, it is fabricated. This is also the conclusion of al-Albānī in his *al-Ḍa*ʿ*īfah*, # 179.

2. The Second Ḥadīth

"When Adam did the sin that he did, he said, 'O Allāh! I ask you by the right of Muḥammad that you forgive me'. Allāh said, 'O Adam! And how do you know Muḥammad and I have still not created him?' He replied, 'O Allāh! When you created me with Your hands, and blew into me Your spirit, I lifted my head, and saw written on the pillars of the throne, '*Lā ilāha illa Allāh Muḥammad Rasūl Allāh.*' And I knew that You would not link with Your name except the most beloved of creation to You'. So Allāh said, 'You have told the truth O Adam! He is the most beloved of creation to me, so make *du'ā* to Me by his rights, and I have forgiven you. And were it not for Muḥammad, I would not have created you.'"

This ḥadīth is narrated by al-Ḥākim (2/615), and al-Dhahabī said of it, 'It is fabricated!' This was also the opinion of Ibn Ḥajr, Ibn Taymiyyah, Ibn Kathīr and others. (See *al-Ḍa'īfah* of al-Albānī, # 25.)

Even the wordings of the ḥadīth clearly indicate so, for they contradict the Qur'ān. The purpose of creation is so that mankind can worship Allāh, and that is why they were created. Yes, the Prophet (ﷺ) is the most beloved of mankind to Allāh, but the exaggerations present in this ḥadīth are not a part of Islām. This ḥadīth is used by those who justify *tawassul* with the status of the Prophet (ﷺ), but it is not possible to base our religion on fabricated ḥadīth!

3. The Third Ḥadīth

"When matters overwhelm you, then seek help from the people of the graves."

This is another ḥadīth whose fabrication can be detected immediately from its contents. This because it is commanding the believers to commit *shirk* by asking the dead to fulfil their needs!

In fact, this ḥadīth does not even have an *isnād* (chain of narrators) to it, so it has no basis whatsoever. (See *al-Tawassul* of Ibn Taymiyyah, p. 25.)

4. The Fourth Ḥadīth

"Perform *tawassul* with my status, for verily my status in the sight of Allāh is exalted."

This ḥadīth too has no *isnād* to it, nor is it narrated in any of the source books of the Sunnah. Despite this fact, it is used by many people in order to justify *tawassul* through the status of the Prophet (ﷺ).

There is no doubt that the status of the Prophet (ﷺ) is higher than the status of any other person, but this does not necessitate performing *tawassul* through him, as *tawassul* is an act of worship which cannot be based on desires or logic, as has already been stated. (See *al-Ḍaʿīfah*, # 22.)

5. The Fifth Ḥadīth

"When Ibrāhīm was thrown into the Fire, Jibrīl asked him, 'Do you need any help?' He replied, 'From you, no!' So Jibrīl said, 'Ask your Lord'. Ibrāhīm replied, 'It is sufficient asking that my Lord knows my situation'".

Again, this ḥadīth has no basis to it, as it is not found with any *isnād* in any of the books of the Sunnah. On the contrary, it is based on Judaeo-Christian narrations, and its meaning contradicts the Sharīʿah. The Qur'ān is replete with the *duʿās* of the prophets and believers, so how can it be claimed that *duʿā* is not required just because Allāh knows the situation of the servant? Of course Allāh is aware of the situation of His slaves, but this does not give the slave an excuse not to make *duʿā* to Him! The evidences for all this have also already been documented above. (See also: *Majmūʿ al-Fatawā*, 8/539).

6. The Sixth Ḥadīth

"When one of you leaves his house to go to the *masjid*, and says, 'O Allāh! I ask You by the right that those that ask have over You, and I ask You by the right (that I have over You) because of this walk of mine… (*to the end of this long* ḥadīth).'"

This *ḥadīth* is narrated by Ibn Mājah (# 778) and others. However, its *isnād* is extremely weak, and therefore al-Būṣayrī said, 'It is full of weak narrators,' and Ibn Taymiyyah, Aḥmad Shākir and al-Albānī all agreed with him. (See *al-Ḍaʿīfah*, # 24.)

This ḥadīth contains an inappropriate meaning, and that is that the one who asks has a *right* over Allāh that He respond to the *duʿā*.

No one has any right over the Creator; it is only Allāh that can legislate any rights upon Himself! Yes, it is true that Allāh has promised that He will respond to the *du'ā* of a person (as long as it is performed properly), but this is a promise that Allāh has given, and not a *right* that creation has over Him, and the difference between these two concepts is clear.

7. The Seventh Ḥadīth

It is narrated that the people of Madīnah, after the death of the Prophet (ﷺ), were afflicted with a severe drought. So they complained to 'Ā'ishah, the Prophet's (ﷺ) wife, about it. She said, "Look at the grave of the Prophet (ﷺ), then place a window (in the roof) facing the sky, so that there is no cover between it and the sky". This they did, and it rained so plentifully that the plants sprouted forth, and the camels became fat.

This narration is not reported in any of the famous works of ḥadīth; it is found in al-Dārimī's *Sunan* (# 92), with a very weak chain. In addition, as Ibn Taymiyyah pointed out, the content of the ḥadīth contradicts historical facts, as it is well known that the small window built in the roof of the Prophet's (ﷺ) house was placed there long after 'Ā'ishah's death, and not during her lifetime. So this ḥadīth cannot be taken as evidence, especially since it is authentically narrated in al-Bukharī that when the people suffered a drought, 'Umar asked al-'Abbās to make a *du'ā* for them, and had they known that it would rain by building a window over the Prophet's (ﷺ) grave, they would not have done what they did. (See *al-Tawassul* of al-Albānī, p. 139.)

Conclusion

What has preceded, dear reader, is merely a glimpse at some of the many facets of *duʿā*. *Duʿā* is a treasure that all people can possess, yet so few strive to achieve. It is a light that one can use to guide oneself out of the darkest dilemma that one may be in. It is the wind that lifts the sails of one's hope and pushes one forth to one's destination. It is the sword that he can use to fight any and every enemy impeding one's path.

Duʿā is the heart of worship, and its foundation. It is the crux of one's relationship with Allāh, for it demonstrates, in clear and certain terms, the inherent helplessness of man, and his continual, desperate need of *al-Raḥmān*.

So ask yourself: what the status is of this affair in your life? How often do you turn to Allāh? And for what matters do you turn to Him? How sincere are you in your requests? And do you ask Allāh properly, conforming with the pre-requisites and etiquettes of *duʿā*? Or do you ask and ask, but not care about the ways that you have blocked its response? Are you heedless of Allāh, and only turn to Him at times of need, only to forget Him when your *duʿā* is answered? Or do you despair of His Infinite Mercy and Wisdom when your *duʿā* is not responded to, forgetting and ignoring the countless other blessings that He has given you, and presuming of Allāh evil thoughts?

Ponder over the answers to these questions, and change your life accordingly to better the situation that you are in.

O you who does not turn to Allāh at all, feeling himself too sinful to merit a response! Are you worse than Iblīs – the accursed devil? For verily, if Allāh can respond to his *duʿā*, then surely you have more right to be responded to. Are you not aware of the vast treasures of Allāh, and that He is *al-Karīm,* the Ever-Generous? Did he not create you out of nothing, and guide you to Islām, and bless you with so many blessings that you cannot even count them? And if He gave all that to you, without you even asking Him, then how much more will He give you when you raise your hands up to Him, seeking His Pleasure, believing in Him as your *Rabb*? So ask Him, and continue to ask Him, and the first matter that you should ask Him for is guidance, for verily it is the primary goal that you strive for.

O you who are in distress! Despair not of finding a solution to your problems. Verily, there is nothing that can overcome a sincere *duʿā*, for Allāh is capable of all things. And know that the response to the *duʿā* will be proportionate to your sincerity to Allāh. If you desire your goal with such fervour and passion, then take the necessary precautions to obtain it. Make sure that you have asked Allāh having fulfilled the conditions of *duʿā*, and ensure that you have removed any obstacles and impediments in the way of the response.

O you whose *duʿā* is yet to be answered! Do not let *Shayṭān* come between you and the response of your *duʿā*. Be certain and have full faith that Allāh will, of a surety, respond to you, but only if *you* have fulfilled the proper conditions of *duʿā*. Examine your own situation, and see if perhaps you have not blocked the response to your *duʿā* by your own sins and actions. Ponder over the goal that you desire, and see whether it is possible that what you desire is in fact harmful for you, and Allāh, in His Infinite Wisdom and Mercy, is depriving you of it for your own good. Realise that Allāh's Kingdom is so vast that if He were to give you all that you ever desired, or could possibly desire, it would not affect His Kingdom an atom's weight, and believe fully with your heart that Allāh is *al-Mannān* – the One Who Gives Continuously and Generously. So when you are dealing with One whose characteristics are these, then what do you fear?

O you who has had his *duʿā* answered, and has seen the effects of his plea! Beware of forgetting your state when you were calling out to Allāh, hopeful of a response, fearful of rejection. Remember your sincerity to Allāh at that time, and be careful not to let *Shayṭān* cause you to become heedless again. Now that Allāh has answered your *duʿā*, it is incumbent on you to thank Him, by increasing your worship of Him, and leaving the sins that you are doing. And beware of acting like the *kāfir*, who, when he needs Allāh, calls out to Him in all sincerity, but when his *duʿā* is answered, forgets the state that he was in, and leaves his worship of Allāh.

O Muslim! Realise that your honour lies in humbling yourself before *al-ʿAzīz* (the One Full of Honour), and your strength and power comes from admitting your total helplessness and dependence on *al-Qawī, al-Qadīr* (the Ever-Powerful, the All-Capable). And know that the strongest channel of communication between yourself and your *Mawlā* (Protector) is the channel of *duʿā*.

Verily, your journey is long, and the perils are many. Your destination is far, and the path is treacherous. So utilise your *duʿā*. Use it to ward off the evil of yourself, and the evil of your enemies, and the evil that is destined for you. And use it as you strive to reach your every goal, and struggle to arrive at your desired destination.

Duʿā is your sharpest sword, and your strongest weapon.

All Praise is due to Allāh, the Creator of all, the Giver of everything.
And He is far Exalted above what others ascribe to Him.
And May Peace and Blessings be upon the perfect
worshipper of Allāh, the Final Messenger,
Muḥammad ibn ʿAbdillāh (ﷺ)
and all those
who follow
him.

Glossary of Arabic Terms

Abū (or **Abī**): Literally 'the father of'. It was a custom of the Arabs to add a pre-fix (known as *kunya*) to their first names consisting of the title "Abū" and then their oldest son's name, or any of their children. Although this was the general rule, sometime they would add this pre-fix without necessarily using the name of one of their children.

Adhān: The call to prayer, given before every single of the five prayers.

'Aqīdah: The faith, creed and beliefs of the Muslims.

Arafāt: A plain outside of Makkah which the pilgrims worship in. The most important feature of the Ḥajj is the standing at Arafāt.

'Aṣr: The name given to the afternoon prayer.

Āyah (pl. **āyāt**): A verse of the Qur'ān.

Bid'ah: A religious innovation or practice that has no basis in the Qur'ān or Sunnah.

Dīn: The religion of Islām.

Dhikr: The remembrance of Allāh.

Ẓuhr: The name given to the noon ṣalāt.

Dhul-Ḥijjah: The twelfth month of the Muslim calendar. The Ḥajj is performed during this month.

Dirham: A gold coin.

Fāsiq: An evil person.

Fitnah: A trial or test.

Fiṭrah: The innate nature that Allāh created in all of mankind.

Ḥadīth (pl. **aḥādīth**): The statements and actions of the Prophet

Muḥammad (ﷺ). These, along with the Qur'ān, form the basis for the religion of Islām.

Ḥadīth Qudsī: A ḥadīth of the Prophet (ﷺ) in which he narrates from Allāh.

Ḥajj: The 'major' pilgrimage that is obligatory for Muslims to perform at least once in their life-time. It can only be performed during the month of Dhul-Ḥijjah.

Ḥarām: Any prohibited act in Islām.

Ḥasan: A ḥadīth that is reliable and sound. It is one level below that of Ṣaḥīḥ.

'Ibādah: The Arabic word for worship.

Iblīs: The name of Satan himself.

Ibn: Literally 'the son of'.

Īmām: The one who leads the congregational prayer.

Īmān: The Arabic term for 'Faith'.

Iqāmah: This is a 'second' call to the prayer, given after the Adhān, and immediately before the congregation starts the prayer.

Inshā-Allāh: An expression used in Arabic which means, "If Allāh wills".

Isnād: The chain of narrators connected to every ḥadīth.

Jāhiliyyah: The name given to the time-period before the advent of the Prophet (ﷺ). It signifies the ignorance and superstition that was prevalent at that time.

Jamarah (pl. **Jamarāt**): Three pillars located inside Mina that Muslims stone during the days of Ḥajj.

Jihād: Literally, striving for the sake of Allāh. It primarily refers to fighting an enemy for religious reasons.

Jinn: The *jinn* are spirit-like creatures that, in general, cannot be seen by men. Since they have free-will, like humans, there are

Muslim *jinn* and non-Muslim *jinn*.

Kāfir: A non-Muslim.

Ka'bah: The 'House of Allāh' located in Makkah, Arabia. It was built by Ibrāhīm.

Khuṭbah: The Friday sermon given before the Friday prayer.

Laylat al-Qadr: The 'Night of Decree;' a blessed night which occurs on one of the odd nights of the last ten nights of Ramaḍān.

Marwa: One of two mountains located next to the Ka'bah. Muslims must walk between these mountains during the rituals of Ḥajj and 'Umrah.

Masjid: The place in which Muslims offer their daily ṣalāt.

Mina: An area outside of Makkah which the pilgrims live in for a number of days during the rituals of Ḥajj.

Mu'adhin: The one who says the *adhān* (call to prayer)

Muzdalifah: A large plain located outside of Makkah, which the pilgrims performing Ḥajj must camp in for one night.

Qiblah: The direction that a Muslim must face when he prays (i.e. the direction of Makkah).

Qunūt: A prayer that is offered during special occasions while in ṣalāt. It is commonly offered during the *wiṭr* ṣalāt.

Rabb: One of the names of Allāh. It signifies that Allāh is the Cherisher, Sustainer and Creator.

Rak'ah: A 'unit' of prayer. Every ṣalāt is composed of a number of *rak'ahs*.

Ramaḍān: The ninth, and holiest, month in the Muslim calendar. During this month, the Muslims must fast throughout the day.

Rukū': The act of bowing down during the ṣalāt.

Ṣadaqah Jāriyah: A type of charity in which the rewards continues to last after the act has been done; for example, building a mosque.

Ṣaḥiḥ: correct; an authentic narration.

Ṣafa: One of two mountains located next to the Ka'bah. Muslims must walk between these mountains during the rituals of Ḥajj and 'Umrah.

Sajdah (pl. **Sujūd**): The act of prostrating on the ground.

Salām (salutations): The greeting that Muslims give one another when they meet.

Salām (upon finishing the prayer): The final movement of the ṣalāt, by which the ṣalāt comes to an end. It is the moving of the head to the right, and then to the left.

Salām (upon the Prophet (ﷺ): The act of sending salutations and a prayer for peace upon the Prophet (ﷺ).

Salāt: The name given to the ritual prayer performed five times a day by Muslims.

Sharī'ah: The legal laws of Islām.

Shayṭān (pl. **Shayāṭīn**): The Arabic word for devils.

Shirk: To associate partners with Allāh by directing an act of worship to other than Him, or by describing a created object with god-like powers and attributes. It is the greatest evil in Islām.

Ṣūfi: A sect of Islām; commonly translated as 'mystics.' They believe, amongst other things, that the Qur'ān has an 'outer' meaning known to all, and an 'inner' meaning known only to them.

Sunnah: The practice of the Prophet (ﷺ).

Sūrah: The name given to a chapter in the Qur'ān. The Qur'ān is composed of 114 sūrahs of various lengths.

Tābi'ī (pl. **tābi'īn**): The generation of Muslims after that of the Companions.

Takbīr: The uttering of the phrase, "Allāh Akbar," or "Allāh is Great".

Taqwa: The fear and consciousness of Allāh.

Tashahhud: The final invocation said before the end of every ṣalāt.

Tawassul: The act of seeking a means of nearness to Allāh. A person can, for example, perform *tawassul* through his good deeds, since he comes closer to Allāh by these deeds.

Tawḥīd: The concept of Islamic monotheism.

Umm: Literally 'the mother of'. Women would add this pre-fix, along with one of their children's names, the same way that men would use 'Abū.'

Ummah: The nation of Muslims.

'Umrah: A 'minor' pilgrimage to Makkah. It can be done at any time of the year.

Wiṭr: Typically the last prayer of the night, it consists of an odd number of rakʿāt. It is common to offer the *qunūt* during the *wiṭr* prayers.

Wuḍū: The ablution that a Muslim performs before offering his prayers.

Zakāt: the third of the five pillars of Islām, it is a mandatory charity that must be given annually.

Zam-Zam: The water that springs forth from the well located infront of the Kaʿbah at Makkah. It is the most blessed water on earth.

Select Bibliography

Abū Zayd, Bakr. *Taṣḥīḥ al-Duʿā*. Dār al-Āsimah, Riyādh. 1419 A.H.

Abū Zayd, Bakr. *Marwiyyāt Duʿā Khatm al-Qur'ān*. Dār al-Sumay'ī, Riyadh. 1416 A.H.

Al-Awāyishah, Ḥusayn. *Kitāb al-Duʿā*. Dār Ibn Hazm, Beirut. 1413 A.H.

Al-Ḥamad, ʿAbd al-ʿAzīz ibn ʿAbdullāh. *Al-Duʿā: Mafhūmuhu, aḥḳāmuhu, aḳhtā taqaʿ fīhi*. Dār Ibn Khuzaymah, Riyadh. 1418 A.H.

Al-Hilālī, Salīm ibn ʿĪd. *Al-Nubadh al-Mustatābah fī al-Daʿwāt al-Mustajābah*. Dār Ibn al-Jawzī, Dammām. 1413 A.H.

Ḥusayn, Abū Anas ʿAlī ibn. *Al-Tawassul Ḥuḳmuhu wa Aqsāmuh*. Dār Ibn Khuzaymah, Riyadh. 1417 A.H.

Al-Khudarī, Abdullāh ibn Aḥmad. *Al-Duʿā*. Dār al-Fatah, Sharjah. 1415 A.H.

Al-Qaḥtānī, Saʿīd ibn ʿAlī. *Shurūṭ al-Duʿā wa Mawaniʿ al-Ijābat*. Mu'asasat al-Juraysī, Riyadh. 1416 A.H.

Ibn al-Qayyim, Shaykh al-Islām Shams al-Dīn Muḥammad ibn Abī Bakr. *Badā'i al-Fawā'id*.

Ibn al-Qayyim, Shaykh al-Islām Shams al-Dīn Muhammad ibn Abī Bakr. *Al-Dā' wa ad-Dawa'*. Ed. By Āmir Yāsīn. Dār Ibn Khuzaymah, Riyadh. 1417 A.H.

Ibn al-Qayyim, Shaykh al-Islām Shams ad-Dīn Muhammad ibn Abī Bakr. *Madārij as-Sāliḳīn*. Ed. By Muhammad al-Baghdadī. Dār al-Kitab al-Arabī, Beirut, 1417 A.H.

Ar-Radi, Samīr Jamīl. *Al-Duʿā wa al-'Itiḳāf*. No publishing details available.